A New Parent's
Guide to Astrology

RAISING BABY BY THE STARS

MARESSA BROWN

ARTISAN | NEW YORK

Library of Congress Cataloging-in-Publication Data

Names: Brown, Maressa, author.
Title: Raising baby by the stars / Maressa Brown.
Description: New York : Artisan, an imprint of Workman Publishing Co.,
Inc., a subsidiary of Hachette Book Group, Inc., [2023] | Includes
index. | Summary: "This book is meant as introduction to a time-honored,
powerful tool: your baby's astrological blueprint, known as their natal,
or birth, chart"—Provided by publisher.
Identifiers: LCCN 2022033376 | ISBN 9781648290954 (hardback)
Subjects: LCSH: Natal astrology. | Birth charts.
Classification: LCC BF1719 .B76 2023 | DDC 133.5—dc23/eng/20220812
LC record available at https://lccn.loc.gov/2022033376

Design by Jennifer K. Beal Davis

Artisan books are available at special discounts when purchased in bulk for
premiums and sales promotions as well as for fund-raising or educational
use. Special editions or book excerpts also can be created to specification.
For details, please contact specialmarkets@hbgusa.com.

Published by Artisan,
an imprint of Workman Publishing Co., Inc.,
a subsidiary of Hachette Book Group, Inc.
1290 Avenue of the Americas
New York, NY 10104
artisanbooks.com

Artisan is a registered trademark of
Workman Publishing Co., Inc.,
a subsidiary of Hachette Book Group, Inc.

Printed in China on responsibly sourced paper

First printing, January 2023

1 3 5 7 9 10 8 6 4 2

RAISING
BABY
BY THE
STARS

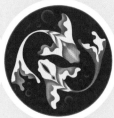

To my parents, Stuart and Irene,
whose study of astrology led to
a thriving marriage and
three babies fortunate to be
raised by the stars

CONTENTS

INTRODUCTION

MAYBE YOU'RE ABOUT TO EXPERIENCE this or you know the feeling all too well, but a particular type of shock hits most new parents in the first few days following the birth of their child. It's the realization that you now have a front-row seat to watch your tiny human grow, learn, and evolve into who they're meant to be. Yet there's no manual, app, or online course that's perfectly tailored to helping you raise your child. As with any new relationship, you will get to know them—and what they need—one day at a time. Along the way, you'll create your own toolbox for making that process a bit more harmonious. This book is meant to introduce you to a time-honored, powerful tool for that box: your baby's astrological blueprint, known as their natal, or birth, chart.

Well before my own parents were handed the first of their three bundles of joy (that would be yours truly) and expected to just figure it out, they already understood how useful astrology could be. In fact, it's possible that without it, they never would have met. My dad had been studying astrology since 1969. When he learned that his ideal match would have been born when the sun was in Pisces (complementing his moon sign—which rules emotions and intuition—also in the sign of the Fish), he asked a family friend if she knew a woman born under the water sign whom she could set him up with. As it turned out, her best friend—my mom—fit that description. When she and my dad went out, their connection was instant and, to date, has led to nearly fifty years of happy marriage.

On September 6, 1983, almost seven years after they tied the knot, I was born while the sun, moon, and Mercury were all in Virgo. Learning about my birth chart was a priority for my parents. Around age thirteen, I found a cassette tape marked "October 12, 1983" on which my parents' astrologer discusses uncanny details about my personality and dreams, for example, my love of writing and desire to make a living as a wordsmith. In the background of the recording, you can hear five-week-old me "chatting" and squealing away, as if to confirm her take.

Although my parents had this celestial intel, they filed it away and allowed me the space to grow into the person being described on that tape. When, at five years old, I told my dad that I was going to be an author one day, he wasn't exactly surprised, given all that cerebral Virgo energy, but he was certainly amused. And since I was born with three other personal placements (my rising sign, Venus, and Mars) in outgoing fire sign Leo, of course I was instantly infatuated with basking in the spotlight.

Flower children boomers like my parents were excited to use astrology to better understand their kids. Now, many millennial and Gen Z parents are not only interested in astrology but are also embracing gentle parenting, which, according to parenting expert Sarah Ockwell-Smith, is based on respecting a child's unique feelings and personality.

As the current or future parent of a little one, you're likely fired up about the fact that your child is a whole, individual person you've been granted the gift of meeting and learning from. You're already taking a holistic view, and it makes sense to explore not only your baby's sun sign but also their full astrological birth chart, which is entirely their own.

This book is a primer on interpreting the key highlights of that chart— details that will help you get to know, nurture, and engage with your child.

HOW TO MAKE THE MOST OF THIS BOOK

Whether you're new to astrology and mostly here for the parenting tips, you're fluent in the language of the sky, or your knowledge falls somewhere in between, this book was written to offer you concrete, accessible insights that'll make it a bit easier to guide your little one from infancy through toddlerhood.

It's broken up into several sections, each of which is meant to bolster your understanding of both astrology and your little one.

Your Baby's Story, as Told by the Sky introduces astrology basics and building blocks, such as what a natal chart actually looks like, how it works, and what your baby's sun sign is versus their moon, rising, and other personal planetary placements. You'll also get familiar with the elements (fire, earth, air, water) and the qualities (cardinal, fixed, mutable), all of which play a part in shaping your child's—and your own—personality.

Part 1, The Twelve Signs (page 30), presents overviews that serve as a starting point for understanding each sign. This is the section you'll want to flip to first to read what it means if your child is an Aries born on April 9 (when the sun was in the dynamic fire sign, symbolized by the Ram) or a Scorpio born on October 29 (when the sun was moving through the intense water sign, symbolized by the Scorpion). Of course it's completely possible to find that a specific placement's attributes don't align with your child's personality. I've of heard of plenty of little ones born with a Libra sun who are anything but social or peace-loving. And you'll meet many fire sign kids whom you would expect to be gregarious, open books who turn out to be quite private. That's because individual placements don't tell you the whole story of a person's astrological blueprint—and natal astrology is just one piece in a complex puzzle of influences on a child's strengths, challenges, and unique lens.

Part 2, A Guide to Your Little One's Mind, Spirit & Well-Being (page 104), is split into two chapters: In Self-Expression & Learning, you'll learn more about how you can support your baby or toddler in finding their voice and sharing who they are with the world. And in Health & Vitality, you'll find details on how to meet resistance from your child as well as the best wellness activities to try.

Part 3, Parent & Child Relationships: Bonding with Your Growing Star (page 182), offers specifics on how you parent, based on your own astrological identity, and how you'll connect with your little one. And because self-nurturing will only serve to strengthen your parenting game, you'll also find self-care suggestions here.

Tips and notes to bear in mind as you get into the weeds:

Explore your child's—and your own—sun sign as well as other personal placements. This book is designed to provide you with a nuanced, useful tapestry of information that you can best weave together by reading about not only your baby's sun sign, which represents their core identity and self-image, but their other personal placements as well. Throughout the book, be sure to read the overview of their "big three," and also their Mercury, Venus, and Mars (which round out the "big six").

In each section intro, you'll get a heads-up on which placements might be particularly useful to dive into. For instance, in "Self-Expression & Learning" (page 106), consider your child's Mercury sign as well as their sun sign, as the former colors how they communicate and think. And whether you're reading the basics on each sign in Part 1 or unpacking your relationship with your little one in part 3, you'll want to consider the main placements in your baby's chart *and* your own. After all, expanding your self-awareness will strengthen your ability to connect with your child.

Embrace contradictions. As you read about various aspects of your child's astrological profile, you might notice that one trait seems to contradict another. As my mentor, April Elliott Kent, puts it in her *Essential Guide to Practical Astrology* (a must-have for astrology students of all levels), contradictions mean "you're complicated, and astrology is complex enough to reflect that. Sometimes, and in some situations, you behave one way; and in other situations, you behave differently. You want different things from different areas of your life. You contain multitudes."

This book is for everyone. The pronouns used throughout the book are gender-neutral. And it was written for anyone who's playing an active role in raising a baby or toddler, whether you're a parent, grandparent, caregiver, aunt, uncle, or best friend.

Astrology can help your little one feel seen. Leos, for example, are often pegged as self-involved. But that self-focus drives one of Leo's superpowers (every sign has many, as you'll soon read). Leos innately understand how important it is to know yourself—and for others to see you as you are. As a Leo stellium (aka three or more placements in one sign), I wrote this book precisely because that understanding is what has fueled my passion for this subject. Parents who are familiar with their child's natal astrology—even if it is just their sun sign—gain more insight into their little one's distinct personality and perspective. And children who feel seen by their parents and loved ones are more likely to grow up to become self-assured, self-aware, happy adults.

Learning about your little one's astrology is just plain fun. The process of getting to know your baby is already ever evolving, educational, and truly gratifying. Incorporating even a bit of astrological wisdom will only serve to make it more so.

YOUR BABY'S STORY, AS TOLD BY THE SKY

THE MINUTE YOU LEARNED YOUR BABY'S DUE DATE, you likely experienced a rush of thoughts and feelings about what that special day and season would feel like. A baby expected in mid-March could arrive on a blustery, icy day, offering hope that springtime is on its way, while a child anticipated in mid-June will arrive when the sun blazes in a big, blue sky and the world is green and brimming with blossoms, as if the universe wants to join in your celebration.

Just as Earth's movement around the sun gives way to changing seasons that are each, in their own way, inspiring backdrops for celebrating new life, the movements of the sun, the moon, and the planets offer a valuable language of their own—the language of the sky, or astrology. From your little one's sun sign, which speaks to their core identity, to their moon sign, which offers intel on how they'll appreciate being nurtured, understanding the various layers of your child's astrology can shed light on their personality, perspective, dreams, behavior, identity, and more.

With your baby's full birth date, time, and place, you can cast a natal, or birth, chart, which serves as a snapshot of the sky. You'll be able to see exactly where the sun, moon, and planets were at the moment of their birth. This snapshot becomes what I like to refer to as a person's "astrological DNA"—a distinctive map that they'll carry with them throughout their life.

Read on for the basics to begin interpreting your baby's distinctive map— an invaluable resource as you embark on the parenting journey ahead.

THE SUN, THE STARS & YOUR BABY: HOW ASTROLOGY WORKS

What does it mean that your little one's sun is "in" a particular sign, and what does it have to do with the constellations in the night sky? We Western astrologers use a primary system called the tropical zodiac, which is based on the sun and its apparent path across the ecliptic, or the band of constellations that surround us here on Earth.

An easy way to think about this system: Imagine you're in the middle of a circular room, surrounded by a 360-degree movie screen that displays all twelve constellations, or zodiac signs. Depending on the time of year, month, or day, the sun, the moon, and all of the planets in our solar system will be projected over those constellations. Because they each move at a different pace and in their own unique pattern, they aren't all clustered in one constellation, or sign, at a time—far from it. The moon, which spends two to two and a half days in a sign, may appear in Aquarius while the sun, which spends about thirty days in a sign, could be a full 180 degrees away from it in Leo.

In other words, although Earth moves around the sun, it appears from our vantage point that the sun—as well as the moon and planets—is moving around us, journeying across the ecliptic. And astrology reflects and speaks to our earthly perspective. It's also based on our experience of the seasons. A new astrological cycle always begins on the first day of spring, when the sun moves into the first sign of the zodiac, Aries, associated with new beginnings, taking initiative, and early childhood.

THE NATAL CHART:
YOUR BABY'S UNIQUE BLUEPRINT

Although you might already know your baby's sun sign, that is just one piece of their natal chart, which denotes which signs *all* the celestial bodies—the moon, Mercury, Venus, Mars, and even outer planets Jupiter, Saturn, Uranus, Neptune, and Pluto—were in when your baby was born.

For example, any baby born on July 31 is a Leo; however, one who was born at 2:00 a.m. on July 31, 2020, in Chicago has a Sagittarius moon and a Gemini rising sign, whereas another born at 1:00 p.m. on July 31, 2022, in Los Angeles has a Virgo moon and a Scorpio rising sign.

To calculate your little one's astrological natal, or birth, chart, you'll need their:

- Birth month, date, and year
- Time of birth
- Place of birth including city, state or province, and country

This integral info can generally be found on a long-form birth certificate. If you don't have this handy, you can request one from the county where your child was born. Then, check out any of the following resources:

- **My site.** Visit MaressaBrown.com, and you'll find a tool that allows you to run a birth chart for free.
- **An app.** TimePassages is a free app on which you can run your baby's— or anyone's—chart. Or if you plan to continue your astrological studies, consider Astro Gold, a paid app that professionals use.
- **A professional astrologer.** Whether they practice locally or you love their work on social media, connect with and hire an astrologer who can cast and provide you with a chart.
- **A sign calculator.** If calculating a whole birth chart feels overwhelming, you can also look up individual placements by searching "moon sign calculator" or "Mercury sign calculator," etc.

Opposite is an example of what a baby's unique astrological map might look like. This one shows the natal chart of heir to the British throne Prince George of Wales.

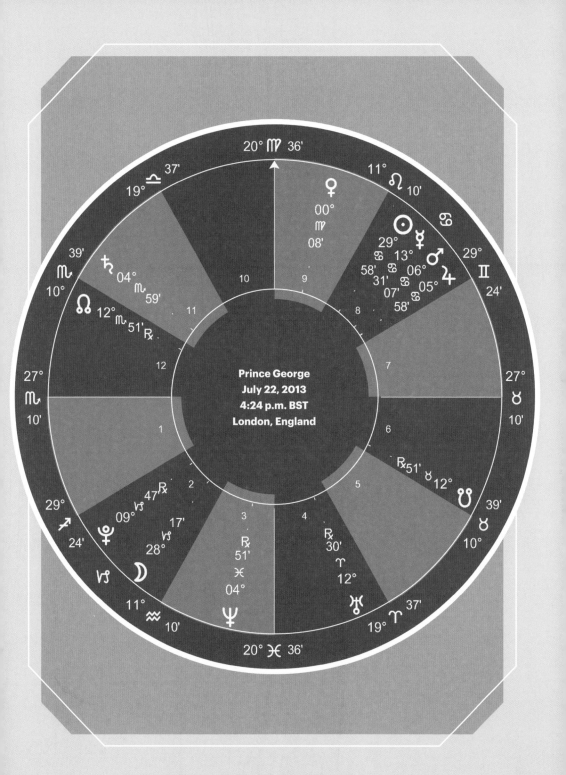

YOUR BABY'S SUN SIGN

Whenever you're asked "What's your baby's sign?" the most straightforward answer will always be their sun sign. The sun sign is a starting point for getting a read on your little one's astrological profile, as it will color their:

- Core identity
- Self-image
- Expression of pride
- Confidence
- Self-esteem
- Life path

HOW TO DETERMINE YOUR BABY'S SUN SIGN

Your child's birth month and day are generally enough to determine their sun sign. If they happened to be born on a day in which the sun moved from one sign into the next, their birth time and year will be key to pinpointing which they claim as their own.

If your child was born within two days of the beginning or end of a sign's date range—aka the cusp of that sign—you can gain clarity by looking at your baby's natal chart or using an online sun sign calculator.

Aries (Ram)
March 21–April 20

Taurus (Bull)
April 21–May 20

Gemini (Twins)
May 21–June 21

Cancer (Crab)
June 22–July 22

Leo (Lion)
July 22–August 22

Virgo (Maiden)
August 23–September 22

Libra (Scales)
September 23–October 22

Scorpio (Scorpion)
October 23–November 21

Sagittarius (Archer)
November 22–December 21

Capricorn (Goat)
December 22–January 21

Aquarius (Water Bearer)
January 22–February 18

Pisces (Fish)
February 19–March 20

YOUR BABY'S MOON SIGN

The gleaming, romantic moon's gravitational pull is known to have an intense effect on the tides—and on all of us down here on Earth. In astrology, the moon possesses a feminine, maternal energy and guides how we feel, intuit, and want to be nurtured.

Every two to three days, it moves from one sign to the next. Say your little one was born on June 5. Because that falls right in the middle of Gemini season, they are, indeed, a Gemini sun. But because the moon moves so much faster through the signs than the sun, it could have been in any one of the twelve signs when your baby was born. And your tyke's moon sign serves as another crucial puzzle piece of their personality.

You can think of your baby's moon sign as their astrological emotional compass, helping to shape how they:

- Express emotion
- Relate to others
- Nurture and want to be nurtured
- Feel a sense of security
- Experience instincts and intuition

HOW TO DETERMINE YOUR BABY'S MOON SIGN

Because the moon slips from one sign to the next so quickly, the easiest way to identify your little one's moon sign is by consulting their natal chart or using an online moon sign calculator (see Resources, page 347).

YOUR BABY'S RISING SIGN (AKA ASCENDANT)

Your child's rising sign, or ascendant, is a detail of their astrological profile that can be determined only with a correct birth time. The rising sign represents the zodiac sign that was rising—aka ascending—on the eastern horizon at the time of your little one's birth. And because of the way Earth rotates on its axis, the rising sign is the part of the birth chart that changes the fastest: approximately every one to two hours. Children born just a couple of hours apart in the exact same location can have different rising signs.

The rising sign rules your child's First House of Self (see page 27) and speaks to how they present themselves to the world. It's the sign that people will guess your little one is based on how they appear at first blush. For instance, if your child was born with their sun in fiery, unfiltered Sagittarius but they have a more private, emotional Scorpio ascendant, they could initially seem more reserved than the average Archer.

Your baby's rising sign or ascendant also reflects their:

- Skills
- Talents
- Pursuit of innermost desires

HOW TO FIND YOUR BABY'S RISING SIGN

Because the rising sign changes throughout the day and is also based on birth location, the fastest way to pinpoint it is by casting a natal chart with your child's exact birth time. Since it's already familiar territory, let's use Prince George's chart (page 17) to illustrate this.

When the heir to the British throne was born, the constellation that was rising over the eastern horizon from the vantage of his birthplace (London, England) was Scorpio, making his rising sign, or ascendant, Scorpio. Had he been born just over two hours earlier, his rising sign would have been Libra. Had he happened to arrive a bit later, his rising sign would have been Sagittarius. But because he was born at 4:24 p.m., his natal chart begins with Scorpio ruling his First House of Self. In turn, the way he is initially perceived by others is not so much as his sun sign—sentimental, tenderhearted Cancer—but as a magnetic, mysterious Scorpio.

On your own child's chart, you can pinpoint their rising and ascendant in this very same spot: on the left-hand side, which represents the eastern horizon.

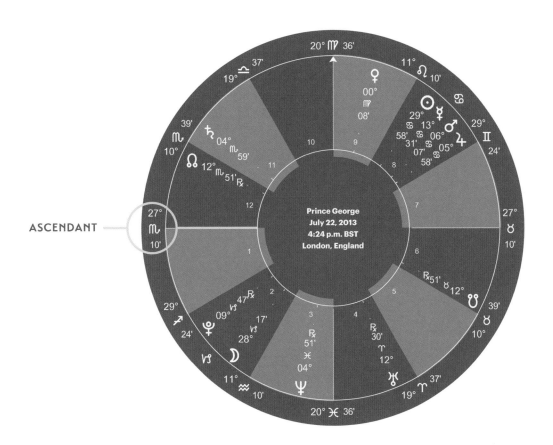

ASCENDANT

THE RULING PLANETS

Every sign has a planetary ruler that colors the sign's expression. This matters whether you're looking at your child's sun, moon, or Mercury sign, or any other placement. For instance, say your little one's Mars (representing their energy and how they take action and assert themselves) is in cardinal air sign Libra. Libra is ruled by Venus, the planet of beauty. They are inclined to act in a social, relationship-oriented (aka Venusian) way.

A quick cheat sheet on each sign's ruling planet:

Aries: Mars

Taurus: Venus

Gemini: Mercury

Cancer: The moon

Leo: The sun

Virgo: Mercury

Libra: Venus

Scorpio: Mars and Pluto

Sagittarius: Jupiter

Capricorn: Saturn

Aquarius: Uranus

Pisces: Neptune

THE ELEMENTS

The twelve zodiac signs are categorized into four elements—fire, earth, air, and water—each of which has its own unique characteristics.

 FIRE

(Aries, Leo, Sagittarius)
Dynamic, action-oriented, adventurous, and driven

 EARTH

(Taurus, Virgo, Capricorn)
Pragmatic, grounded, rational, and analytical

 AIR

(Gemini, Libra, Aquarius)
Social, cerebral, information-seeking, and communicative

 WATER

(Cancer, Scorpio, Pisces)
Empathic, sensitive, intuitive, and artistic

MERCURY, VENUS & MARS: THE OTHER PERSONAL PLANETS

Your baby's "big three" (sun, moon, and rising) can serve as a helpful jumping-off point for understanding their core identity (sun), emotional compass (moon), and outward personality (rising sign). Together with Mercury, Venus, and Mars, these round out what's often referred to as the "big six," all puzzle pieces that offer useful intel on what makes your little one tick.

 MERCURY

The planet of communication, transportation, and technology influences their:

- Communication style
- Thought processes
- Approach to learning
- Decision-making
- Information-gathering and sharing

 VENUS

The planet of love, beauty, and values influences their:

- Artistic self-expression
- Perception of beauty
- Relationship to money
- Experience of pleasure and contentedness
- Way of expressing affection

 MARS

The planet of energy influences their:

- Action style
- Inner drive
- Self-assertion
- Motivation
- Anger and aggression

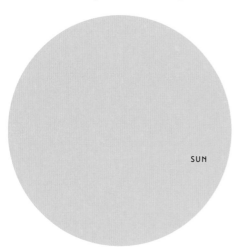

SUN

MERCURY

VENUS

MOON

EARTH

MARS

THE QUALITIES

Understanding the quality of your child's astrological placements can shed light on their innate temperament and approach to tasks and challenges. The three qualities are cardinal, fixed, and mutable. Each has its own distinct powers, and under each element (fire, earth, air, water), there is one sign of each quality (also referred to as modality or triplicity).

 CARDINAL

(Aries, Capricorn, Libra, Cancer)

Key strengths: Taking the initiative, thinking in a big-picture way, leading the charge

Main weakness: Follow-through

 FIXED

(Leo, Taurus, Aquarius, Scorpio)

Key strengths: Committing to a game plan and seeing it through; being resolute, persistent, and consistent

Main weakness: Obstinance

 MUTABLE

(Sagittarius, Virgo, Gemini, Pisces)

Key strengths: Being open-minded and flexible, enjoying experimentation, gathering information

Main weakness: Indecisiveness

HOW THE SEASONS FACTOR IN

A sign's quality correlates with where it falls within the four seasons. Cardinal signs, eager go-getters, kick off each season. The fixed signs land in the middle, their resolute nature embodying the tone of a season. Mutable signs wrap up each season, their flexibility helping to prepare for transition. Note: In the Southern Hemisphere, the seasons are reversed, so the spring signs are fall signs there, and winter signs are summer signs.

SPRING	SUMMER	FALL	WINTER
Aries (cardinal)	Cancer (cardinal)	Libra (cardinal)	Capricorn (cardinal)
Taurus (fixed)	Leo (fixed)	Scorpio (fixed)	Aquarius (fixed)
Gemini (mutable)	Virgo (mutable)	Sagittarius (mutable)	Pisces (mutable)

THE ASPECTS

Once you know your baby's main placements, you can look at how they relate to one another. These are referred to as planetary aspects. How their moon sign interacts with their sun sign or how their Venus sign and their rising sign "talk to each other" in their chart can present you with a new layer of insight into their distinctive personality and perspective.

When reading a natal chart, the strongest, most notable relationships between placements fall under five major aspects.

 ## Conjunction

This means two placements are the same. Say your baby's sun and moon are both in the same sign; they're conjunct each other, indicating that their sense of purpose and their emotions are in sync, which can strengthen self-assuredness.

 ## Trine

When placements are 120 degrees apart, they fall under the same element, leading to a natural harmony. If your baby's moon is trine their Venus, the way they want to be nurtured matches how they show affection.

 ## Square

Placements that are 90 degrees apart indicate friction but also present opportunities to learn, be challenged, and act. Perhaps your baby's moon is square their Mercury. They might need a little extra support around putting their emotions into words.

 ## Sextile

Placements that are 60 degrees apart make for an easygoing vibe. Take a little one whose moon is sextile their rising sign: It's effortless for them to identify and express how they're feeling.

 ## Opposition

Placements that are 180 degrees apart indicate a spot where one detail of your child's chart is at odds with another, but again, like the square, an opposition offers a chance for growth. If your baby's sun sign is opposite their moon sign, they'll be especially drawn to understanding both sides of an argument or all their options before making a decision.

THE HOUSES

Every birth chart is split into twelve pie slices called houses. Houses are a way to map the sky and show where the sun, the moon, and the planets were when your baby took their first breath. Imagine your little one in the center of the chart. The points and planets and symbols above them (in houses seven through twelve) represent the celestial bodies that could be seen in the sky when they were born. Everything at the bottom (houses one through six) is what wasn't quite visible from your vantage point on Earth but which could be seen by someone in the opposite hemisphere. Each house oversees a particular area of life.

Each house is also associated with one of the twelve signs, which further colors its expression and how we interpret planetary placements in the house.

Noting which house your baby's planetary placements fall in offers more detail on where in your baby's life those placements will manifest. For example, if your baby's sun is in the Fifth House, they'll enjoy fun-loving, artistic pursuits. Or if their moon is in the Eleventh House, playdates with several kids will be particularly soothing for them.

BABY'S SUN & MOON HOUSE PLACEMENTS

Regardless of which sign your baby's sun, moon, or any planet was in when they were born (that can be factored in later), you can get solid info on how their personality will shine in different areas of their life simply by identifying which of the twelve houses a particular celestial body inhabited.

 YOUR BABY'S SUN THROUGH THE HOUSES

By looking at your baby's natal chart, you can learn which house the sun was in when they were born. This will tell you that their core identity will be most illuminated when:

Sun in First

They're comfortable in the spotlight or a leadership position and making a bold impression.

Sun in Second

They're emotionally secure and feel valued.

Sun in Third

They're satiating their curiosity through lively, animated social interactions.

Sun in Fourth

They're cozy at home, surrounded by family, and pouring energy into nurturing their security.

Sun in Fifth

They're involved in playful, creative, self-expressive pursuits and soaking up the limelight.

Sun in Sixth

They have a reliable daily routine and feel like they're proving themselves useful to others in small but meaningful ways.

Sun in Seventh

They're establishing and tending to harmony in relationships—particularly partnerships—and working toward goals with a companion.

Sun in Eighth

They're able to fully explore the mysteries of life and connect with others in a deeply emotional way.

Sun in Ninth

They're soaking up knowledge, able to express themselves in a free-spirited and jovial way, and feeling like life's an adventure.

Sun in Tenth

They feel like they have authority and are slowly, steadily working their way toward achieving a big-picture goal for which they'll be recognized.

Sun in Eleventh

Their friendships are thriving, they're able to

express what makes them unique and even quirky, and they're involved in humanitarian causes.

Sun in Twelfth

They're connected with their inner selves and channeling their sensitivity and empathy toward supporting others emotionally.

YOUR BABY'S MOON THROUGH THE HOUSES

Your baby's natal chart shows you the house the moon was in when they were born. This will tell you that they seek the most nurturing and security through:

Moon in First

Having direct, intense emotional interactions with others; they'll lead with their feelings, wearing their heart on their sleeve.

Moon in Second

Collecting material possessions, gifting others, being gifted, and filling up their piggy bank.

Moon in Third

Socializing, communicating, learning, and intellectualizing their feelings.

Moon in Fourth

Nesting, exploring their roots and family traditions, and spending time with loved ones.

Moon in Fifth

Enjoying playful, even theatrical activities, making art, and spending time with friends and family—especially other children.

Moon in Sixth

Following a routine; being helpful and organized.

Moon in Seventh

Spending one-on-one time with you, family, and playmates, enjoying close relationships, and mediating conflicts that may arise.

Moon in Eighth

Feeling exceptionally emotionally connected and intimate with others, and nurturing intuitive, almost psychic bonds.

Moon in Ninth

Soaking up knowledge, adventure, and eye-opening experiences.

Moon in Tenth

Achieving goals, being in the limelight, and being recognized for hard work.

Moon in Eleventh

Celebrating individuality, working as part of a team, and feeling like they're standing up for the greater good.

Moon in Twelfth

Appreciating all things otherworldly and enjoying an abundance of peaceful, meditative moments.

PART 1

The Twelve Signs

W hen you found out that your baby's due date was May 15, you may have thought, *I'm having a Taurus!* and envisioned raising a little one who would be as stubborn as they are down-to-earth. Or when you heard that the child you would be adopting came into the world on August 3, you pictured setting the stage for a spotlight-loving, charismatic Leo. Either way, completely fair! Your baby's sun sign is a powerful, important piece of their astrological puzzle, coloring their core identity, self-image, confidence, and more. But as you'll discover from your child's birth chart, there are many moving parts—or, shall we say, planets—and layers to a person's natal astrology. For example, if you're looking for the best way to soothe your child when they're upset, you'll want to explore their moon sign, which speaks to how they want to be nurtured. Looking for nursery design ideas? Consider baby's Venus sign, as Venus is the planet of beauty. The more you know, the easier it will be to navigate your child's unique astrological map and to understand their distinct behaviors, motivations, and perception of the world around them.

ARIES

SUN SIGN DATES: MARCH 21–APRIL 20

SYMBOL: RAM

ELEMENT: FIRE

QUALITY: CARDINAL

RULER: MARS, THE PLANET OF ACTION

HOUSE: FIRST HOUSE OF SELF

PLANTS: POPPIES, RED ROSES, TIGER LILIES, CAYENNE

GEMS: FIRE AGATE, RED AVENTURINE, AQUAMARINE

Aries is the first sign of the zodiac. Guided by the crimson-hued, go-getter planet Mars, which oversees how we take action and express our energy, Aries little ones are active, direct, competitive, innately athletic, and independent-minded, and derive pleasure from moving through life at lightning speed.

HAPPY ARIES

BABY

A wide-eyed little Ram enjoys being on the go as much as possible. They're thrilled by new experiences, from riding in a jogging stroller to soaking up the sights and sounds at the playground.

Mini Aries are action-oriented to the core. They love participating in high-energy activities like clapping along to a song or making lots of noise with a rattle. They also tend to enjoy physical humor, so slapstick tricks, like pretending to fall, might entertain your infant Ram.

TODDLER

Aries little ones are initiators and go-getters, wired to forge ahead and take on the world through dynamic action. They have a keen sense of self, eagerness, and independence. It's typical for them to grab a favorite toy and assert that it's time to play with it—*stat*! They'll charge around at the park and be enthralled by athletics—playing catch, learning to ride a tricycle, or being a daredevil on the playground. These rambunctious, fiery kids are impulsive and bold, so let them explore their adventurous side. Just remember that they'll still need you to catch them when they tumble.

CRANKY ARIES

BABY

Tiny Rams might be frustrated by activities that feel too slow or limiting. Anything that requires a bit of extra patience—like waiting for you to prepare homemade baby food—could lead to an explosion of fussiness. Because they're apt to speed through just about every moment, you'll notice that they get irritated if a particular exercise (like, say, tummy time) feels like it's taking longer than they'd prefer.

Their restless, energetic, and very active nature might also make winding down for naptime and bedtime a challenge.

TODDLER

From walking to jumping, your Aries toddler wants to do everything fast and furious—and, given their cardinal nature, to take the initiative.

They might be especially good candidates for the patience-stretching technique developed by Harvey Karp, MD, in which you ask them to wait five, ten, and increasingly more seconds until they receive that snack or iPad. In turn, your Ram is rewarded for being patient, and they learn that you mean what you say.

And because your little Aries wants to conquer any challenge presented to them, feeling like they did anything less than that—or, gasp, lost—could spur devastation. (See page 109 for more on communicating with your little Aries.)

ARIES MUST-HAVES

- Toys that let them jump, like a bouncy chair or trampoline
- Any kind of game in which a player is declared the winner
- Raucous music, like your favorite classic rock tunes (try "We Will Rock You" by Queen, "Hit Me with Your Best Shot" by Pat Benatar, or "I Love Rock 'n' Roll" by Joan Jett), that would serve as the perfect backdrop for rowdy play
- Stories about daring adventures or athletic feats

FAMOUS ARIES SUN KIDS	ARIES SUN CELEBRITIES
Jessica Biel and Justin Timberlake's son Silas (April 8)	Reese Witherspoon (March 22)
Khloé Kardashian and Tristan Thompson's daughter, True (April 12)	Lady Gaga (March 28)
Hoda Kotb and Joel Schiffman's daughter Hope (April 12)	David Oyelowo (April 1)
John Legend and Chrissy Teigen's daughter, Luna (April 14)	Chance the Rapper (April 16)
Dwayne "The Rock" Johnson and Lauren Hashian's daughter Tiana (April 17)	Jennifer Garner (April 17)

THE STORY BEHIND THE STARS: ARIES, THE RAM

Aries—and its symbol, the Ram—comes from the Greek myth of the golden ram. Aries, a golden ram with wings, rescued a prince named Phrixus. Zeus, the king of the gods, embedded the ram's image into a constellation to honor its heroism.

The symbol is also associated with:

- Persistence
- The vibrant energy of springtime
- Courage
- Impulsivity

PREPARING FOR A MINI RAM

ARIES-INSPIRED BABY NAMES

Short and/or spirited names that nod to bravery, speediness, and strength:

Aiden: **Little fire**

Archie: **Brave**

Ares: **The ancient Greek god of courage**

Athena: **The ancient Greek goddess of courage**

Audrey: **Noble strength**

Flyta: **Fast**

Javin: **Swift**

Poppy: **Red flower**

Valentina: **Strength, health**

THE ARIES BABY SHOWER

Try these details to celebrate the vibe of your tiny Ram:

- Fiery flowers like roses, marigolds, and celosia

- Competitive games, such as bowling with baby bottles for pins or relay racing with baby dolls in strollers

- Lots of red to celebrate your Mars-ruled baby

- Decor that touts the logo and colors of your favorite sports team

- Spicy foods like buffalo wings or anything that tastes better with a dash of Cholula

NURSERY DESIGN IDEAS

- Bright, bold, primary colors—especially red (like Mars)

- Sports details—a lamp shaped like a baseball mitt or a mural that incorporates the logos of your family's favorite sports teams

- Wall art featuring mountainous landscapes like the ones rams inhabit

BEYOND BABY'S SUN SIGN: OTHER ARIES PLACEMENTS

If one or a few of your baby's "big six" are in the sign of the Ram (for example, they have an Aries sun and Mercury in Aries—or even a Virgo sun and Mars in Aries), here's what you can expect.

Aries Rising: Pint-size Ram risings will first act—in a fast-paced, enthusiastic way—and think later. They appear incredibly self-sufficient, even as little ones.

Moon in Aries: Little ones whose moon is in the sign of the Ram could lose their cool quickly but will be on to the next thing before you've even had a chance to figure out how to soothe them. Connecting through high-energy activity, games, and playtime is comforting for these fiery kids.

Mercury in Aries: Expect a passionate but direct, to-the-point thought process and communication style.

Venus in Aries: They're straightforward, incredibly playful, and action-oriented in their relationship with you as well as other loved ones and friends.

Mars in Aries: Apt to act speedily and in a fearless manner, they're also prone to bore in a flash.

TAURUS

SUN SIGN DATES: APRIL 21–MAY 20

SYMBOL: BULL

ELEMENT: EARTH

QUALITY: FIXED

RULER: VENUS, THE PLANET OF LOVE

HOUSE: SECOND HOUSE OF SELF-WORTH AND INCOME

PLANTS: LILACS, DAISIES, VIOLETS

GEMS: EMERALD, AVENTURINE, CALCITE

Ruled by Venus, the social planet that oversees love—as well as beauty, art, and values—and symbolized by the Bull, Taurus children are down-to-earth and particularly in tune with all five senses, and tend to be quite deliberate in how they act.

HAPPY TAURUS

BABY

A grounded little Bull is bound to be blissful when they can take their sweet time with just about everything. Tauruses love being held; whether nestled in a swaddle, cuddled up in your arms during a feeding, or getting their first taste of fruit, they'll gaze at you lovingly, soaking in the moment. Your little Taurus is also tactile and will revel in a massage—perhaps with a soothing lavender-scented lotion. You might notice that your little Earth sign is especially content while surrounded by nature (think: babywearing your tiny Bull on a picnic or on a walk through a nature preserve).

TODDLER

Thanks to their Venusian influence, your toddler Bull adores art and music, so being surrounded by both is bound to stimulate their creativity and keep them centered. They'll enjoy listening with you to a playlist of soaring pop love songs (like tracks by Adele, whose sun is in Taurus, or Celine Dion, whose Mars is in Taurus), creating a favorite animal out of paper plates, and getting their hands dirty by playing in nature or helping you tend a garden (which will tap into their earthiness to boot).

And given their fixed nature, your growing Bull is a creature of habit, most content when they know what to expect, whether it's being read the same books before bed or enjoying a consistent lighting scheme in their nursery. This trait goes hand in hand with mini Taurus being a homebody who would prefer to spend the day engaging with the sights, sounds, smells, tastes, and tactile sensations they're accustomed to. They're rarely in a rush as they take in the world around them and are happiest when they're allowed plenty of time and space to move from one activity to the next or warm up to a new experience.

CRANKY TAURUS

BABY

Because your tiny Bull is happiest when life is moving at a slower, steadier pace, being surrounded by frenetic activity (perhaps at a crowded social gathering or in a bustling grocery store) and being off schedule could throw them into a fussy tailspin.

Not fully understanding object permanence can be an especially big deal for a little Taurus, as they're the sign associated with the Second House, which, in addition to involving income and values, oversees material things. If you show them a toy, and then it suddenly disappears, they could be particularly perturbed.

TODDLER

Your pint-size Taurus will likely be very attached to a lovey—this may be in the form of an especially soft, fuzzy, cozy toy or blanket that feels and smells like you and like home. And if it has to stay home or accidentally gets lost, they won't be as quick as some kids to channel their inner Queen Elsa and "let it go." Apply that mentality to just about anything they're accustomed to—a bedtime routine, a regular phone call from the grandparents, a favorite meal—going *poof*! (See page 112 for more on communicating with your little Taurus.)

TAURUS MUST-HAVES

- Opportunities to dig in the dirt
- Art classes
- Books with lots of vibrant illustrations, textures, and prompts that allow them to flex their creative muscle

- Stories about friendship, playing dress-up, or food
- A wide variety of music that's easy for them to sing along with

FAMOUS TAURUS SUN KIDS

Jessica Simpson and Eric Johnson's daughter Maxwell Drew (May 1)

Prince William and Catherine, Duchess of Cambridge's son Prince Louis (April 23) and daughter, Princess Charlotte (May 2)

America Ferrera and Ryan Piers Williams's daughter, Lucia Marisol (May 4)

Amy Schumer and Chris Fischer's son, Gene David (May 5)

Prince Harry and Meghan, Duchess of Sussex's son, Archie (May 6)

TAURUS SUN CELEBRITIES

Queen Elizabeth II (April 21)

Channing Tatum (April 26)

Lizzo (April 27)

Dwayne "The Rock" Johnson (May 2)

Rosario Dawson (May 9)

THE STORY BEHIND THE STARS: TAURUS, THE BULL

Taurus—and its symbol, the Bull—comes from the Greek myth of Princess Europa, who was wooed by the king of the gods, Zeus, after he appeared to her as a white bull with glowing horns at the Phoenician waterside.

The Bull is also associated with:

- Perseverance
- A calm disposition, mirroring that of a bull that's happily grazing
- Strength
- Power

PREPARING FOR A LITTLE BULL

TAURUS-INSPIRED BABY NAMES

Monikers that pay tribute to our planet, beauty, art, and being steadfast:

Adam: From *adama*, the Hebrew word for earth

Chloe: Blooming

Daisy: A flower ruled by Venus

Dimitri: Earth lover

Dion: Child of heaven and Earth

Ekon: Strong

Isa: Strong-willed

Liam: Resolute protector

Vale: Valley by the stream

THE TAURUS BABY SHOWER

Think about bringing these Taurean elements into your fete:

- Daisies everywhere—it's the flower of Venus

- Lots of emerald green, a reference to one of the sign's gems and the verdant Earth

- A spa where guests can be pampered

- Music-driven games: e.g., play songs in which the word "baby" appears in the lyrics—whoever guesses the title of the track first wins

- Especially decadent treats (like mini crème brûlées or chocolate soufflés) befit for a Venus-ruled affair

NURSERY DESIGN IDEAS

- Music-inspired features like a cool retro turntable or mobile of instruments

- Air-purifying plants like a bird's-nest fern or Calathea beauty star

- Hand-painted bulls or bucolic scenes in soothing earth tones

BEYOND BABY'S SUN SIGN:
OTHER TAURUS PLACEMENTS

If one or a few of your baby's "big six" are in the sign of the Bull (for example, they have a Taurus sun as well as Mercury in Taurus—or even a Sagittarius sun and Mars in Taurus), here's what you can expect.

Taurus Rising: With their rising in the sign of the Bull, your little one appears steadfast, calm, and determined. They're also slow to act, cautious, and might struggle to go with the flow.

Moon in Taurus: Your baby feels nurtured by predictable practices (like hearing the same lullaby every night) and concrete objects (their favorite blanket or most loved snack). And because they're so in tune with all five senses, they'll find emotional centeredness in cozy textures, relaxing scents, yummy treats, beautiful surroundings, and soft music.

Mercury in Taurus: Your child will take their time to reach any decision, but once they've made up their minds, they're prone to digging their heels in. They're direct and pragmatic.

Venus in Taurus: Your baby was born with Venus in a sign it rules—and is therefore at home, aka "in domicile," meaning they're extra balanced and comfortable when it comes to Venusian activities, such as expressing themselves artistically. They adore connecting with others and are endlessly loyal. The buddy they make on the playground today could be their BFF well into adulthood.

Mars in Taurus: Patient and determined when pursuing their goals, your child has a long fuse when it comes to losing their cool. They'll also shy away from multitasking, as they'd prefer to zero in on one to-do at a time.

GEMINI

SUN SIGN DATES: MAY 21–JUNE 21

SYMBOL: TWINS

ELEMENT: AIR

QUALITY: MUTABLE

RULER: MERCURY, THE PLANET OF COMMUNICATION

HOUSE: THIRD HOUSE OF COMMUNICATION

PLANTS: LILACS, LAVENDER, LILIES OF THE VALLEY

GEMS: AGATE, TIGER'S-EYE

Ruled by Mercury, the messenger planet that oversees communication, transportation, and technology, your Gemini child is a curious, bubbly information-gatherer who loves to be on the go. Symbolized by the Twins, they're innately dualistic, often revealing two sides of most personality traits—such as super social versus reserved or focused versus scattered.

HAPPY GEMINI

BABY

Your Twins baby will be a social butterfly from the start. They're at their most content when they're taking in information, moving and shaking in a bouncy seat or accompanying you on errands, and feeling like part of a buzzy, lively, social environment. Your Gemini baby thrives on being around throngs of people at the farmers market or a family party. A supercommunicator in the making, they'll also be gleeful when they can hear and test out different sounds, be that coos, giggles, or first words.

TODDLER

Because they're so joyful and can flit from appearing sweet and innocent to acting like a capricious trickster, your Gemini toddler is basically the equivalent of a sprite or elf. Ruled by Mercury, they're wide-eyed, playful, and friendly to the max. If they're not talking up a storm, they'll be singing, doing impressions of you and their favorite characters, flaunting an appreciation for creative fashion, or aiming to learn something new from a book, an app, or any other medium they can get their hands on. After all, their goal, as a mini Mercury-ruled person, is to absorb as much information from as many sources as possible.

Given their mutable nature, little Gemini values the ability to perpetually switch gears. Anytime they're given free rein to fly from one playful activity to the next—especially if it involves other people and stimulating sights and sounds—they'll be over the moon.

CRANKY GEMINI

BABY

Because their Mercury rulership has them wired to seek stimuli at every turn, lacking interactive time with you or other loved ones, playmates, or even their favorite mobile or rattle will leave baby Gemini bored and showing signs of frustration and restlessness. The more opportunities they're given to explore and take in new information, the more at peace your Twins-influenced baby will be.

Geminis are known to be particularly adept at using their hands to learn and express themselves, so they could get aggravated if they're curbed from using their little fingers to discover objects around them. Supporting their ability to do this safely can be a boon for their mood—and development.

TODDLER

As an innately adaptable mutable air sign, your little Gemini will want the freedom to change their mind or switch up a game plan on a dime. For that reason, stringent routines and anything they interpret as mundane could set off a tantrum or naughty behavior. They might also get sulky when something—or someone, like a similarly talkative and attention-seeking sibling—stands in the way of their ability to express themselves verbally. The good news: Experimenting with activities that serve as opportunities to investigate and disseminate what they've learned can preempt moodiness. (See page 115 for more on communicating with your little Gemini.)

GEMINI MUST-HAVES

- Playtime with any tech device (e.g., pretending to call or FaceTime relatives)
- Stories or songs about flying (cue the Tom Petty)
- Transportation-inspired toys (airplanes, trucks, buses, cars)

- Playdates with a group of peers
- Interactive books that can be turned into a game
- Word games, like "I spy" or guessing which animal name rhymes with a particular word

THE STORY BEHIND THE STARS: GEMINI, THE TWINS

The story behind Gemini—and its symbol, the Twins—comes from the Greek myth of twin half brothers named Castor and Pollux, who were known as the Dioscuri. King of the gods Zeus honored the twins' relationship with a constellation in their image.

The Twins are also associated with:

- Duality
- Adaptability
- Interaction
- Sharing ideas

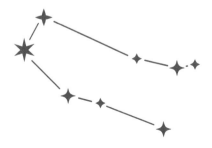

PREPARING FOR A TINY TWIN

GEMINI-INSPIRED BABY NAMES

Whimsical names that nod to being inquisitive, lighthearted, and social:

Alvin: Friend of the elves

Aria: Air; song or melody

Dakota: Friendly

Hugo: Mind

Gil: Happiness

Ilma: Air

Puck: Mischievous

Siofra: Sprite

Zephyr: West wind

THE GEMINI BABY SHOWER

Consider incorporating these Twins-influenced elements into your soiree:

- Brain-teasing games, like trivia, a crossword, a word scramble, or bingo, that center around baby- and parenting-related words (like "swaddle," "nursing," "high chair") as well as Gemini themes (anything to do with transportation, technology, communication)

- Centerpieces that incorporate lilacs and lilies of the valley, both of which are Gemini-ruled blooms and evoke the sign's season: late spring and the dawn of summertime

- A DIY onesie station—Geminis are super style-conscious

- "Twin" tapas—foods that are frequently paired, like grilled cheese and tomato soup or milk and mini cookies

NURSERY DESIGN IDEAS

- Wall art displaying your favorite children's book quotes you hope your Mercury-ruled baby, sure to be a voracious reader, will love as much as you do

- Lavender plants or even lavender-hued walls, as the air sign rules the herb

- Airplanes, birds, fairies, bees, or any other object or being that takes to the air incorporated into mobiles and other details, as your little one will frequently fantasize about flying

- A baby swing with a variety of high-tech bells and whistles, like different songs you can play or motions and directions they can be soothed by

BEYOND BABY'S SUN SIGN: OTHER GEMINI PLACEMENTS

If one or a few of your baby's "big six" are in the sign of the Twins (for example, they have a Gemini sun as well as Venus in Gemini—or even a Pisces sun and Mercury in Gemini), here's what you can expect.

Gemini Rising: Your child comes off as super social, busy, active, playful, and quick-witted. They'll easily attract a wide variety of playmates and take an interest in numerous activities and hobbies.

Moon in Gemini: Your baby's emotional identity is wrapped up with their high mental energy and perpetual need to express what's on their mind. For that reason, talking about feelings brings about a sense of inner peace for these mercurial children. Connecting intellectually—think narrating new discoveries and heartfelt one-on-one moments—will also feel nurturing to them.

Mercury in Gemini: Because your baby was born with Mercury in one of the two signs it rules, they're even more of a "natural" in the themes of this planet: communication and information-gathering. They're

energetic learners who might struggle with focusing on one task at a time if only because they're intensely excited to see, do, and experience everything around them (yes, even more than the average little one!).

Venus in Gemini: They'll rely on words (versus touch or other languages of affection) to express their love, enjoy bonding with family members through lively conversation, and be open to making all different types of playmates, from the kid who's the reigning royal of the playground to the shy one who's always working on their coloring book or a craft.

Mars in Gemini: Your child will want to experiment with a variety of directions before settling on one—and even then, settling isn't their forte. What is: being constantly in motion and switching things up. They'll also appreciate the opportunity to hear you talk through actions—whether that's a bath or a trip to the doctor—well before they ultimately verbalize it themselves.

CANCER

SUN SIGN DATES: JUNE 22–JULY 22

SYMBOL: CRAB

ELEMENT: WATER

QUALITY: CARDINAL

RULER: THE MOON, THE EMOTIONAL COMPASS

HOUSE: FOURTH HOUSE OF HOME LIFE

PLANTS: WATER LILIES, JASMINE, JUNIPER

GEMS: MOONSTONE, PEARL, ROSE QUARTZ

Symbolized by the Crab and born under the influence of the emotional moon, which represents maternal energy in astrology, sensitive and sentimental Cancer babies are especially fond of cuddles, food, and laughter and tend to be especially attached to their mom or a mother figure.

HAPPY CANCER

BABY

The most playful, exploratory water sign, infant Crabs are big on taking baths, splashing in the pool, and going on trips to the beach. They'll also take a keen interest in mealtime, finding joy in trying new flavors and textures at your urging. But while they might be go-getters from the time they're tiny, they're also deeply emotional and sensitive. They'll take quickly to—and adore—being worn in a baby sling or carrier or held close in a skin-to-skin snuggle session and will be especially engaged with you during a feeding. And though sweet coos and I love yous are sure to benefit any little one, warm, fuzzy sounds and actions that reassure your Cancer baby that you're there for them go especially far to helping them feel truly blissed-out.

TODDLER

Because they were born under a big-picture-oriented cardinal sign, Cancer little ones have huge ideas and imaginations. As an artistic water sign, they can't help but daydream and get swept up in the most magical moments of everyday life, from story time to holiday celebrations.

Because they are born nurturers, they might be thrilled by play with baby dolls and animal toys. They'll also shower family pets and younger siblings with lots of love, doting on them and wanting to be involved in or take the reins on all aspects of their care. With a little brother or sister, they might even assume the role of a mini parent, helping with anything from diapering to teaching their sibling how to walk or swim and expressing eagerness to help with grocery shopping and food prep, even cleanup.

CRANKY CANCER

BABY

As an emotional water sign, a Cancer baby might appear moodier and cry more than the average little one, but it's simply because they're ruled by the moon. You might want to track how they're feeling under each moon sign, as they're particularly sensitive to lunar phases. (See Resources, page 347.) They tend to be even more attached to you and crave your presence more than other infants, so moments in which they feel disconnected can spur fussing. Play peekaboo to let them know that even when you go away, you'll be back, or come up with a sweet routine—say, leaving them with a special kiss or funny song when it's time to drop them off with a caregiver.

Even the tiniest Crab will thrive when they feel most secure, and you can provide them with a solid foundation for this by ensuring that they have their favorite lovey, a comfort food they're enamored with, and a tranquil nursery for downtime.

TODDLER

When your little Crab is upset, they're bound to retreat into their shell for self-protection. They might act especially shy, need an extra nap that day, or appear, well, crabby. They're also apt to seek extra comfort from a caregiver in times of distress and during times of transition, such as a move or heading off to day care. Being around or in water can be therapeutic for a little Cancer, so consider prioritizing bath time when they're feeling blue. (See page 118 for more on communicating with your little Cancer.)

CANCER MUST-HAVES

- Lots of bath time and bath toys
- Creative outlets like water coloring or "helping" in the kitchen with pretend food prep
- Being swaddled or worn in a sling
- Stories about family, caregiving, and love
- Music with sweet, heartfelt lyrics they'll want to sing back to you
- A baby doll or a furry dog or cat toy for practicing nurturing on

FAMOUS CANCER SUN KIDS

Stephen and Ayesha Curry's son, Canon (July 2)

Lauren Conrad and William Tell's son Liam (July 5)

Liv Tyler and David Gardner's daughter, Lula Rose (July 8)

Cardi B and Offset's daughter, Kulture (July 10)

Mario Lopez and Courtney Laine Mazza's son Santino (July 7)

CANCER SUN CELEBRITIES

Mindy Kaling (June 24)

Busy Philipps (June 25)

Kevin Hart (July 6)

Tom Hanks (July 9)

Malala Yousafzai (July 12)

THE STORY BEHIND THE STARS: CANCER, THE CRAB

Cancer—and its symbol, the Crab—originates from a Greek myth in which Hera, the queen of the gods, sent a huge crab to battle on her behalf. Legend has it that Hera created a constellation in the image of the crab to honor its sacrifice.

The Crab is also associated with:

- Sensitivity
- Defending and protecting loved ones
- Tenacity
- Family, home, and roots

PREPARING FOR A TEENSY CRAB

CANCER-INSPIRED BABY NAMES

Monikers that channel the romanticism of the moon and the ocean:

Bader: Full moon

Chantara: Moon water

Cynthia: Greek moon goddess

Gareth: Gentle

Kai: Sea

Luna: Moon

Morgan: Sea-born

Rita: Pearl

Zira: Moonlight

THE CANCER BABY SHOWER

Think about adding these Crab-centric ideas to your party plan:

- A waterside venue, whether it's a local beach, lake, or pond

- Moon pies, crescent moon–shaped sandwiches, balloons and centerpieces crafted to look like the moon and shimmery stars

- "Ocean water" mocktails made with a blue punch

- A playlist of classic, sentimental love songs (like "Unforgettable" by Nat King Cole or "La Vie en Rose" by Édith Piaf)

- A menu packed with time-honored treats like a favorite childhood cookie recipe, go-to pizza order, or type of pie, befitting of a sentimental, foodie Cancer's appetite.

NURSERY DESIGN IDEAS

- Walls and other details sporting baby crabs and seaside elements like ocean waves, sandcastles, sailboats, beach umbrellas

- Lamps or art decorated with pearls or moonstones (gems associated with Cancer) or rose quartz, which can help protect your sensitive Crab's heart

- Lunar elements, like art of the moon phases or glowing, shimmering stars

BEYOND BABY'S SUN SIGN: OTHER CANCER PLACEMENTS

If one or a few of your baby's "big six" are in the sign of the Crab (for example, they have a Cancer sun as well as moon in Cancer—or even a Taurus sun and Cancer rising), here's what you can expect.

Cancer Rising: Your baby or toddler appears tenderhearted, self-protective, and sensitive to their surroundings. They're quick to show how much they care for people and creatures—from a bird in the backyard they'll want to put out a feeder for to their newborn sibling.

Moon in Cancer: Because your baby was born with the moon in the sign it rules, the themes of this luminary— emotions and intuition—come organically to them. They are extra sentimental and imaginative, are easily caught up in their feelings, and desire lots of nurturing from their parents and caregivers. They'll be especially attached to you and their home life and find a lot of comfort in spending quality time with the people and things they love.

Mercury in Cancer: Your little one is thoughtful, sentimental, reflective, often holding tight to events, conversations, and details from the past. They can easily pick up on the mood of any interaction and are naturally funny in a goofy, endearing way.

Venus in Cancer: Your child is wired to be incredibly nurturing and sweet when expressing how they feel. They'll get super snuggly with you and be loving with younger children or pets. Feeling connected and secure only serves to boost these awe-inspiring traits.

Mars in Cancer: Your baby will likely express the desire to protect you and everything they cherish. They'll take action in a big-picture way, and their ability to move forward will be especially colored by their mood.

LEO

SUN SIGN DATES: JULY 23–AUGUST 22

SYMBOL: LION

ELEMENT: FIRE

QUALITY: FIXED

RULER: SUN, THE LUMINARY OF SELF

HOUSE: FIFTH HOUSE OF SELF-EXPRESSION

PLANTS: SUNFLOWERS, MARIGOLDS, CHAMOMILE

GEMS: RUBY, PYRITE, CITRINE

Ruled by the brilliant, shimmering sun, which oversees core identity and confidence, and symbolized by the Lion, Leo little ones are self-aware, assertive, bighearted, and fun-loving and thrive on being the center of attention.

HAPPY LEO

BABY

As a dynamic fire sign, your Leo is immediately outgoing, confident from the time they're teeny, and people can't help but respond to this royal of the jungle's magnetism. You might notice early on that your Lion infant can easily captivate onlookers with an innate charisma. Your child will be a major fan of working it—and will very clearly revel in attention from you, other family members, and strangers alike.

They'll also be gleeful when soaking up the rays of their ruler, the sun—safely, with plenty of SPF, of course—or exploring a scene filled with potential admirers, whether that's the nearest beach or a neighborhood block party. Independent-minded and active, they're most content when they're given plenty of space to investigate their surroundings on their own, but they're also total lovebugs who'll appear to light up even more than usual when they're in your arms.

TODDLER

Born to lead, your growing Lion will be elated by any opportunity to run the show. On a playdate, you could find that your little Leo takes to directing their peers to participate in a game they've chosen—or dreamed up themselves. And chances are, those games will be impressively imaginative, as Leo rules the Fifth House of Self-Expression.

Your Leo kid will also be blissed-out whenever drama is called for. If you tell them you're taking a video for social media or want to cast them in a play with their friends, they'll adore stepping into the spotlight, intent on earning a round of applause.

And thanks to their fixed nature, you'll notice that when your little Lion finds something they love—a show, a movie, an outfit—they'll love it with all their might. They'll be especially pleased when you support and even join in on their infatuation.

CRANKY LEO

BABY

When lions aren't ruling their terrain, they can often be found enjoying a snooze in the sun. That penchant for plenty of z's will translate to your tiny Leo, who could be noticeably more aggravated and tearful than the average child when their sleep schedule is off or they're overdue for a nap. And being wired to act—and then follow through on that action at any cost—they could get irked if their attempts to get into, well, just about everything are curbed.

TODDLER

As a fixed sign, a little Lion can find it tough to switch gears from one activity to the next. They might also need a little extra time to embrace a transition like welcoming a younger sibling or moving from a crib into a big-kid bed.

And as a leadership-oriented fire sign, Leo toddlers are even more prone to the typical bossiness that strikes when kids are two and three. When you tell them they're not in charge, you might be subjected to a whole lot of roaring. And don't forget that because they thrive on attention, feeling ignored could provoke frustration and upset. (See page 121 for more on communicating with your little Leo.)

LEO MUST-HAVES

- Plenty of praise and opportunities to pose for the camera
- Props and costumes for theatrical playtime
- Stories about being a star, loving yourself, leadership
- Toys that tap into their interest in expressing themselves, like a sing-along microphone
- Music that's high-energy and fun to make up silly dances to

THE STORY BEHIND THE STARS: LEO, THE LION

The constellation of Leo is said to honor a brave, fearless Nemean lion in Greek mythology that fought Heracles, the son of the king of the gods, Zeus.

The Lion symbolizes:

- Sovereignty
- Courage
- Nobility
- Magnanimity

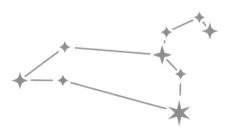

PREPARING FOR A PINT-SIZE LION

LEO-INSPIRED BABY NAMES

Bright, upbeat monikers inspired by warm, radiant sunshine and the most regal feline around:

Apollo: Greek and Roman god of sunlight, prophecy, music, and poetry

Ari: Lion

Aurora: Dawn

Helen: Sunray or shining light

Kiran: Sunbeam

Lev: Heart, lion

Lionel: Young lion

Sol: Sun

Zariel: Lion princess

THE LEO BABY SHOWER

Consider weaving these Leo-esque elements into your summery celebration:

- A dance competition set to a playlist of your favorite '80s or '90s throwback hits

- Karaoke

- Lots of luxurious pampering, like a nail bar

- Citrusy drinks (think mocktail mimosas or margaritas) and spicy foods (tacos)

- Capturing photos and videos of the party that your tiny rising star will be fired up to watch someday

NURSERY DESIGN IDEAS

- Lots of natural sunshine and other glowing, bright elements like twinkle lights

- Summertime icons (popsicles, sunglasses, beach umbrellas) painted on the walls or incorporated into details like blankets and lamps

- Shimmery gold (or yellow or orange) accents to incorporate Leo's ruling colors

- A jungle or *Lion King* theme with baby cubs—or Simba and Nala—as the stars of the show

BEYOND BABY'S SUN SIGN: OTHER LEO PLACEMENTS

If one or a few of your baby's "big six" are in the sign of the Lion (for example, they have a Leo sun as well as Mercury in Leo—or even an Aquarius sun and Mars in Leo), here's what you can expect.

Leo Rising: With their rising sign in outgoing, sunny Leo, your little one will face the world with an undeniable self-awareness, confidence, and charisma. You could be wondering if you're raising the next Selena Gomez or Nick Jonas (both Leo risings!), and hey, you might very well be.

Moon in Leo: Being born with their emotional and intuitive compass in the proud, boisterous sign of the sun means your little one will be exceptionally demonstrative and confident when it comes to expressing how they're feeling, and they'll appreciate being nurtured in a playful, exuberant way (think: having an impromptu dance party in the kitchen while you wear them close in a sling or singing along with them to their favorite song in the car).

Mercury in Leo: This cub thinks in a bold, outspoken way. They'll easily claim the spotlight—even if just among friends and family with the charming, engaging way they express themselves.

Venus in Leo: Your child expresses love and creative impulses in a warm, effusive, even theatrical way. Hearing words of affirmation reminding them how smart, kind, and loved they are will have them positively radiating from the inside out.

Mars in Leo: Thanks to the planet of action's placement in the fixed fire sign, these little ones are action-oriented, and once they've trained their eye on an objective, will rarely let an obstacle curb their success.

VIRGO

SUN SIGN DATES: AUGUST 23–SEPTEMBER 22

SYMBOL: MAIDEN

ELEMENT: EARTH

QUALITY: MUTABLE

RULER: MERCURY, THE PLANET OF COMMUNICATION

HOUSE: SIXTH HOUSE OF WELLNESS

PLANTS: NARCISSUS, HONEYSUCKLE, LICORICE

GEMS: SAPPHIRE, LAPIS LAZULI, BLUE TOURMALINE

Symbolized by a harvesting Maiden and ruled by buzzy, curious Mercury, which fuels our ability to gather information and pinpoint details, Virgo kids are cerebral, innately helpful, whip-smart critical thinkers with busy minds, an eye for detail, a preference for tidiness and organization, and sensitive hearts.

HAPPY VIRGO

BABY

Mercury's influence on this earth sign means that even when your Virgo child is tiny, their mind is likely going a mile a minute. Just like their symbol, the Maiden, usually depicted as a woman holding the wheat she's harvested, mini Virgos search far and wide to gather as much information as possible, often in an effort to help others. You'll notice that they're tuning in to even the slightest details.

Thanks to their mutable nature, not only are they innately flexible but also eager to please. You might find that your Virgo is up for going with the flow more than other kids.

TODDLER

As the sign associated with the Sixth House, which oversees routine and the habits of everyday life, your little Maiden will be thrilled with any opportunity to help you, whether that's with laundry, food prep, or a younger sibling. Pitching in—and putting their organizational skills to work—is how Virgo children show they care, and being recognized for those efforts will have your growing Maiden gleaming with pride.

And with messenger Mercury as their guide, your little Virgo is as excited by story time as some kids are by a trip to the toy store. These supercommunicators generally ask to be read to—and read themselves—voraciously, broach thoughtful conversations, and ask lots of questions from an early age.

CRANKY VIRGO

BABY

Given the Maiden's attention to detail, your tiny Virgo is acutely aware of the most minute aspects of life that could go right over your head, whether that's a certain type of fabric they're not the biggest fans of wearing or a particular feeding position. In other words, a specific detail may seem inconsequential in the grand scheme of things, but if it feels off as far as your tiny Virgo is concerned, they could get fussy, aggravated, or tearful.

TODDLER

Although the plus side of a mutable child is their ability to adapt, they can also struggle to make up their minds.

And your Maiden toddler instinctively wants to soak up all the information available before committing to a plan. Being pressured to act before they've had a chance to process all the details may spur a tantrum.

And being so analytical and cerebral goes hand in hand with being worrisome. Little Virgos might think so much that they end up concocting stressful scenarios for themselves so they'll often need a bit of reassurance and coaxing to stay present as much as possible. They're perfect candidates for kid-friendly breathing exercises or yoga! (See page 124 for more on communicating with your little Virgo.)

VIRGO MUST-HAVES

- A bookshelf brimming with stories about Mercury-ruled transportation (from trains to cars to yellow submarines) and technology, as well as Virgoan acts of kindness and service-oriented characters
- A notebook, pencils, or apps (like the handwriting game iWriteWords) that will foster their communication skills
- Organization (such as a toy storage system) that supports their need to maintain order and curb clutter
- Gardening-, grocery store–, or cleaning-themed toys that play into Virgo's love of nature and daily routine

FAMOUS VIRGO SUN KIDS

Katy Perry and Orlando Bloom's daughter Daisy Dove (August 26)

Lucy Liu's son, Rockwell Lloyd (August 27)

Chance the Rapper and Kirsten Corley's daughters, Marli Grace (August 29) and Kensli (September 16)

Michael Phelps and Nicole Johnson Phelps's son Maverick (September 9)

Adam Levine and Behati Prinsloo's daughter Dusty Rose (September 21)

VIRGO SUN CELEBRITIES

Ava DuVernay (August 24)

Melissa McCarthy (August 26)

Beyoncé (September 4)

Idris Elba (September 6)

Prince Harry (September 15)

THE STORY BEHIND THE STARS: VIRGO, THE MAIDEN

The Greek goddess of innocence, purity, and precision, Astraea, dwelled with humans during the Golden Age of Greek mythology, but when the following era, marked by lawlessness, dawned, she became the last of the deities to leave Earth. King of the gods Zeus honored her with the Virgo constellation, which takes the form of a Maiden holding an ear of wheat.

The Maiden symbolizes:

- Innocence
- Inner beauty
- Self-sufficiency
- Resourcefulness

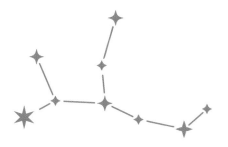

PREPARING FOR A MINI MAIDEN

VIRGO-INSPIRED BABY NAMES

Monikers that nod to high mental energy as well as being of service and in tune with Mother Nature:

Akira: **Bright, intelligent**

Avani: **The good earth**

Cody: **Helpful**

Elisabelle: **Helpful**

Evangeline: **Bearer of good news**

Hugh: **Mind, intellect**

Minnie: **The mind**

Kaj: **Earth**

Sophia: **Wisdom**

THE VIRGO BABY SHOWER

Try bringing these Virgoan details into your pre-baby festivities:

- A botanical mocktail bar where you and your guests can make your own drinks with fresh, herbal elements like lavender, chamomile, and mint

- Bingo or trivia games with a literary twist, featuring answers that are details from your favorite books

- A guest book or another way for guests to write heartfelt notes to the baby for them to read (or have read to them) down the road

- Nourishing bites made from fresh produce— perhaps from a local farmers market

NURSERY DESIGN IDEAS

- A windowsill herb garden, which can turn into an educational opportunity for your earth sign toddler

- A harvest theme incorporated into prints and wall art

- Art displaying favorite quotes or excerpts from classic literature

- Lots of drawers and shelves that make it easy to corral clutter

BEYOND BABY'S SUN SIGN:
OTHER VIRGO PLACEMENTS

If one or a few of your baby's "big six" are in the sign of the Maiden (for example, they have a Virgo sun as well as Mercury in Virgo—or even an Aries sun and Virgo rising), here's what you can expect.

Virgo Rising: These little ones come off as grounded, talkative, and seeking any chance to support others and solve problems with their communication skills.

Moon in Virgo: With their emotional compass in the sign of the Maiden, your child can find it tough to separate their head from their heart. Hyperaware of even the most minor details, they're sensitive and thoughtful. And they'll feel most cared for and seen by receiving recognition and praise for being helpful.

Mercury in Virgo: With the planet of information-gathering in a Mercury-ruled sign, your child finds that expressing themselves—through

speech and writing—is something that comes to them naturally.

Venus in Virgo: Having the planet of love in thoughtful earth sign Virgo can translate to being exceptionally aware of even the slightest details— especially those that matter the most to you or another loved one. If you've professed your love for clementines or sunflowers, your incredibly thoughtful Venus in Virgo tot will present you with one out of the blue or make you an "I love you" card just because. They will also strive to be helpful—pitching in on age-appropriate chores or simply doing their best to be well-behaved—to show you they care.

Mars in Virgo: Born with the planet of action in the sign of the pragmatic Maiden, your child can easily multitask and will generally want to understand how the actions they're taking prove useful to themselves and others.

LIBRA

SUN SIGN DATES: SEPTEMBER 23–OCTOBER 22

SYMBOL: THE SCALES

ELEMENT: AIR

QUALITY: CARDINAL

RULER: VENUS, THE PLANET OF LOVE

HOUSE: SEVENTH HOUSE OF PARTNERSHIP

PLANTS: ROSE, GARDENIA, PENNYROYAL

GEMS: AMETRINE, OPAL, KUNZITE

Symbolized by the Scales of Justice and ruled by Venus, the planet that oversees relationships, beauty, and values, Libra children are social, balance-seeking, peace-loving, and artistic.

HAPPY LIBRA

BABY

Venus's effect on this air sign means your little Libra enjoys being around people and feeling like they're a part of an experience that's buzzy and interactive. They'll be particularly alert and engaged at gatherings, like a neighborhood barbecue or family dinner. And symbolized by the Scales, they're born sensitive to both harmony and conflict. They'll light up when they feel surrounded by love, peacefulness, and beauty, which is helped by extra time with you or activities that foster their artistic impulses.

TODDLER

As the sign related to the Seventh House of Partnership—which revolves around one-on-one bonds—your Scales kid will naturally join forces with loved ones and friends. They might make their first best friend on their initial day of preschool or request special time with just you, your partner, a sibling, or an imaginary friend.

Appreciative of music, dance, and any form of creative self-expression, your little Libra may find a great deal of pleasure in choreographing a dance routine to their favorite songs, playing dress-up, singing, or coloring to their heart's content. And if they're doing any of these things along with you, they'll be even more elated.

CRANKY LIBRA

BABY

Wired to seek balance at every turn—they are symbolized by the Scales, after all—your tiny Libra could get emotional when they sense any kind of discord, even if that's just a raised voice or a car alarm going off nearby. But, on the flip side, while they do love peace and calm, they aren't big fans of *too much* quiet time, as social energy is practically their life force.

TODDLER

Born under the harmony-seeking Scales, your Libra little one will avoid conflict at all costs. But when it comes to their own needs, they can get irritated and passive-aggressive if things don't go their way. For example, if a playmate takes their favorite toy, your Libra might fight back tears to avoid outward headbutting but be resentful and grouchy.

As a social, free-spirited air sign, they tend to crave as much time with friends as possible. Saying it's time to go home from a playdate or being unable to go to the playground could fuel a lot of big feelings for your growing Libra. (See page 127 for more on communicating with your little Libra.)

LIBRA MUST-HAVES

- Soothing music (like classical or lullaby versions of folk songs) played at a low volume
- Lots of playdates
- An array of art supplies from watercolors to crayons and colored pencils, blank notepads, and construction paper
- A grooming kit—perhaps featuring a comb/brush and mirror—because thanks to their ruler, beauty-loving Venus, your little Libra is especially driven to develop their personal style

FAMOUS LIBRA SUN KIDS

Shenae Grimes-Beech and Josh Beech's daughter, Bowie Scarlett (September 27)

Tyrese Gibson and Samantha Lee Gibson's daughter, Soraya (October 1)

Kate Hudson and Danny Fujikawa's daughter, Rani Rose (October 2)

Jason Biggs and Jenny Mollen's son Lazlo (October 2)

Amber Rose and Alexander Edwards's son, Slash Electric Alexander (October 10)

LIBRA SUN CELEBRITIES

Donald Glover (September 25)

Serena Williams (September 26)

Hilary Duff (September 28)

Cardi B (October 11)

John Mayer (October 16)

THE STORY BEHIND THE STARS: LIBRA, THE SCALES

In Greek mythology, the goddess of justice was Themis, the mother of Astraea (aka the goddess who became the Virgo constellation). Themis is generally depicted as a blindfolded woman who holds a scale. In turn, her constellation represents weighing scales.

The Scales symbolize:

- Balance
- Justice
- Harmony
- Equilibrium

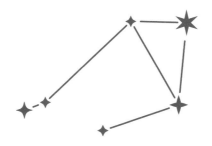

PREPARING FOR A SCALES BABY

LIBRA-INSPIRED BABY NAMES

Airy, graceful names suited to a little one who will pursue peace, harmony, and connection:

Alana: Harmony

Axel: Father of peace

Elden: Noble friend

Irvin: Handsome

Levi: Joined in harmony

Olivia: Olive tree, which symbolizes peace

Paloma: Dove

Solomon: Peace

Tula: Tranquil

THE LIBRA BABY SHOWER

Try incorporating these Scales-inspired elements into your celebration:

- Plus ones for guests to bring along their significant other, given Libra's ruling house

- Games that involve pairing off—like a Baby Shark game in which guests team up and are given a cup of gummy sharks. One tosses the candy to the other, attempting to land it in their partner's mouth. Then, the catcher and thrower switch roles. The couple who catches the most overall wins.

- An artistic activity, such as designing your own cookie

- A beauty bar for guests to create their own body product (like hand cream)

- Romantic bites that utilize flower essences, like cupcakes with rose-infused buttercream

NURSERY DESIGN IDEAS

- Serene colors like lavender or baby blue

- Floral or lush botanical—perhaps specifically their ruling flower, rose—blankets and art

- Warm, soothing lighting (for example, a lamp with a pretty pearl or cloud design)

- Romantic details like lace curtains or a fluffy rug

BEYOND BABY'S SUN SIGN:
OTHER LIBRA PLACEMENTS

If one or a few of your baby's "big six" are in the sign of the Scales (for example, they have a Libra sun as well as Mercury in Libra—or even a Gemini sun and Venus in Libra), here's what you can expect.

Libra Rising: Your Libra rising kid will come off as gentle, relaxed, stylish, and interested in keeping everything around them aesthetically appealing and harmonious.

Moon in Libra: Kids who have their natal moon in the sign of the Scales gravitate to one-on-one bonding time with loved ones. Feeling like one half of a pair, whether with you, a sibling, or a best buddy, gives them a sense of security.

Mercury in Libra: When the messenger planet falls in the sign of the Scales in a little one's chart, you can expect their communication style to be diplomatic above all else. If they're feeling sad or angry, they might beat around the bush or downplay what they're experiencing to keep the peace.

Venus in Libra: A child who has the planet of love in Libra—one of two signs it rules and therefore is "at home" in—will show affection in classic ways, like picking and bringing you a bouquet of daisies from the backyard or drawing a picture of the two of you together.

Mars in Libra: Born with the planet of aggression in balance-seeking Libra, your child will channel their passion into standing up for what they see as right. Justice and equality are key for these little ones.

SCORPIO

SUN SIGN DATES: OCTOBER 23–NOVEMBER 21

SYMBOL: SCORPION

ELEMENT: WATER

QUALITY: FIXED

RULER: PLUTO, THE PLANET OF POWER, AND MARS, THE PLANET OF ACTION

HOUSE: EIGHTH HOUSE OF CLOSE BONDS

PLANTS: GERANIUM, RHODODENDRON, ALOE VERA

GEMS: LABRADORITE, CLEAR QUARTZ, BLOODRED CARNELIAN

Co-ruled by powerful Pluto and go-getter Mars and symbolized by the Scorpion, Scorpio little ones are emotionally intelligent, intuitive, resolute, even a bit mysterious (which only adds to their innate charisma), family-oriented, fearless, and in tune with the mystical side of life.

HAPPY SCORPIO

BABY

While most children are curious, you'll find that your Scorpio child is intensely engaged in various layers of the world around them. Endlessly perceptive, they'll be captivated when they're playing with a toy or book that puts investigation at the heart of the activity (think: a board book that has flaps under which your little Scorpion can discover illustrations or elements).

And for the fixed water sign, having access to certain security-bolstering elements—from a favorite blanket to reliable, designated snuggle time with you—at *all times* will be reassuring and mood-boosting.

TODDLER

While they try to figure the world out in their head, incredibly observant Scorpios tend to be rather quiet—or at least particular about their self-expression. That said, they'll be most content when they're not feeling nudged to open up about what they're experiencing or seeing. Don't worry; they'll do it in their own time.

And influenced by action-oriented Mars and commanding Pluto, a magnetic little Scorp will seek out opportunities to take charge; they'll beam at the chance to set the dinner table, choose the weekend activity, or be deemed your chief assistant in looking after a baby sibling.

CRANKY SCORPIO

BABY

From a young age, even when they're completely silent, your emotionally intelligent Scorpio baby, a deeply feeling water sign, is tuned in to the undercurrent or subtext of a particular situation playing out before their eyes. If they sense that something is off, tense, or stressful, they could respond with a monsoon of tears—or even physical woes like gas or a fussy tummy.

Fixed signs are not thrilled by change, so your Scorpio baby might react poorly if you attempt to switch up their go-to evening routine or even the type of infant cereal you've been feeding them. Peach or apple won't cut it when they're attached to banana.

TODDLER

Given that their sign rules the Eighth House, which involves complex emotions, your Scorpio tot could be intuitively aware of the less airy and bright aspects of life, like physical or emotional pain, grief, and loss.

One of Scorpio's co-rulers, Pluto, is the planet of power and control—two things your little Scorpion needs to feel like they have. Most toddlers despise the word *no*, but your resolute child, in particular, will be determined to make sure their desires have at least been acknowledged, if not fulfilled. (See page 130 for more on communicating with your little Scorpio.)

SCORPIO MUST-HAVES

- Their go-to security blanket or lovey, best designed in a soothing, rich color like chocolate brown or royal purple
- Sea life–themed puzzles
- Stories that involve mystery and magic, themes they're innately drawn to (they enjoy uncovering secrets and delving into the unknown)
- Bath time activities like tub painting
- A musical instrument (a continuous learning tool and an outlet for expressing intense emotions)

FAMOUS SCORPIO SUN KIDS

Hilary Duff and Matthew Koma's daughter Banks Violet (October 25)

Kevin and Danielle Jonas's daughter Valentina Angelina (October 27)

Mookie Betts and Brianna Hammonds's daughter, Kynlee Ivory (November 6)

Dwyane Wade and Gabrielle Union's daughter, Kaavia James (November 7)

Kevin and Eniko Hart's son, Kenzo Kash (November 21)

SCORPIO SUN CELEBRITIES

Julia Roberts (October 28)

Tracee Ellis Ross (October 29)

Ryan Gosling (November 12)

Travis Barker (November 14)

Adam Driver (November 19)

THE STORY BEHIND THE STARS: SCORPIO, THE SCORPION

The scorpion that became the symbol for Scorpio appears in the Greek myth of Orion, the son of Poseidon, the god of the sea. The creature was honored by Gaia, the goddess of Earth, with a constellation in its image.

The Scorpion symbolizes:

- Power
- A strong will
- Magnetism
- Intuition

PREPARING FOR A LITTLE SCORPION

SCORPIO-INSPIRED BABY NAMES

Mystical, bold names that bring to mind water, shadows, and magic:

Duncan: Dark warrior

Ethan: Strong, firm

Jason: To heal

Jett: Black gemstone

Kali: Goddess of destruction and enlightenment

Maya: Water

Morgan: Sea-born, sea song

Talia: By the water

Rune: Secret

THE SCORPIO BABY SHOWER

Consider adding these Scorpion-esque details to your fete:

- A personalized scavenger hunt (perhaps finding a photo from the parents-to-be's wedding or a onesie in their favorite color)

- Halloween-inspired details, like costumes or tarot card readings

- Big, lush, red (Mars-inspired!) geraniums

- Rich, flavorful comfort foods, like a truffle mac 'n' cheese or flourless chocolate cake

- A DIY virgin Bloody Mary bar with lots of spice options (hot sauce, red pepper, horseradish)

NURSERY DESIGN IDEAS

- Elements inspired by the deep sea and ocean floor like octopuses, coral, whales

- Linens or even walls in striking jewel tones like emerald green or aubergine

- A designated area they can visit to find their inner calm with sensory toys

- Blackout curtains and a sound machine or fan for white noise, as Scorpios slumber best with absolute dark and quiet

BEYOND BABY'S SUN SIGN:
OTHER SCORPIO PLACEMENTS

If one or a few of your baby's "big six" are in the sign of the Scorpion (for example, they have a Scorpio sun as well as Mars in Scorpio—or even a Pisces sun and a Scorpio moon), here's what you can expect.

Scorpio Rising: Your Scorp ascendant appears magnetic, reliable, and laser-focused on whatever goal they've trained their eye on, whether that's grasping a block or mastering an athletic technique.

Moon in Scorpio: Children born with their natal moon in the sign of the Scorpion emote deeply and want to feel cared for and connected with the same level of intensity that they feel inside. They'll be masters of seeing the truth beneath a façade, so it's a must to engage in real talk with them—age-appropriately, of course.

Mercury in Scorpio: Possessing the planet of communication in the sign of the Scorpion, a child will be innately private and will express themselves in their own way and on their own timetable. But with a particularly investigative mindset, they're also game for discussing topics that other kids might be less inclined to tackle, like how it's going with potty-training or even just straight-up bathroom humor.

Venus in Scorpio: When the planet of love falls in magnetic Scorpio, a child is extremely intuitive, capable of pinpointing how you're feeling even if you aren't talking about it. They can also be possessive and particularly set on certain family traditions and routines.

Mars in Scorpio: Born with the go-getter planet in determined Scorpio—one of the signs it rules— a little one will see any challenge or roadblock as an opportunity to test themselves and win, as they're passionately action-oriented and focused on success.

SAGITTARIUS

SUN SIGN DATES: NOVEMBER 22–DECEMBER 21

SYMBOL: ARCHER

ELEMENT: FIRE

QUALITY: MUTABLE

RULER: JUPITER, THE PLANET OF FORTUNE

HOUSE: NINTH HOUSE OF ADVENTURE

PLANTS: PEONIES, CROCUSES, BURDOCK

GEMS: TURQUOISE, BLUE TOPAZ, ZIRCON

Ruled by lucky Jupiter—our solar system's largest planet, known for its magnifying, fortune-bringing impact in astrology—and symbolized by the Archer, a mythical creature that's half human, half horse, Sagittarius children are courageous, entertaining, and often hilarious, direct, truth-seeking, fiercely independent, and free-spirited.

HAPPY SAGITTARIUS

BABY

Jupiter's influence means spirited, knowledge-seeking Sagittarian babies will be more upbeat than the average child when traveling, whether you're thinking of taking a day trip to see the grandparents or bringing them with you on a long-distance flight. It'll be the first clue that unlike siblings or peers who are homebodies, your Sag baby is ready to take on the world, preferring to shrug off tried-and-true routines for eye-opening moments.

And as the mutable fire sign, they'll not only be more capable of taking a different, action-oriented approach midstream but they'll welcome it. You may find that they're even more blissed-out by a different sleep schedule than you are.

TODDLER

Children born under the sign of the Archer will assert their independence early and often. They'll be excited to take the reins on their wardrobe choices, pulling together a boldly hued, eyebrow-raising look that's uniquely their own. And they'll be up for any activity or field trip you can dream up, from horseback riding (a Sag favorite) to spending a day at a museum.

No matter what they're doing, they'll be most gleeful when they're learning new skills or honing existing ones. Sag, after all, is associated with the Ninth House, which oversees not only adventure but higher learning, so children who have their natal sun or other personal placements in the fire sign will be on a perpetual mission to broaden their horizons.

CRANKY SAGITTARIUS

BABY

As a brave and ambitious fire sign, your Sag little one will exhibit what can feel like an overflowing reserve of jubilant energy, which as an infant, will manifest with lots of wiggly, excitable movin' and shakin', giggling and shrieking. They might loathe times when they're expected to be quiet or still—like naptime.

And given Sag's mutability, your baby prefers to have opportunities to adapt and constantly push the bar further, so they might get bored— and in turn, noticeably frustrated—if routines start to feel too humdrum. Taking them to different parks or playgrounds for a change of scenery and letting them try new foods can preempt aggravation.

TODDLER

As the sign related to the Ninth House of Adventure, which also oversees long-distance travel, a growing Sag will exhibit wanderlust from the time they learn what it means to get in a car or on an airplane and be somewhere other than home. That daring streak means they're wired to push boundaries, and if they feel limited or fenced in from doing an activity they've set their fiery little heart on—usually something wild and physical—they'll be driven to a big, loud tantrum.

Jupiterian energy can be summed up with "go big or go home," so your Sag could also react poorly when they feel that their world is made smaller in any way, such as by having to focus on a task that they see as dull, like cleaning up. (See page 133 for more on communicating with your little Sag.)

SAGITTARIUS MUST-HAVES

- Adventurous make-believe
- Stories about truth-seeking leaders (see page 134)
- Maps, a compass, a pretend passport, or their own luggage set
- A playlist of silly songs (like "On Top of Spaghetti") to support their burgeoning sense of humor
- A wide-open play space (like a huge field for your Jupiterian kid to run free in)

FAMOUS SAGITTARIUS SUN KIDS

Daphne Oz and John Jovanovic's daughter Domenica (December 4)

Kim Kardashian and Kanye West's son Saint (December 5)

Cassie and Alex Fine's daughter Frankie (December 6)

Mick Jagger and Melanie Hamrick's son, Deveraux (December 8)

Enrique Iglesias and Anna Kournikova's twins, Nicholas and Lucy (December 16)

SAGITTARIUS SUN CELEBRITIES

Scarlett Johansson (November 22)

Don Cheadle (November 29)

Britney Spears (December 2)

Jenna Dewan (December 3)

Taylor Swift (December 13)

THE STORY BEHIND THE STARS: SAGITTARIUS, THE ARCHER

Greek mythology tells the story of a kindhearted centaur called Chiron who was quite knowledgeable, was a wonderful teacher, and took a keen interest in medicine. Jupiter, the god of the sky, honored him by placing him among the stars as the constellation Sagittarius.

The Archer symbolizes:

- Truth telling
- Bravery
- Wisdom
- Personal growth

PREPARING FOR A TINY ARCHER

SAGITTARIUS-INSPIRED BABY NAMES

Spirited, fiery, wanderlust-inspired monikers befitting of a vivacious, buoyant adventurer:

Actaeon: Hunter

Bridget: from Brigid, Celtic goddess of fire, poetry, and wisdom

Evander: Bow warrior

Fletcher: Arrow-maker

Kymani: Adventurous traveler

Nina: Fire

Robin: Bright fame

Scott: Wanderer

Seraphina: Ardent, fiery

THE SAGITTARIUS BABY SHOWER

Think about incorporating these Archer-informed elements when celebrating a Sag on the way:

- Fireball cocktails or spicy, cinnamon-flavored mocktails

- A live performer, like a comedian or dance teacher

- A passport-themed guest book

- Flavorful bites from all over the world (like Korean fried chicken, spanakopita, or samosas with mint chutney)

NURSERY DESIGN IDEAS

- Horses, ponies, or unicorns everywhere to tap into that Archer spirit

- A prominently displayed globe or world map

- Lots of natural light and fresh air, which will give your future globe-trotter a taste of the great big world beyond their walls

- A kid-friendly smart speaker that a Sag toddler can use for learning, story time, and even to add structure to their day with alarms or reminders

- A colorful organizational system that'll encourage little Sag to corral their toys and other belongings, as they tend to prefer to focus on exuberant, imaginative play over being tidy

BEYOND BABY'S SUN SIGN: OTHER SAGITTARIUS PLACEMENTS

If one or a few of your baby's "big six" are in the sign of the Archer (for example, they have a Sagittarius sun as well as Mercury in Sagittarius—or even a Capricorn sun and Sagittarius rising), here's what you can expect.

Sagittarius Rising: A Sag ascendant child shows the world how much they want to be on the go by being unable to sit still and sharing their big, whimsical dreams. Their joy and liveliness are downright infectious.

Moon in Sagittarius: Children born with their natal moon in the sign of the Archer need to feel like they have free rein to be unapologetically themselves, which is boisterous, giddy, and fun-loving. They'll feel most nurtured by being exposed to lots of new experiences that satisfy their impressive appetite to see, do, learn, and grow.

Mercury in Sagittarius: Born when the planet of communication fell in the sign of the Archer, this child is eager to soak up knowledge of all kinds and travel as far and wide as possible, even from an early age. They are also quite opinionated and unfiltered.

Venus in Sagittarius: Possessing the planet of love in bold Sagittarius, your baby or toddler's love language is action-oriented. They most enjoy bonding with you by being out in the world and shrugging off their everyday routine (whether that means heading to the zoo—or to another country). They are also direct about how they feel.

Mars in Sagittarius: With the planet of action in optimistic, brave Sagittarius, this little one is a go-getter through and through, wisely using the powers of persuasion and a direct, fearless approach to pursue a goal. But they're also restless and can struggle to follow through.

CAPRICORN

SUN SIGN DATES: DECEMBER 22–JANUARY 19

SYMBOL: SEA GOAT

ELEMENT: EARTH

QUALITY: CARDINAL

RULER: SATURN, THE PLANET OF HARD WORK

HOUSE: TENTH HOUSE OF PUBLIC IMAGE

PLANTS: CYCLAMEN, PANSIES, CARNATIONS

GEMS: GARNET, HOWLITE, MALACHITE

Symbolized by the Sea Goat and ruled by Saturn—the planet of responsibility, maturity, and tradition—Capricorn children are precocious, wise, serious, industrious, and pragmatic, and exhibit a work ethic that will allow them to reach the peak of any mountain they want to climb. Old souls even as tots, they have a deep reverence for their elders and history. And as the cardinal earth sign, they find that being active in the great outdoors supports their overall well-being.

HAPPY CAPRICORN

BABY

With taskmaster Saturn informing your little Capricorn's energy, you may notice how serious, reserved, and even practical they are from the start. You'll be able to tell when they're content because they'll be especially quiet and focused on whatever "work" is required of them in each moment, whether that's checking out new shapes and colors, attempting to roll over, or chowing down at mealtime. That's because your little Cap is most content when they feel they're facing a new challenge and working toward an accomplishment—ideally, a milestone that will earn them recognition.

TODDLER

Little ones born under the sign of the Sea Goat are some of the most precocious in all the zodiac, often exuding a mature energy that's wise beyond their years. Not only are they serious about their chores and responsibilities, but "taking care of business" is fun for them. They'll be among the first tots on the block to volunteer to help you set the table, fold laundry, or help with a work-related task (like taking inventory of your office supplies).

And as a cardinal earth sign, they're pragmatists who take the initiative and plan ahead; they'll enjoy picking out an outfit for preschool or talking through the agenda for their first big-kid birthday party well in advance. You can trust that they'll set their sights on ambitious goals throughout their lives and prefer to lead the charge, possibly pursuing entrepreneurship one day.

CRANKY CAPRICORN

BABY

As a grounded, no-nonsense earth sign, your Cap infant isn't a fan of being around loud, bustling crowds or especially excitable people. All that might feel like a bit too much for this little one, who prefers low-key, serious, and straightforward activities; being overstimulated could set off the waterworks.

And born under stern Saturn's home sign, your Cap baby is a fan of meeting goals—say, working on crawling or trying to sit up on their own—in a very calculated way. But if they're pushed to accelerate their process too quickly, you can bet they'll show signs of frustration.

TODDLER

As the sign connected to the Tenth House of Public Image, your little Cap is conscious of how they appear to others and wants to command respect from the time they're tiny. How this could manifest: They try their hand at running, kicking, or jumping but slip and fall. Worry that they'll be seen as incompetent—or worse, "foolish"—will spur a quiet, gloomy storm inside your growing Sea Goat.

You'll want to frequently and gently remind them that mistakes and accidents happen to us all—and can make them stronger in the long run. (See page 136 for more on communicating with your little Cap.)

CAPRICORN MUST-HAVES

- Opportunities to foster their budding business savvy, like mirroring you at your yard sale
- Working on an outdoor project, like planting herbs or helping rake leaves
- Big-picture goals and an organizational system for achieving them (like a potty-training chart)

- Books about influential leaders throughout history (see page 137)
- Activities, games, and toys that teach financial skills (think: a singing piggy bank that comes with fake coins)

FAMOUS CAPRICORN SUN KIDS

Nick and Vanessa Lachey's son Phoenix (December 24) and daughter, Brooklyn (January 5)

Pink and Carey Hart's son, Jameson Moon (December 26)

Bryson Tiller and Kendra Bailey's daughter, Kelly Jade (December 26)

Beyoncé and Jay-Z's daughter Blue Ivy (January 7)

Carrie Underwood and Mike Fisher's son Jacob Bryan (January 21)

CAPRICORN SUN CELEBRITIES

John Legend (December 28)

LeBron James (December 30)

Kate Middleton (January 9)

Lin-Manuel Miranda (January 16)

Michelle Obama (January 17)

THE STORY BEHIND THE STARS: CAPRICORN, THE SEA GOAT

In Greek mythology, the god Pan was a half man, half goat who ruled over forests, flocks, shepherds—and, eventually, all of nature. He also had the ability to transform into a half goat, half fish—in other words, a sea goat. King of the gods Zeus honored him by creating the Capricorn constellation.

The Sea Goat symbolizes:

- Wisdom
- Responsibility
- Steadiness
- Intelligence

PREPARING FOR A MINI SEA GOAT

CAPRICORN-INSPIRED BABY NAMES

Enchantingly grounded, earthy names befitting of a determined little one:

Aaron: High mountain

Aja: Goat

Beaumont: Beautiful mountain

Diana: Divine, Roman goddess of hunting and forests

Emery: Industrious

Liana: To climb like a vine

Peter: Rock

Sage: Wise and knowing

Yukio: Snow

THE CAPRICORN BABY SHOWER

These details will bring the spirit of the Sea Goat to your festive fete:

- Games that incorporate throwback photos, such as displaying old pictures of relatives and asking guests to guess which parent they're related to

- Classic cocktails like old-fashioneds, sophisticated wine, and their nonalcoholic equivalents, which nod to Cap's traditionalist, old-soul vibe

- Physical activities that leave guests feeling accomplished (think: a prenatal yoga session)

- Time-honored family recipes, like Grandma's go-to chicken parm or your uncle's tamales

NURSERY DESIGN IDEAS

- Goat and/or mountain prints and elements

- Clean, grounding colors like neutrals and earthy tones

- Wall art displaying a beloved quote or two from respected Capricorn leaders (such as Dr. Martin Luther King Jr. and former FLOTUS Michelle Obama)

- Compartments and cubbies to bring Cap-loved order to any space

BEYOND BABY'S SUN SIGN: OTHER CAPRICORN PLACEMENTS

If one or a few of your baby's "big six" are in the sign of the Sea Goat (for example, they have a Capricorn sun as well as Mars in Capricorn—or even a Libra sun and moon in Capricorn), here's what you can expect.

Capricorn Rising: A Cap ascendant child leads with their ability to take care of whatever it is they're tasked with—efficiently and seriously. They want to appear capable and "grown-up"—even as a little one.

Moon in Capricorn: Kids who come into the world when the moon is in the sign of the Sea Goat feel—and want to be—nurtured in a deeply practical, coolheaded way. Engaging through simple, everyday moments like mealtime or on a stroll through your favorite park can truly deepen their sense of security and emotional well-being.

Mercury in Capricorn: With the planet of communication in the sign of the Sea Goat, this child is cautious and analytical with their thinking and self-expression. They'll generally opt for an approach that's tried-and-true and rational (well, as much as any toddler can be).

Venus in Capricorn: Having the planet of love in earthy, Saturn-ruled Cap gives a child a strong affinity for tradition and goal-setting. They'll enjoy connecting through acts of service or by building something together over time. Working with you to nurture a plant or bake a cake can strengthen a heartfelt bond.

Mars in Capricorn: A little one born while the go-getter planet was in hardworking, driven Capricorn is wired to take logical, controlled action—one step at a time—to reach the peak of any figurative mountain. A set game plan helps them feel secure and on track.

AQUARIUS

DATES: JANUARY 20–FEBRUARY 18

SYMBOL: WATER BEARER

ELEMENT: AIR

QUALITY: FIXED

RULER: URANUS, THE PLANET OF CHANGE

HOUSE: ELEVENTH HOUSE OF FRIENDS

PLANTS: BIRDS OF PARADISE, GLADIOLUS, LADY'S SLIPPERS

GEMS: ANGELITE, APATITE, RHODONITE

Symbolized by the Water Bearer and ruled by Uranus—the planet of rebellion, sudden change, the future, and electricity—Aquarius kids are social team players who are science-oriented, forward-thinking, inventive, tech-savvy, and humanitarian. Preferring to march to the beat of their own drum, they'll reject anything they perceive as conventional. This goes hand in hand with their strong contrarian side (all toddlers have one, but your Water Bearer's on another level) and desire to pinpoint concrete evidence of anything they're asked to believe.

HAPPY AQUARIUS

BABY

As the sign related to the Eleventh House of Friends, even the smallest Aquarius is super social and interested in connecting with different types of people—from their loved ones to strangers they pass on an afternoon walk. They'll light up during music classes, playdates, or anytime they're in a crowd, making eye contact with and engaging anyone within sight. It'll be the first sign that you're raising a tiny humanitarian with an innate interest in being a part of a community.

And as a cerebral, rational, future-thinking air sign, an Aquarian infant will be most delighted when they have toys, puzzles, or games that foster their love of science. It's really never too soon to introduce your Water Bearer baby to STEM (Science, Technology, Engineering, Mathematics) concepts (see page 140).

TODDLER

Ruled by rebellious Uranus, the game-changer planet, Aquarian kids are most elated when they're seeing or doing things in their own electrifyingly different way. This could mean wanting to wear their favorite T-shirt backward or preferring to use the most out-there, neon-hued crayons.

Although they enjoy striking out on their own, their Eleventh House influence paired with their air sign energy means your growing Water Bearer thrives when they feel connected to a group or part of a team effort.

CRANKY AQUARIUS

BABY

Air signs might be more easygoing in general, but because your infant was born under the fixed air sign, they could get stuck on particular routines—especially any that involve social time. If they're used to getting a bedtime story with you and their big sister but it's suddenly with Grandpa instead, they could be taken aback and launch a full-scale, red-faced fit.

You could also notice that your infant Aquarian's gloomy mood rolls in like a tropical thunderstorm—out of nowhere, there's lightning and a gasp-worthy downpour—then, they're almost eerily calm. That's the work of their ruling planet, Uranus, the planet of sudden change.

TODDLER

It might sound like a paradox, but your free-spirited Aquarius child is equally extremely social—thriving on playdates and family parties—and fiercely independent. That said, two scenarios are most likely to set them off: Being required to do something they feel impinges on their sense of freedom (like wear a formal outfit or stay strapped into their car seat) or feeling left out of time with friends or loved ones. Whether their bedtime falls in the middle of a family get-together or they find out that their regular playtime with a pal isn't happening this week, your little Aquarius is at risk of FOMO. (See page 139 for more on communicating with your little Aquarius.)

AQUARIUS MUST-HAVES

- Toys and games that nurture their innate curiosity around technology and electricity
- Group playdates and classes
- Opportunities to flex their humanitarian muscle, like selling lemonade to raise funds for a local charity
- Entertainment that involves futuristic and/or STEM themes, like *StoryBots* and *Space Racers*
- Books about social, political, and scientific progress and leaders in these fields (like Martin Luther King Jr. or Sally Ride)

FAMOUS AQUARIUS SUN KIDS

Criss Angel and Shaunyl Benson's son Xristos (January 22)

James and Kimberly Van Der Beek's daughter Annabel Leah (January 25)

Kylie Jenner and Travis Scott's daughter, Stormi (February 1)

Andy Cohen's son, Benjamin Allen (February 4)

Adam Levine and Behati Prinsloo's daughter Gio Grace (February 15)

AQUARIUS SUN CELEBRITIES

Oprah Winfrey (January 29)

Harry Styles (February 1)

Shakira (February 2)

Laura Dern (February 10)

Michael Jordan (February 17)

THE STORY BEHIND THE STARS: AQUARIUS, THE WATER BEARER

According to Greek mythology, Ganymede was a prince who was taken by king of the gods Zeus to become cup-bearer to the gods, providing them with wine. He was then placed among the stars as the constellation Aquarius.

The Water Bearer symbolizes:

- Humanitarian action
- Flowing energy
- Healing and cleansing
- Learning

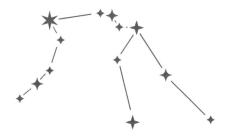

PREPARING FOR A LITTLE WATER BEARER

AQUARIUS-INSPIRED BABY NAMES

Unique, electrifying monikers that suit an individualistic, humanitarian activist in the making:

Advaita: Unique

Alexander: Defender or helper of mankind

Barak: Lightning

Bellamy: Fine friend

Darwin: Dear friend, also the surname of the nineteenth-century scientist

Emma: Universal

Isa: Strong-willed

Miro: Peace, world

Nadira: Rare

THE AQUARIUS BABY SHOWER

Incorporate these details to infuse your wintry fete with Water Bearer vibes:

- A futuristic theme with decor inspired by the guest of honor's favorite sci-fi TV show or movie (like *The Jetsons* or *Back to the Future 2*)

- A volunteer effort or raising money for your favorite nonprofit

- Live music, maybe performed by a local indie band the parents-to-be adore

- Apps or meal options made with vegan and/or sustainable, eco-conscious foods

NURSERY DESIGN IDEAS

- A space theme with glowing stars or a projector night-light that beams the moon and stars onto the ceiling to appeal to their love of technology and science

- A sound machine that offers up white noise, lullabies, or other relaxing sounds

- A photo collage of your Water Bearer baby's extensive network of family and friends that you can grow over time

- Ultramodern silver and chrome details, which echo their futuristic Uranian energy

BEYOND BABY'S SUN SIGN: OTHER AQUARIUS PLACEMENTS

If one or a few of your baby's "big six" are in the sign of the Water Bearer (for example, they have an Aquarius sun as well as Venus in Aquarius—or even a Taurus sun and Mars in Aquarius), here's what you can expect.

Aquarius Rising: An Aquarius rising child will come off as very personable and open-minded, eager to connect with all kinds of people in a variety of scenarios. They're also incredibly inventive and appear self-possessed.

Moon in Aquarius: Children who are born with their natal moon in the sign of the Water Bearer believe that they feel differently from others, are very protective of their independence, and have a strong inner pull to create positive change in the world. They'll feel most nurtured when their eccentricities and free-spiritedness are seen and celebrated.

Mercury in Aquarius: With the planet of communication in the sign of the Water Bearer, your child aims to think and express themselves in a unique, out-of-left-field way. Just wait for all the innovative, quirky inventions they come up with!

Venus in Aquarius: Born with the planet of love in friendly Aquarius, this child will express their affection in an intellectual way, whether that's by having long, thoughtful conversations or by collaborating with you or their playmates on activities that help them better understand how the world works. The spirit of friendship—which comes naturally to them—will be at the heart of all their most meaningful bonds.

Mars in Aquarius: A kid born when the action planet was in future-minded, humanitarian Aquarius will dig their heels in on their ideals. They're happiest when they can assert their independence and idiosyncrasies.

PISCES

SUN SIGN DATES: FEBRUARY 19–MARCH 20

SYMBOL: FISH

ELEMENT: WATER

QUALITY: MUTABLE

RULER: NEPTUNE, THE PLANET OF DREAMS

HOUSE: TWELFTH HOUSE OF SPIRITUALITY

PLANTS: VIOLETS, ORCHIDS, IRISH MOSS

GEMS: AQUAMARINE, AMETHYST, CELESTITE

Symbolized by the Fish and ruled by Neptune, the planet of imagination, illusion, spirituality, dreams, and compassion, Piscean children are deeply empathic, artistic, emotional, and perhaps even a bit psychic. As an incredibly intuitive water sign ruled by the most mystical planet in astrology, Pisces little ones pick up on other people's emotions and energy and therefore connect easily with anything happening between the lines. Neptune's influence also makes them highly active dreamers, when asleep or awake.

HAPPY PISCES

BABY

Ruled by mystical Neptune, Piscean infants are tenderhearted, perceptive dreamers from the start. Your little Fish will be happiest when they can pick up on your love, support, and sense of calm. They'll light up when their actions are met with a soothing, reassuring tone that can serve as a balm for their sensitive spirits.

And while all water signs will benefit from plenty of bath time, pool time, or moments spent by the shore, your Pisces baby will find any opportunity to engage in any form of hydrotherapy especially centering. One of the best ways to deal with tears might be a luxurious sink bath, which will go far toward resetting a baby Fish's mood.

TODDLER

As your Pisces child grows, the influence of dreamy Neptune will have them feeling at their most content when they're putting their vivid imagination to work. Little Fish might find that the best way for them to process and channel their emotions is through an artistic outlet, be that dance, finger painting, singing, whimsical storytelling, or getting lost in a book.

At times overwhelmed by emotions and more easily swept away by them than other signs, they'll gain confidence by being empowered to acknowledge, explore, and own what they're feeling. Teaching them about empathy versus sympathy can boost their centeredness (see page 179).

CRANKY PISCES

BABY

All babies pick up on the emotional energy around them, but your infant Fish is highly sensitive to it. Whether your family pup starts whimpering to be let out or you're clearly stressed by a text you just read, they may show their empathy by getting distressed as well. And because their imagination is so highly charged, they could be fearful of strangers or even of you walking out of the room. They might need extra reassuring and coaxing to be comfortable with anything—or anyone—unfamiliar and daunting. But because these early days of life are jam-packed with introductions and uncertainties for your little Fish, they'll do best when their nerves and blue moods are met with your grounded reassurance and love.

TODDLER

Your growing Pisces might be overwhelmed by all the emotions they can't help but feel at any given time, and big, tough ones could serve to take their already active imagination to the next level, causing them to have nightmares. This is a case for creating and practicing calming rituals—meditation, breathing exercises, kid yoga—that can teach your little Fish to self-soothe.

Because they're dreaming 24/7 and love to space out, they might also struggle with super-logical, step-by-step directions, so finding imaginative ways to teach them new lessons could preempt frustration and tears. (See page 142 for more on communicating with your little Pisces.)

PISCES MUST-HAVES

- A beginner's musical instrument, like a toddler guitar or toy piano
- Watercolors or finger paints and blank canvases
- Their own tranquil space for dreaming, creating, and working through big feelings
- Books (see page 143) or TV shows (like *Doc McStuffins and Daniel Tiger's Neighborhood*) that center on Piscean themes like understanding your emotions and showing compassion
- Poetry—they'll love to read it and learn how to write it themselves

FAMOUS PISCES SUN KIDS

Jennifer Lopez and Marc Anthony's twins, Max and Emme (February 22)

Gwen Stefani and Gavin Rossdale's son Apollo (February 28)

Tori Spelling and Dean McDermott's son Beau (March 2)

Jenna Dewan and Steve Kazee's son, Callum (March 6)

Jessica Simpson and Eric Johnson's daughter Birdie Mae (March 19)

PISCES SUN CELEBRITIES

Rihanna (February 20)

Elliot Page (February 21)

Drew Barrymore (February 22)

Josh Groban (February 27)

Stephen Curry (March 14)

THE STORY BEHIND THE STARS: PISCES, THE FISH

In Greek mythology, Aphrodite, the goddess of love, and Eros, the god of love, were turned into fish by the king of the gods, Zeus, who later immortalized this incident with the Pisces constellation, in which two fish are swimming in opposite directions.

The Fish represents:

- Open-mindedness
- Illusion versus reality
- Deep emotions
- Mysticism

PREPARING FOR A TEENSY FISH

PISCES-INSPIRED BABY NAMES

Poetic, otherworldly, aquatic names that are rooted in the beauty of water and its connection to emotion:

Adrian: Sea or water

Cherith: Winter stream

Cordelia: Heart or daughter of the sea

Dylan: Son of the sea

Gareth: Gentle

Mira: Ocean

Triton: Son of Poseidon

Zale: Power of the sea

THE PISCES BABY SHOWER

These elements will bring Pisces vibes into your celebration:

- A poetry slam that challenges guests to write and present their own fun or heartfelt poems

- A waterside venue and/or lots of ocean colors and decor as well as Neptune-ruled water lilies

- A guest tarot card reader or psychic

- Seafood- and nautical-themed drinks, like a Sea Breeze or Dark 'n' Stormy

NURSERY DESIGN IDEAS

- An aquarium theme with colorful fish displayed on the walls—and perhaps ultimately a tank of real fish that your little Fish will love to help care for

- Mermaid-themed toys, mobile, and art

- Lots of cozy blankets and rugs in calming ocean hues

- A sound machine or speaker that offers a variety of water sign–approved ocean, river, and rain sounds

BEYOND BABY'S SUN SIGN: OTHER PISCES PLACEMENTS

If one or a few of your baby's "big six" are in the sign of the Fish (for example, they have a Pisces sun as well as a Pisces moon—or even a Capricorn sun and Mars in Pisces), here's what you can expect.

Pisces Rising: A Pisces rising child will appear extremely artistic, open-minded, huge-hearted, gentle, and content to roll with life from moment to moment. They might struggle to make decisions and to opt for a rational versus emotional approach.

Moon in Pisces: Children who are born with their natal moon in the sign of the Fish are extremely intuitive, sensitive, and escapist. They'll feel most supported and nurtured when they have a calm, safe space to talk through their deep-rooted emotions and daydreams.

Mercury in Pisces: With the planet of communication in the sign of the Fish, this child sees the world through the lens of art and compassion. While rationality and details might not be their strong suit, they excel at expressing creativity and empathy.

Venus in Pisces: Born with the planet of relationships in tender Pisces, this child is quick to tune in to and respond to other people's emotions. It can be tough for them to separate how they feel from how a loved one is feeling. Their imagination informs how they show affection (think: making up fanciful stories and crafting whimsical art projects).

Mars in Pisces: A kid born when the action planet was in emotional Pisces won't be the most proactive, preferring to float from one activity to the next and see where the tide takes them. They'll steer clear of conflict but might have to contend with repressed anger.

PART 2

A Guide to Your Little One's Mind, Spirit & Well-Being

Your child's birth chart not only provides insight into their nascent personality, but it also serves as a wonderfully useful tool for supporting their contentment and growth. By tapping into the power of their natal placements, you can better understand their communication style and empower them to express themselves in their own special way or offer them learning strategies that suit their disposition. You can also gather intel on how their emotional and physical needs may manifest as well as pinpoint the wellness-boosting pastimes they'll love most based on their unique interests.

Consider this part of the book a road map for supporting your baby's mind, body, and spirit, based on their starry blueprint.

SELF-EXPRESSION & LEARNING

EVEN BEFORE YOU MEET YOUR LITTLE ONE, you'll wonder, what might make them belly laugh? Will they wiggle, dance, or hum when you put on your go-to playlist? Which books will they cherish right off the bat? How will they interact with others, convey their ideas, and discover the world around them? And what will they dream of becoming when they grow up? You might not be able to see into the future to answer these questions, but you can look to your baby's natal placements for invaluable insight.

The following sign profiles can help you better understand your baby's distinctive communication and learning styles. You'll also find tailored tips for nurturing their voice and supporting their growth. As you move through the chapter, be sure to check out not only your baby's "big three" (sun, moon, and rising) signs but also their Mercury sign (as the planet rules how we think and communicate).

ARIES

Your bold little Ram will share their thoughts and opinions in a direct, to-the-point, and action-oriented way, thanks to their ruling planet, go-getter Mars. They might make statements like "I want to play with you," "No diaper change," or "I need to use the potty."

They are also pros at asserting their independence. They want to *do* versus discuss, and at the swift pace they prefer (yep, buckle up!). Whether their heart is set on running, jumping, playing with their friends, learning their ABCs, or trying a new snack, they'd prefer to get right down to it *stat*.

They'll use their bold, authoritative energy to command your attention and to ensure that their needs are met, whether by shrieking, yelping, thrashing around in their crib, or barreling around their play space. And having to wait is the worst thing ever for an impatient Aries, so don't be surprised if they make it very obvious that they want to try what you're having for dinner, perhaps by sitting up tall in their high chair and squealing at top volume.

But it bears noting that as the first of all twelve signs, Aries is considered the baby of the zodiac, so they might surprise you with bursts of dependency that could manifest as an all-out wailing fest when they feel they're not getting the attention they need. And if a moment is proving too low-energy for your dynamo Ram, they won't shy away from "telling" you that they need more stimulation by simply setting out to drum it up themselves.

HOW TO NURTURE YOUR MINI RAM'S VOICE

Talk to your Aries baby about big-picture plans. You may find that even the smallest Aries, with their innate athleticism, takes a shine to competition, so adopting sports-related language when you talk about their milestones can be very effective. Offer a play-by-play of the "game plans" they'll want to follow to hit different goals, whether that's moving from their crib to a big-kid bed or learning how to ride a tricycle. They'll be empowered anytime they feel like they've crossed a finish line and won at any particular challenge, athletic or otherwise. At the same time, it can help to celebrate the concept of achieving their own personal best—versus comparing themselves with others.

Applaud their assertiveness while offering appropriate guardrails. Since they're apt to demand a certain toy or food, or more of your undivided attention, you can commend their ability to speak their minds and also remind them to be patient and to say "please."

Connect the dots between communication and action, especially when they're fired up. Because your little Aries is less likely to speak than to act, show them how talking through a particular task or challenge can bolster their ability to take care of business. Help them put words to their feelings by first acknowledging their emotions, then fostering a vocabulary of words for expressing themselves. You can do this by creating flash cards or signs to match with a word that describes that emotion, like "angry," "frustrated," or "disappointed."

POSSIBLE FIRST WORDS FOR AN ARIES

"I win!"	"Throw"
"Ball"	"Fast"
"Go!"	"Vroom!"

TOOLS TO HELP YOUR TINY ARIES LEARN & GROW

Clear rewards. Stock up on lots of trophies—large or small, like stickers that are part of a bigger reward system. Your little Aries is wired to work toward a win, so framing any achievement in that context will keep them motivated.

Competitive games. When they display a fascination with animals, take your adventurous Ram to the zoo and come up with a game, like counting how many llamas or giraffes they see or quizzing them on animal names. Keep a score card, and promise a reward for hitting a particular goal (like naming five creatures you come across or finding the correct number of animals in three exhibits).

Speed. Working against a clock—and knowing they can do something quickly—psychs up your tiny Ram, so embrace any opportunities to incorporate a timer into any lesson plan. How many colors can your little Aries name in a minute? Can they count from one to ten faster now than they could a month ago?

INSTANT CLASSICS FOR AN ARIES

Titles that celebrate springtime (which encompasses Aries season and serves as the kickoff of a new astrological cycle) as well as your Ram's feisty, brave, and passionate personality:

- *A Spring Stroll in the City* by Cathy Goldberg Fishman
- *Sheila Rae, the Brave* by Kevin Henkes
- *She's Got This* by Laurie Hernandez
- *Evie's Field Day: More Than One Way to Win* by Claire Noland
- *I Choose to Calm My Anger* by Elizabeth Estrada
- *Llama Llama Time to Share* by Anna Dewdney

DREAM CAREERS FOR AN ARIES

Pro athlete	Sports reporter
Litigator	Lawmaker
First responder	Emergency room doctor

TAURUS

Your grounded little Bull is wired to share what they think in a deliberate, pragmatic, and gentle way that's informed by their ruling planet, social Venus. Because Venus is the planet of beauty, and a Taurus, as the earth sign that's known for being deeply in tune with their senses, will often engage with you around any opportunity to touch, taste, see, smell, or hear something breathtaking and awe-inspiring, it's easy to understand why they're content taking their time. Taurus babies know that it's best to savor the moment—whether it's snuggling with a parent or caregiver, listening to beautiful melodies, being mesmerized by vivid colors, or reveling in delicious foods.

On the flip side, as the fixed one of the earth bunch, your baby Bull is persistent, plenty stubborn at times, and will dig their heels in if pushed to open up when they're not quite ready. At the same time, the influence of Venus makes them personable, often relying on personal style, music, or coloring to convey their thoughts.

Your little one is a creature of habit more than the average child, so once they find a particular way to show you what they want, they'll generally stick to it. For that reason, consider striving for early reliance on big-kid language (for example, descriptive words that are usually reserved for toddlers, like "clean," "gentle," "soft"). This can lay the groundwork for healthy, clear communication.

They will be apt to share when they've had a powerful sensory experience, for example noting, "I liked seeing the pretty flowers on our walk" or "That snack was so sweet and yummy."

HOW TO NURTURE YOUR MINI BULL'S VOICE

Keep it low-key. Nudging your tiny Taurean to clear a hurdle more quickly than they might be up for will only create more resistance, so it can help to reassure them that taking any new interaction or learning opportunity as slowly as they need is A-OK.

Talk them through creative projects. As the fixed earth sign, your little Taurus finds it grounding to take any mission one step at a time, and ruled by the planet of beauty, they're naturally artistic. Bring those two qualities together for your tiny Bull by talking through anything from picking out their outfit for the day to gathering supplies for a craft project.

Strive for consistency. Your Bull tot is a creature of habit, so stick to a schedule. Discussing plans for the day or reading the same book before bed will help them open up. Creating rituals can be centering and communication-bolstering for your Taurus toddler.

POSSIBLE FIRST WORDS FOR A TAURUS

"Gentle"   "Pretty"

"Soft"   "Blanket"

"Yum"   "Cookie"

TOOLS TO HELP YOUR TINY TAURUS LEARN & GROW

Step-by-step game plans. As a steadfast earth sign who thinks in concrete, pragmatic terms, your tiny Bull is a fan of building blocks—figurative and literal. Break major goals into bite-size steps.

Soothing treats. Think about rewarding your little Taurus for a job well done with an activity or object that adds to their sense of security with lots of coziness, like an extra snuggle session or new lovey.

Empowering, tangible reminders. When they're struggling with new experiences and shake-ups, offer them a tactile, comforting reminder that appeals to their senses. For example, when they're weaning, let them hold a shirt that you were wearing and that smells like you, and if they're nervous about their first day at preschool, put a photo of the two of you together in their backpack.

INSTANT CLASSICS FOR A TAURUS

Taurean titles that pay tribute to friendship, being strong-willed, and taking your time to embrace change and see the beauty in everyday life:

- *Olivia* by Ian Falconer
- *It's Show and Tell, Dexter!* by Lindsay Ward
- *The Story of Ferdinand* by Munro Leaf
- *Little Blue Truck* by Alice Schertle
- *The Very Hungry Caterpillar* by Eric Carle
- *Rosie Goes to Preschool* by Karen Katz

DREAM CAREERS FOR A TAURUS

Candymaker	Spa owner
Makeup artist	Landscaper
Sommelier	Realtor

GEMINI

As not only a personable air sign but one of two signs ruled by Mercury, the planet of communication (the other being earth sign Virgo), your little Gemini is eager to experience the world around them and express that in words. While this doesn't mean they won't have shy moments, they are generally comfortable expressing themselves verbally and interacting animatedly with everyone they encounter. They're inherently playful and quick to make friends.

In fact, your baby Gemini might surprise you by just how easily self-expression comes to them. They'll show you that they're hungry by emphatically pointing at the food they want or exuberantly trying out a new word over and over again. Their curiosity and enthusiasm for figuring out the world around them is off the charts. You'll find that they enjoy pretend chats on their toy phone (or your device when it's not being used), craft their own silly songs, and look forward to bedtime if only because it's an opportunity to hear or—better yet—tell stories. And it wouldn't be unheard of for them to quickly pick up baby signing or a second language.

Twins kids will be early to respond to you through imitation—more so than the average tyke. A master of mimicry and mirroring, your mini Gemini will offer up their own eerily accurate, albeit pint-size, version of a sweet lullaby, warm words of affection, or even distraught disapproval.

You could be surprised when your Twins-influenced kid quickly goes from proudly mouthy, asking a gazillion questions, and confidently asserting themselves to notably soft-spoken, quiet, and reserved. This is one of the first indications of their innately dualistic, mercurial nature.

HOW TO NURTURE YOUR MINI GEMINI'S VOICE

Chat with your baby Gemini about people and travel. Even if they're mere weeks old and can respond only with cute noises, smiles, and wiggles, strike up a conversation; for example, while on a drive, narrate what's happening along the way. Talking about the world around them—specifically, Mercury-esque social situations and transportation (like telling them about the guests who will be attending your summer barbecue or giving them a play-by-play of what happens when your partner takes the train to work)—is something Geminis will rarely get enough of. And the more sounds and words they hear, the faster their language skills will develop.

Turn story time into a creative exercise. Storytelling comes naturally to your Gemini, and having opportunities to practice will boost their confidence. Kick off the activity by asking them to give you just one word (like "dog" or "juice") that you then craft into a bedtime story,

encouraging them to chime in with additions at will.

Prioritize playdates early on. People with a strong Twins influence—even the tiniest among them—would gladly connect with others 24/7. They're wired to seek out opportunities to soak up information and forge a bevy of social bonds, so providing them with plenty of opportunities to interact with their peers, loved ones, and members of your community out in the world whenever possible will help them hone these innate skills and grow into their übersocial selves.

POSSIBLE FIRST WORDS FOR A GEMINI

A friend's name	"Silly"
"Choo," "car," or anything else that relates to Mercury-ruled transportation	"Book"
	A word in a second language

TOOLS TO HELP YOUR TINY GEMINI LEARN & GROW

A restful reading ritual. All little ones benefit from lots of story time, but your little Gemini, with their perpetually buzzing brain, craves the intellectual stimulation that only reading a book can bring. From the time they are a newborn, listen to audiobooks together. As they grow, they'll be head over heels for their own bookshelf brimming with a range of titles. Not only does reading together present an opportunity for them to sharpen their verbal skills, but it's also centering and a curiosity fix. Conversations about what you read are sure to spur an interaction that thrills your child.

Listening exercises. Chatter isn't the only sound that piques a Gemini's curiosity. They often have an auditory learning style and are tuned in to everything from birds chirping to cars whizzing by. Urge them to tap into their sensitivity to sound by asking what they think the birds at the park are saying. In the process, you'll nurture their learning potential and cultivate their listening skills.

Try mindfulness. It could be challenging for your information-gathering Gemini to concentrate at times. Try engaging them in mindfulness activities, like rainbow breathing (reach arms overhead as you inhale; as you exhale, spread your arms out like the arc of a rainbow) or focusing on a slowly moving object (like clouds or a glitter jar, a calming tool you can make with distilled water, glitter, and clear glue) for two to three minutes.

INSTANT CLASSICS FOR A GEMINI

Stories that touch on Twins-esque themes like mimicry, self-expression, good cheer, and curiosity:

- *Mr. Brown Can Moo! Can You?* by Dr. Seuss
- *A Color of His Own* by Leo Lionni
- *My Mouth Is a Volcano!* by Julia Cook
- *This Is Sadie* by Sara O'Leary
- *Wordy Birdy* by Tami Sauer
- *Curious George* by H. A. Rey

DREAM CAREERS FOR A GEMINI

Talk show host	Transportation engineer
Publicist	
Social media manager	Music producer
	Event planner

CANCER

Thanks to their ruler, the shimmering, intuitive moon, your sensitive Cancer leads with their heart, and as a cardinal sign, they're initiators who enjoy plotting out the big picture.

While your little Cancer is known to be mushy, emotional, and perceptive—all of which might manifest in their being passive and quiet—you'll learn that they're more assertive than you think.

One of the main forces informing and fueling your little Cancer's developing voice is their sensitivity. Crabs can't help but be in their feelings, which is reflected in their self-expression. Even if you've checked off every possible box—feeding, diapering, naptime—the energy of a given moment might just be a lot for your Crab, who will default to seeking extra snuggles and support.

Just as their ruler looms awe-inspiring over Earth at its most full, your growing Cancer can't help but share their thoughts in a meaningful and engaging way. They are a dreamer and doer, so when they say they're going to make up their own dance to the latest Taylor Swift track, you can trust that they will.

On the other hand, when they are struggling with big emotions, don't be surprised if they retreat into their protective rock-hard shell, and go silent. Little—and big!—Crabs often need their alone time to process difficult feelings, and nudging them for information might only strengthen their resolve to stay tight-lipped. You can trust that whenever they're ready, you'll get an earful.

Expect that their rants and raves—stemming from any mood, gloomy or sunny—will have an entertaining edge. Crabs are naturally funny and excel at comedic timing, goofy impressions, and physical comedy. (Famous comedian Cancers include Robin Williams, Amanda Seales, Will Ferrell, and Mindy Kaling.)

HOW TO NURTURE YOUR MINI CRAB'S VOICE

Introduce your Crab baby to the kitchen. To many of us, there's nothing more homey than preparing a traditional family recipe—Sunday sauce, matzo ball soup, or Grandma's cookie recipe—then gathering around the table to enjoy the fruits of your labor. As the sign connected to the Fourth House of Home Life, Cancers have a natural penchant for making and sharing food. They might love helping you cook—or trying new dishes. Talk through recipes, show them cookbooks and photos of the food you're making together, and ask them questions about ingredients or how something tastes. Connecting with your tiny foodie in this way is a fast track to fostering their voice.

Create space for comedic play. Whether you do silly voices for different characters in your Cancer baby's bedtime story or encourage your Crab toddler to act out a hilarious scene from their favorite TV show, be sure to nurture their inner comedian. They'll feel more confident about their ability to connect with others by leaning on humor, and bonus: they'll leave you in stitches.

Emphasize language for big emotions. Beyond recognizing, validating, and empathizing when your little Crab is in the midst of an emotional experience, you can try to teach them how to label their feelings when they're struggling to find the right words, for example, "You're sad because we can't go to the park today," or "You're so excited to start sleeping in your big-kid bed!"

POSSIBLE FIRST WORDS FOR A CANCER

"Mama"	Your family pet's name or a sound they make
"Lovey"	
"Yummy"	The name of their favorite food
"Eat"	

TOOLS TO HELP YOUR TINY CANCER LEARN & GROW

Mini benchmarks. Cancers' cardinal quality makes them naturals at tackling large-scale projects, so tap into this skill from an early age by mapping out milestones for your little Crab. Learning shapes and colors, potty-training, or even creating an organizational system for their toys, they'll see how following through on the small steps adds up to the end result—something you can illustrate on a progress chart.

Music to suit their moods. Your sentimental Cancer will associate sensory experiences with specific moments, routines, and memories, and music is a biggie. Show them the therapeutic value of their favorite songs by taking a class together or introducing them to tunes that fit different feelings, so they learn to use music as a tool for recognizing and working through tough emotions—as well as looking back on happy ones.

Animated brainstorming sessions. As a natural initiator, your little Crab is inspired by big, bold intentions—and the opportunity to come up with them. So whether you're meal planning for the week or considering booking a family vacation, involve your toddler in the idea stage. Encourage them to scribble down their suggestions to fuel their inner visionary.

INSTANT CLASSICS FOR A CANCER

Books about family, food, compassion, and crabs that will speak to your Cancer:

- *Are You My Mother?* by P. D. Eastman
- *Llama Red Pajama* by Anna Dewdney
- *What Pet Should I Get?* by Dr. Seuss
- *Bee-Bim Bop!* by Linda Sue Park
- *Strictly No Elephants* by Lisa Mantchev
- *A House for Hermit Crab* by Eric Carle

DREAM CAREERS FOR A CANCER

Nurse

Child care provider

Chef

Psychotherapist

Baker

LEO

Your little Lion, ruled by the vibrant sun, is a natural at soaking up the spotlight, and this goes hand in hand with how they communicate. Little Leo adores being onstage—even if that stage is their bassinet and you're their sole devoted admirer. At times insistent to the point of domineering, your regal kid will make bold moves to get what they want and claim your undivided attention. They can be stubborn and must learn that although they might see themselves as the Littlest Royal of the Jungle, life's not just about sitting in their throne—ahem, high chair—and getting their way.

Still, their assertiveness can come in handy. Whether they need a diaper change or a meal, your tiny Lion will usually be vocal and direct about their needs.

For the most part, though, you'll notice that your Leo baby is often smiley and giggling. With the gleaming, vitality-bringing sun as their ruler, your positive, driven Lion has a natural sense of optimism and is in love with life, which shines through in their enthusiasm and confidence.

A Leo toddler will roar their emotions and thoughts loudly and proudly. They'll tell you they're "in love" with everything from their favorite movie to a younger sibling. Stormy feelings will be equally intense. You can anticipate dramatic statements or thunderous temper tantrums.

Given their adoration of all things theatrical, your Leo will gravitate to eye-catching costumes in bold, sparkly hues (all the gold!) and regal accessories.

Your Leo toddler is also a major lovebug who will offer up hugs, kisses, and declarations of love without prompting.

HOW TO NURTURE YOUR MINI LION'S VOICE

Support their love of theatrics with lots of showy make-believe. Supplying your Lion toddler with plenty of items that will allow them to step into a role and on a stage—literal or figurative—is a wonderful way to ensure that they're getting their spotlight fix. Think: sewn capes, tiaras, or pajama onesies that you simply add a tail to and turn into a costume inspired by their favorite feline, like a Black Panther mask to morph into the King of Wakanda. Then, perhaps you can decide that a particular corner of the room is for dress rehearsals and performances. Having a dedicated space that's their own can satiate their appetite for being in the limelight while inspiring even more creativity.

Have lots of impromptu dance parties. A Leo stellium myself (my natal Mars, Venus, and rising are all in the sign of the Lion), I remember loving kitchen dance parties set to the tune of the latest '80s pop hits—"I'm So Excited" by the Pointer Sisters was a favorite. Put on some favorite bops, and watch your playful little Lion express themselves through smooth and silly moves.

Encourage performing on the fly. Your Lion could have a flair for public speaking when they get older. Channel their imaginative, self-expressive energy into a spontaneous performance, which will also help your fixed sign kid get comfier with being adaptable. Ask them to come up with a topic (anything from summertime to a beloved book character or their favorite color) and urge them to tell a story about it. They thrive on regaling an audience, whether that's simply you or you, a sibling, and their lovey.

POSSIBLE FIRST WORDS FOR A LEO

"Me"	"Lion"
"Sun"	"Love"
"Dance"	"Kitty"

TOOLS TO HELP YOUR TINY LEO LEARN & GROW

Listening games. One possible drawback of having a little one who's so self-assured and vocal is that it's not always their first instinct to tune in to what others have to say. Fostering this skill can be as easy as prioritizing simple games or activities that emphasize listening, like urging your little Lion to mimic you when you're singing your favorite lyrics or after you imitate the sound of your family pet.

New rules for tried-and-true activities. Whether your little Lion is in the midst of a rollicking good time playing catch or Candy Land, encourage your fixed sign child to adopt more flexible thinking by changing up the rules of any given game. And because their instinct is to go first—they are the Littlest Royal of the Jungle, remember?—working on taking turns won't hurt either.

Performance-based activities. Your Leo loves to show and tell so you can encourage them to process new info and demonstrate comprehension by doing either. You might encourage them to sing a song about what they learned in preschool that day or to create a music video that shows how they're feeling certain big emotions.

INSTANT CLASSICS FOR A LEO

Stories that tackle Leo-esque themes like generosity, parties, leadership, and lions:

- *Dragons Love Tacos* by Adam Rubin
- *The King of Kindergarten* by Derrick Barnes
- *Think Big, Little One* by Vashti Harrison
- *When Your Lion Needs a Bath* by Susanna Leonard Hill
- *The Giving Tree* by Shel Silverstein
- *Giraffes Can't Dance* by Giles Andreae

DREAM CAREERS FOR A LEO

Movie star	Anchorperson
Senator	Chief creative officer
Advertising copywriter	Film director

VIRGO

Your Virgo is naturally analytical and observant of the slightest details, which is made abundantly clear when they express themselves. They'll point out a tiny bird or fluttering leaf you may have never noticed otherwise or ask to use a specific writing utensil to scribble with. As one of two signs ruled by messenger Mercury (the other being Gemini), Virgos adore words, and as a practical earth sign, they're motivated to gather information for the purpose of being helpful—especially to the people they cherish most. For instance, your Virgo toddler will parrot the weather report, because they sense knowing that it'll be rainy could be useful as you go about planning your to-dos.

Budding perfectionists, your little Virgo wants to not only share what they're thinking but do so in just the right way. They'll benefit from being encouraged to experiment and learning that mistakes are OK—particularly when it comes to language and self-expression.

Associated with the Sixth House of Wellness, Virgo toddlers—even more than other toddlers—are observant and ask questions about the minutiae that happens in any given day, like how many celery stalks you're going to use in that green juice or which park you're taking the dog to—not to mention why!

You might notice that they're in full-on investigation mode at times, searching your face to get a read on your mood or looking lost in thought as they try a new fruit. The more information they have on a particular situation, the more comfortable and connected they'll feel, and the more likely they are to speak up.

Though Virgos are tenderhearted, their instinct is to consider any situation in an intellectual versus emotional way. Remind your Maiden that not everything in life will make sense, and that's OK.

HOW TO NURTURE YOUR MINI MAIDEN'S VOICE

Cultivate their love of storytelling. As the sign connected to the Sixth House, which governs routine, Virgos are particularly entranced by stories that revolve around everyday life. Offer them the opportunity to chime in and recall what they did, saw, and felt that day, either in conversation or by dictating a tale you'll write for them on a pad of paper or in a journal, which is sure to appeal to their particularly tactile nature.

Encourage them to zoom out to see the big picture. Your Virgo's tendency to zero in on all the moving parts will make it tough for them to take in a wider perspective at times. You can help them steer toward this, though, by talking to them about your own goals or initiating a game of make-believe that involves stepping into an authoritative role (say, their teacher) or favorite character (perhaps cheery and gregarious Big Bird) or even an inspiring historical figure (like Ruth Bader Ginsburg).

Create your own book club. Your Virgo toddler will be a proud bookworm, keen to devour every title in their possession again and again—and then connect with others on what they've learned. It's a case for reading and discussing stories together, which will nurture their voice and your bond.

POSSIBLE FIRST WORDS FOR A VIRGO

"Book"	"Icky"
"Uh-oh"	"Clean"
"Help"	"Give"

TOOLS TO HELP YOUR TINY VIRGO LEARN & GROW

Useful tasks. Your Virgo toddler will feel empowered by putting their sleuthing to good use, while developing a sense of independence. Give them a task that requires taking a variety of small steps that add up to a greater result. Maybe you assign them the mission of gathering up all the ingredients for baking cupcakes (they love checking items off a list!) or make a game out of looking for the numbers on highway exit signs when you're on the road.

Lots of room to organize and plan. Because your Virgo aspires to be tidy and organized, give them freedom to create a storage system for their toys or to help plan their breakfast menu for the week. This will give them confidence to make these decisions for themselves as they get older.

Trips to the library or bookstore. The number of options on the shelves will not only thrill your voracious reader but also serve to inspire big-picture thinking and aspirations. And if there are book readings and activities for children you can get involved in, even better!

INSTANT CLASSICS FOR A VIRGO

Stories that honor your Virgo's Mercury-fueled love of reading, writing, learning, and daily routines:

- *Bunny's Book Club* by Annie Silvestro
- *Madeline* by Ludwig Bemelmans
- *The Pigeon Has to Go to School!* by Mo Willems
- *How to Write a Story* by Kate Messner
- *The Curious Garden* by Peter Brown
- *Barnaby Never Forgets* by Pierre Collet-Derby

DREAM CAREERS FOR A VIRGO

Author

Nutritionist

Life coach

Social worker

Professional organizer

LIBRA

Your Scales baby came into this world with a gift for infusing any challenging or messy situation with serenity. As the Venus-ruled air sign, Libras are personable and interested in keeping—or creating—peace and beauty. From the time they're tiny bundles, they'll attract lots of compliments for appearing tranquil. As they get older and start interacting with their peers, you'll notice that your cardinal air sign takes the initiative in play, starting a game that others will be inspired to join in. They're also invested in getting along with everyone, which you might observe when they seem perfectly OK with sharing even their most prized lovey.

But because they're so conflict-averse, a Libra little one might avoid sharing how they feel for fear of rocking the boat—holding back tears or going along with a plan they're not 100 percent on board with for the sake of being agreeable. Getting comfy with disagreements and reframing conflict not as something to be afraid of but as an opportunity to learn and grow is a lifelong lesson for your Scales kid.

This is not to say that your Libra is meek. You'll see a more assertive side of your little Libra when something doesn't seem quite fair—perhaps mediating a conflict between playmates or attempting to cheer up a grouchy sibling by telling Siri to play a happy song.

As the sign associated with the Seventh House of Partnership, they will also love opportunities to interact with you or a playmate one-on-one. In fact, their innate social skills could lead to their becoming one of the most popular preschoolers around.

HOW TO NURTURE YOUR MINI SCALES'S VOICE

Encourage expression through art. Whether you arm them with watercolors or a xylophone, show your little Libra that they can share what they think and feel through a range of art forms. Just know that because their inclination will be to want everything they create to look or sound pretty, it can also be helpful to remind them that there can be as much (or more) beauty in the process of creation as there is in the result.

Embrace any excuse for a party. Even early on, your social Libra baby will show you that they adore being at the center of any get-together. For that reason, they'll benefit from social occasions such as weekly family gatherings, video calls with loved ones, or playdates with your bestie's little one. And because their ruler is beauty-loving Venus, they are also naturals at party planning and decor, so whether you're working on the details for their upcoming birthday fete or an older sibling's graduation, try to include them in the design process, which will foster their innate creativity in this department. They'll love helping you pick out the perfect color napkins, decorating cupcakes, or hanging a celebratory sign.

Prioritize partnership. Urge grown-ups to get down on your Libra baby's level to engage with them in floor play or to partner up with your Libra toddler on any fun or productive task, whether that's watering plants or enjoying a sing-along.

POSSIBLE FIRST WORDS FOR A LIBRA

"Pretty"	"Draw"
"Please"	"Flower"
"Thank you"	"Two"

TOOLS TO HELP YOUR TINY LIBRA LEARN & GROW

Emphasizing the beauty of the endgame. Although your little Libra loves coming up with grand artistic schemes and getting swept up in imaginative play, they're not as thrilled about undertakings that require a challenging, slow, and steady slog to the finish line. It can help to be real with them about how many moments in life will require hard work but that every step of the way leads them to something they can take a lot of pride in.

Exploring one-on-one. Your Libra will feel especially supported when they are working as part of a pair. Consider all variations of tête-à-têtes when teaching new skills. For example, maybe you sing the first line of a song about counting to ten (e.g., "I like to count . . . let's shout it out! One, two—that's your cue . . ."), then urge your little Libra to add a line, and go back and forth.

An eye toward aesthetics. Strive to make textbook lessons a bit more colorful, eye-catching, visual, and of course, social whenever possible. If you're working with your little Libra on learning shapes, go out into the neighborhood and take photos of flowers, plants, rocks, and clouds, then use those as flash cards. Opt for books on a given milestone that feature stunning illustrations or even exciting 3-D elements like pop-ups and textures.

INSTANT CLASSICS FOR A LIBRA

Titles that tackle Libra-esque lessons like the true definition of beauty, prizing balance and justice, and embracing all types of emotions:

- *Malala's Magic Pencil* by Malala Yousafzai
- *A Book of Love* by Emma Randall
- *Sulwe* by Lupita Nyong'o
- *Your Name Is a Song* by Jamilah Thompkins-Bigelow
- *The Color Monster: A Story About Emotions* by Anna Llenas
- *Beautiful Oops!* by Barney Saltzberg

DREAM CAREERS FOR A LIBRA

Interior designer	Mediator
Event planner	School counselor
Personal stylist	Matchmaker

SCORPIO

Your Scorpio baby was born with an undeniable magnetism and the capacity to experience emotions deeply. Co-ruled by both action-oriented Mars and powerful Pluto, Scorpios are commanding, mysterious, intense, and intuitive.

Your Scorpio toddler will be charismatic in a quiet, powerful way. Even as a little one, they'll exude an air of being commanding and in control—particularly of their feelings. But the fact is that their emotions are deep and occasionally stormy, and they are unafraid to swim in them. This could manifest in the form of stunning silence (they'll refuse to respond to you when you ask them questions) or an epic Mars-fueled meltdown that leaves you vowing to do whatever it takes to avoid that again. The whole point of either is to show you who your toddler believes is really the boss. Even when they're upset, your Pluto-ruled kiddo wants to appear 100 percent in control.

On the flip side, your fixed water sign toddler will generally express an equally intense joy when they're engaging with the experiences and people that bring them a sense of security. Sure, all kids love Daniel Tiger at some point, or go through a stage of wearing only dresses (or perhaps just that one Princess Raya dress!). But this isn't really transient for a Scorpio. Once they're into something, they're all in—forever, if at all possible.

And with their co-ruler powerful Pluto at play, they'll attract a crew of playground or preschool buddies without much effort at all. Other kids will be equally intrigued and drawn to your quietly magnetic and ambitious toddler.

HOW TO NURTURE YOUR MINI SCORPION'S VOICE

Honor their pace. From being comfiest in a nursery that's basically pitch-black to despising being prodded for information they're not yet ready to share, your Scorpio is particular and protective of their space and their feelings. You'll do best to give them plenty of time to process on their own. Then, simply remind them that they can tell you anything and you've got their back, and eventually, they'll come around.

Respect their need to tell you private matters in confidence. Scorp wants to know that they can trust you to keep their secrets, which could be that they are struggling to make it to the potty, scribbled on the wall, or think a preschool playmate is sweet and funny. So if they admit to anything like this, it's likely something they'll expect you to keep to yourself. (Of course if you need to tell your partner or another caregiver, you might do so in a low-key way.) If they want to share with someone else, they will.

Spend quality time with loved ones. Considering that Scorpio is associated with the Eighth House, prioritizing emotional bonding time with their VIPs can be particularly useful for helping them to express themselves. After all, when they're surrounded by the people who feel comfortable and familiar to them—especially if those people are speaking openly about how they feel—Scorpio will be even more empowered to speak from the heart.

POSSIBLE FIRST WORDS FOR A SCORPIO

"Bath"	"Quiet"
"Hug"	"Red"
"Mine"	"No"

TOOLS TO HELP YOUR TINY SCORPIO LEARN & GROW

Anything that's a series. "Creature of habit" is an understatement when describing your Scorp. They're one of the signs most likely to want to read the same bedtime story every night. To urge them to spread their wings—er, pincers—a bit: Read about the same characters, in different stories, by finding a book series they adore. Or zero in on a genre that really appeals (like sci-fi or mystery).

A private space. Having the option to learn solo, in a quiet area that's entirely their own, is invaluable to your little Scorp. Whether it's a tent in the corner of a living room or a spot in their bedroom dedicated to books and educational toys, you'll be supporting your fixed water sign's need to shape and feel comfortable in their environment, which will help them be even more confident and excited to explore.

Routine bonding time. Consider blending one-on-one time with eye-opening moments. Establish a weekend tradition of taking a walk along the same trail while learning about different plants and animals together.

INSTANT CLASSICS FOR A SCORPIO

Stories with mysterious, otherworldly, and imaginative plotlines that will appeal to your Scorp:

- *The Miss Spider* board book series by David Kirk
- Eric Carle's Very Little Library
- *Where the Wild Things Are* by Maurice Sendak
- *The Gruffalo* by Julia Donaldson
- *The Darkest Dark* by Chris Hadfield and Kate Fillion
- *Nate the Great* by Marjorie Weinman Sharmat

DREAM CAREERS FOR A SCORPIO

Private investigator

Forensic scientist

Chemist

Couples therapist

CEO of a start-up

SAGITTARIUS

With the sign of the Archer at the helm, your baby is all about exploring and philosophizing. Soaking up knowledge (sometimes pushing their limits in order to do so) is integral to their happiness. If they're not learning, they feel they're missing out. Boredom might be the main trigger for ginormous toddler meltdowns. As the sign connected to the Ninth House of Adventure, they dream of ultimately learning about all corners of the planet, but investigating every nook and cranny of their own little world might have to do for now—and they'll embrace whatever's in their path with a fun-loving, joyful, excitable attitude. Just about everything they do is big—from looking at you wide-eyed to reaching their arms out when they stretch and eating with unparalleled exuberance. This boisterous, buoyant energy is due to the mutable fire sign's ruling planet, go-big-or-go-home Jupiter.

When they're tiny, they'll reveal this Jupiterian influence with a ton of overjoyed, roaring squeals, flailing limbs, and wiggliness. And as a toddler, your fiery Sag will express themselves physically with big hand gestures, waving arms, and huge grins. They'll also be unfiltered about how they're feeling, pulling no punches—yes, even with a limited vocabulary. They'll be the first to tell you what they really think of those homemade chicken nuggets. After all, they'll grow up to value the truth above all else.

And as a natural-born entertainer, your little Sag will vie for your laughter by repeating an eyebrow-raising word they've heard you say accidentally or howling alongside the family pup.

Bear in mind that more is always better for your little Sag. More time spent reading with you, more time with loved ones, more laughter, more seeing, doing, and soaking up all that life has to offer.

HOW TO NURTURE YOUR MINI ARCHER'S VOICE

Praise their penchant for assertiveness while teaching empathy. Fiery, honest, and direct, your Sag has a tendency to spout out whatever it is they're thinking—as a toddler and beyond! You'll want to champion their candidness and desire to be genuine, as those are applause-worthy traits to be sure. But you can also help them work on feeling a situation out before blurting out their take. For example, if your Sag toddler offers up a harsh observation about a friend after a playdate, you can ask them how they think their friend might feel if they heard them say that, which can help foster empathy and hopefully, in turn, diplomacy.

Don't shy away from worldly subjects. Archers have a strong sense of right and wrong and, even as little ones, feel like citizens of the world, so your Sag toddler could express interest in something you might not think to touch on until they're older, like climate change or voting. Involving them in your recycling routine or filling out your ballot could be a way to start an enriching dialogue.

Lean on silliness. Your Archer is naturally funny, and they could find a lot of comfort in sharing how they feel and what they're experiencing through comedy. Goofing around together, urging them to tell jokes, and perhaps even putting on "stand-up" shows as a family can make for lots of hilarious memories—and a solid foundation for your budding comedian to be creative.

POSSIBLE FIRST WORDS FOR A SAGITTARIUS

"More!"	"There"
"Big!"	"Funny"
"Whee!"	"Go!"

TOOLS TO HELP YOUR TINY SAGITTARIUS LEARN & GROW

Lots of adventuring. Sagittarians have a burning wanderlust their whole lives, so if you're big on travel and want to bring your Archer kid, you could be surprised by just how cooperative they'll be when they're being treated to exhilarating new sights and sounds. But even if you're simply buckling into the car versus hopping on a flight together, you can get your little Archer babbling a bunch by driving to neighborhoods they've never seen, exploring local museums, or even going on a camping trip.

Spending time in big, open spaces. Sag will thrive by having as much room as possible to run, play, imagine, and explore. Head out to a field or your own garden and blow bubbles, check out unusual trees and plants, identify wildlife, or fly a kite.

Rituals. As much as your Archer is invested in discovering whatever's new and exciting, they also find a lot of joy in spirited, time-honored traditions, like holidays, birthdays, even special family dinners. Involve your Sag in the prep work (maybe you bake a family recipe or make a festive playlist together) while discussing the history and the meaning behind the event.

INSTANT CLASSICS FOR A SAGITTARIUS

Adventurous tales that touch on a variety of Archer themes from exploring the world to horseback riding and celebrating bigger as better:

- *The Snowy Day* by Ezra Jack Keats
- *Every Cowgirl Needs a Horse* by Rebecca Janni
- *Busy, Busy World* by Richard Scarry
- *Oh, the Places You'll Go!* by Dr. Seuss
- *This Is How We Do It: One Day in the Lives of Seven Kids from around the World* by Matt Lamothe
- *If You Give a Mouse a Cookie* by Laura Numeroff

DREAM CAREERS FOR A SAGITTARIUS

Flight attendant	Publisher
Travel writer	Comedian
Professor	Politician

CAPRICORN

Your small Sea Goat is pragmatic, tradition-loving, and goal-oriented. From early on, they'll equate learning and growing with achievement. The better they can wrap their heads around any aspect of life, the greater the chance they'll be able to make their way up whatever mountain they've set their sights on climbing. This lens is a no doubt practical, studious one, and it's owed to the cardinal earth sign's ruling planet: taskmaster Saturn.

When they're just a sleepy newborn bundle, they might offer up facial expressions that you'd expect to see only on someone older than your child. That wise-beyond-their-years vibe tends to be especially apparent when they're kids, but as they get older—perhaps once they've hit lofty goals—they tend to find more levity.

As the cardinal earth sign, they'll be most content when they're working toward their ambitions. Whether attempting to grab a toy that's just out of reach or mastering a pull-up game that helps them move from a sitting to a standing position, they're constantly striving to master the next level of development.

Your Sea Goat toddler will also be eager to put together a complicated puzzle, create a craft that requires lots of concentration (like making a pasta necklace), and grow their own pint-size garden. And then, sooner or later, they might decide that when they grow up, they're going to be lauded in their chosen field like fellow Cap Lin-Manuel Miranda, or a CEO, or even POTUS.

Your Cap wants to communicate just like you do, so they'll quietly zero in on your lips and hand gestures, those ambitious Cap wheels already spinning, trying to master grown-up behavior. They'll also respect "no" early, because they're wired to recognize authority.

HOW TO NURTURE YOUR MINI SEA GOAT'S VOICE

Give them opportunities to step into an authoritative role. As much as your Saturnian Cap respects rules, regulations, and you as the person in charge of setting and implementing them, they itch to feel like they're in the driver's seat early on. Give them a piggy bank (inserting coins helps with fine motor skills too!), allow them to pick and choose chores they'll help with, or set up a lemonade stand together. Any way in which they're able to feel like they're getting a taste of adulthood and being a boss will fuel confident self-expression.

Create opportunities for them to connect with their peers. Although that precocious Capricorn point of view can make it easier for your little Goat to connect with older siblings and playmates, they might feel a little out of place at times around children their own age. You can set them up for social success by planning group playdates early on. Even if they're just playing side by side with kids their age, it'll help them get comfier with the dynamic that'll be inevitable as they go to preschool and beyond.

Applaud mistakes. If they choose the wrong word, pronounce it incorrectly ("Dad, are we taking the alligator?" versus "elevator"), or offer up the wrong answer ("A, B, C, G . . ."), it'll be best to mirror it back to them the right way ("Yes, we're getting in the elevator"). Then, you can never go wrong with celebrating "oops" moments as you point out that they present an opportunity to learn.

POSSIBLE FIRST WORDS FOR A CAPRICORN

"Climb"

"Slow"

"Shh"

"Grandma," "Grandpa," or an older loved one's name

"Dada" (Cap's planet, Saturn, rules fathers)

"Goat"

TOOLS TO HELP YOUR TINY CAPRICORN LEARN & GROW

Early learning around media literacy and fact-checking. Your Cap wants to engage with authoritative voices (and to ultimately be one), so they'll want to be sure that any information they're soaking up is worthy of their respect. A useful first step: Talk to your Cap preschooler about the fact that what they see and hear on TV, apps, and other forms of media is information that was put out there by people who are just like you and them. Then, you can discuss who the "authority" actually is, laying the groundwork for them to ask more advanced questions on the subject down the road.

Modeling emotional self-care. Your hardworking Cap tends to believe that putting their nose to the grindstone is the best way to get ahead, but as admirable as that work ethic is, they'll also benefit from seeing the importance of tending to emotions. Encouraging them to carve out time to do that will help them develop valuable life skills.

Opportunities to build something tangible. As a practical earth sign, your Cap will appreciate seeing their hard work pay off in the form of something tactile. Get their creative juices flowing and hone a sense of accomplishment by working with play dough, building with LEGOs, or baking together.

INSTANT CLASSICS FOR A CAPRICORN

Titles that star your Sea Goat's symbol or teach crucial lessons about chasing your dreams, leadership, and being human:

- *Goat in a Boat* by Lesley Sims
- *It's Okay to Make Mistakes* by Todd Parr
- *Courageous People Who Changed the World* by Heidi Poelman
- *The One and Only Sparkella Makes a Plan* by Channing Tatum
- *One, Two, Three . . . Climb!* by Carol Thompson
- *Let's Go Explore* by Mimochai

DREAM CAREERS FOR A CAPRICORN

CEO	Financial planner
Secretary of the Treasury	Personal trainer
	Architect

AQUARIUS

Your mini Water Bearer is sociable, forward-thinking, strong-minded, and innovative. They'll strive to show you who they are, as Aquarians can't help but assert their individuality. This stems from the sign's ruling planet, the electrifying planet of change, Uranus.

An Aquarian little one might surprise you with unexpected sounds, gurgles, and facial expressions that portray their nascent but already eccentric point of view. And they might rebel against being cared for in traditional ways. For instance, while some babies adore being swaddled, your baby Water Bearer is the type to resist it. (In fact, anything that feels too confining could lead to a spontaneous downpour of tears.) As the fixed air sign, they'll let you know what they like—and don't like—from the way they're held to a go-to rattle. Your kid will grow up to prize what they see as a rational approach above all else, so when they express how they feel, it's in a "just-the-facts" way.

Feeling like part of a group or a team is very much in your child's wheelhouse, as the sign associated with the Eleventh House of Friends. The expression "it takes a village" applies to every baby, but that's something your Aquarius child will innately understand, open to being cared for by not just you but other relatives or a professional caregiver. And everyone who connects with your Water Bearer could, in some way, feel like they've just forged a lifelong bond with the friendliest baby they've ever met.

They're also at their happiest when they're bringing their own twist to anything they're learning. Your Water Bearer toddler will pride themselves on asking an out-there question or dreaming up a new, unconventional way to play with a toy. And they'll usually find a way to charm and rope anyone around them into whatever undertaking they've come up with. For instance, your Water Bearer will have no trouble getting Grandpa to crawl around with them or throw together a costume from items around the house and become their own made-up superhero.

HOW TO NURTURE YOUR MINI WATER BEARER'S VOICE

Celebrate what makes them unique.
You might want to read stories about historical figures, artists, and scientists who once raised eyebrows but persisted in making their mark on the world. Or applaud your Water Bearer for their unconventional (and brilliant) takes. Either way, they'll be hugely validated by consistently hearing that their sometimes eccentric way of showing up in the world is a gift.

Hold plenty of space for innovation.
Although your Aquarian is keen to connect with others and will generally find it easy to do so, striking out against convention might as well be their favorite pastime, so they'll also want to create their own unique style of communication. This could mean making up words, experimenting with giggle-inducing accents, playing with volume, and telling jokes that make zero sense. The best thing you can do: Go with it!

Spotlight science. Your Water Bearer is likely to take an interest in the factual why and how behind just about anything. No doubt that mini-lessons on the science behind a given interest could quickly provoke excited chatter from your Water Bearer. They'll be especially fascinated by "airy" subjects—a discussion on how kites or airplanes work could turn into a lifelong infatuation.

POSSIBLE FIRST WORDS FOR AN AQUARIUS

"Water"	Something wacky, made-up, and/or totally out of left field
"Silly"	
"Plane"	
A friend's name	"Fly"

TOOLS TO HELP YOUR TINY AQUARIUS LEARN & GROW

Innovative twists on classic lessons. The more off-beat a story, art project, or activity, the more your Aquarius is going to eat it up. Maybe you'll place glowy stickers on the ceiling of your Water Bearer's nursery and have tummy time sessions "under the stars" or make up rules when you play with a ball (think: challenging them to touch their toes before they toss it to you).

Group learning opportunities. While some children will prefer to learn one-on-one (Libra) or from the comfort of a familiar environment (Taurus), your Aquarius will adore being a part of a team—take them to a parent-and-baby music or art class, and they'll have a blast.

STEM activities. Your science-minded Water Bearer toddler will love donning a white lab coat—figuratively and literally—and testing any kind of hypothesis. Show them how vinegar and baking soda react when combined, watch a video that illustrates the metamorphosis of a caterpillar into a butterfly, or create and play with sensory bins.

INSTANT CLASSICS FOR AN AQUARIUS

Titles that pay tribute to the Aquarius symbol, the Water Bearer, being unique, and cherishing community:

- *Thank You, Omu!* by Oge Mora
- *The Day the Crayons Quit* by Drew Daywalt
- *The Water Princess* by Susan Verde
- *Unstoppable* by Adam Rex
- *The Day You Begin* by Jacqueline Woodson
- *We Are Water Protectors* by Carole Lindstrom

DREAM CAREERS FOR AN AQUARIUS

Scientist	Indie rock musician
Nonprofit executive director	Surgeon general
Community organizer	Electrician

PISCES

Your little one, born under the sign of the Fish, is intuitive, sensitive, and artistic. Reading emotions comes naturally to them, and as a mutable water sign, they're a sponge, apt to pick up on your feelings and blend them into their own mood. If you're excited, they'll offer up elated coos. If you groan, they might grimace. It's not that they're mimicking you necessarily. They're just extraordinarily empathic and emotionally receptive.

Ruled by Neptune, the planet of mysticism, your Pisces child will often communicate quietly—think: a dreamy, sweet gaze and gentle sounds that somehow bring the ocean to mind. You may feel like you're developing a psychic connection with your little Fish. But loud noises, too-bright lights, or a stressed-out loved one are all potential triggers for a dramatic display from your tiny Pisces. Your Fish can't help but feel all the things, and they're much better off expressing and releasing those emotions than not.

As the sign associated with the Twelfth House of Spirituality, they'll be at their most content when they have plenty of time and space for make-believe.

They will also be quick studies on creative ways to channel their emotions. Theater, poetry, and music are particularly intriguing to a Fish child. As they begin to learn and use language, they might even sound like a pint-size Amanda Gorman (whose sun is in Pisces, by the way). But they might loathe lessons that require memorization and are taught in a straightforward—and to Pisces, snoozy—way (for instance, with flash cards). Your Pisces would prefer to learn in ways that allow their imagination to run wild. And because they might struggle to believe in themselves, any technique that serves to boost their confidence will help them be an even more engaged learner as well, especially when it comes to anything colorful, musical, poetic, or whimsical play.

HOW TO NURTURE YOUR MINI FISH'S VOICE

Introduce them to every creative outlet imaginable. Although lots of Pisces take to acting or poetry, there's a chance your little Fish will be a big fan of dance, watercolors, playing an instrument, or all of the above. Their capacity for artistic expression is truly phenomenal, and it's one of the best and healthiest ways for them to identify and work through all the big emotions they can't help but pick up on and feel themselves.

Encourage your Fish to tune in to and celebrate their own emotions. Pisces people can't help but pinpoint and swim in other people's thoughts, feelings, opinions, energy! This can be overwhelming and also inhibit their own self-exploration and awareness. But you can empower your Fish early on by encouraging them to turn their focus inward. It

could be as simple as asking your Pisces to draw what happiness "looks" like to them or jointly coming up with their very own power pose (like standing with their hands on their hips or like their favorite superhero, whether that's the Hulk or Wonder Woman) that reflects their inner strength and bravery.

Prioritize make-believe. Just about every toddler benefits from letting their imagination run wild, but creating a magical fictional world that you can exist within for an hour, a day, or longer is 100 percent in your Fish's wheelhouse. Whether you make costumes, sets, and props out of everyday objects or buy them online, your Pisces child will be downright enthralled by the opportunity to act out their vivid daydreams.

POSSIBLE FIRST WORDS FOR A PISCES

"Heart"	"Hug"
"Soft"	"Love"
"Kiss"	"Fish"

TOOLS TO HELP YOUR TINY PISCES LEARN & GROW

Positive self-talk. Every little one has their own blocks that can cloud their ability to think clearly and soak up new information, and for your little Fish, that can be overpowering waves of emotion—and sometimes self-doubt. Help your growing Pisces find inner calm with upbeat mantras, like, "I can do this," "I am strong," "I am powerful."

A more productive naptime. If there's any sign that can prove getting swept away by daydreams is actually conducive—versus counter—to learning and growing, it's Pisces. Nurture your Fish's tendency to let their imagination wander by challenging them to report back on what they thought or dreamed about during their nap. From there, you could turn it into an art or science project.

Spotlighting perseverance. As your Pisces works through a challenging task—like playing a matching game—they might struggle with dedication and begin to drift toward overwhelm. If this happens, they'll benefit from warm words of encouragement, reminding them that they've made it this far, and if they keep at it, they'll prevail and feel accomplished.

INSTANT CLASSICS FOR A PISCES

Books that explore themes and lessons fit for your Fish, like working through overwhelming emotions, boosting confidence, and honing creativity:

- *The Wonderful Things You Will Be* by Emily Winfield Martin
- *Jabari Jumps* by Gaia Cornwall
- *The Boy With Big, Big Feelings* by Britney Winn Lee
- *There, There* by Tim Beiser
- *I Can Do Hard Things: Mindful Affirmations for Kids* by Gabi Garcia
- *Drum Dream Girl: How One Girl's Courage Changed Music* by Margarita Engle

DREAM CAREERS FOR A PISCES

Artist	Stage actor
Astrologer	Poetry professor—
Filmmaker	maybe even a
Yoga teacher	poet laureate

HEALTH

&

VITALITY

WHETHER YOU'RE IN THE MIDST OF preparing for parenthood or learning as you go, there's only so much you can know until you're in the thick of it. And whether you're working on weaning, tummy time, teaching your baby how to walk, or helping your toddler burn off excess energy, one of the greatest variables will always be, well, your little one themselves—their individual strengths, challenges, interests, and emotions. While you'll take note of a lot of this along the way, considering your little one's astrological wiring can equip you with clues on how to best care for their health and vitality. Then, as you work toward milestones, plan outings and games, and even think about the best way to cope with misbehavior, taking the wisdom of your baby's natal chart into account can make for smoother sailing.

ARIES

Your Aries is spirited and action-oriented thanks to their Mars-driven nature, which affects their physical, mental, and emotional well-being. No matter how tiny they are, they'll pretty much always be high-energy and up for any activity that's competitive, fast-paced, potentially reckless, and offers a rush. For this reason, they're notorious for pulling daring tricks during playtime and sticking to a healthy routine as a result of their signature impatience. For example, feeding might be a struggle as they are more likely than other signs to get distracted, squirmy, and fussy. But given their upbeat, carefree attitude, they'll usually brush off any ailment quickly.

On the other hand, the red-hot Mars energy that fuels your baby Ram's insatiable drive also powers their motivation to cross the finish line. Whether it's potty- or sleep-training, you'll score big when you turn a challenge into a game they can win. Just be aware of the fact that their propensity for speed and impulsivity can make them one of the most accident-prone tykes of the zodiac.

As the first sign, an Aries child is innately playful, innocent, and rambunctious (even more so than the average little one). By holding their wide-eyed, fun-loving perspective in mind, you can come up with go-getter twists on healthy habits that'll benefit their growing heart, body, and mind. For example, if you want them to try a healthy snack or activity, use their desire to be first or declared number one to your advantage by talking up just how new and cool it is.

Because your fired-up Ram is so inclined to charge through one activity after the next at such a rapid pace, you can potentially preempt "oops" and "ouch" moments by prioritizing chill-out time. It will help your little Aries to be consistently reminded of the benefits of slowing down, like being able to recognize and process emotions and connect in a heartfelt way with you and other loved ones.

HOW TO MEET RESISTANCE FROM YOUR ARIES

Your Aries baby wants to move, push their limits, play, and claim the number one spot in any group setting. Asking them to slow down or work on their patience could lead to turbulence. Help them work through rocky emotions with these techniques:

Create a calm-down space. As wonderful as Mars energy is for helping your little Aries get motivated and moving, it can be tough for them to wind down. For that reason, it may help to have a dedicated space where your Aries toddler can retreat when frustration strikes. Include objects that you know soothe your toddler, like a fidget toy.

Make it easy for them to blow off steam. Sometimes your fired-up Aries needs to go, go, go until they're totally tuckered out. Try refocusing their energy for use in very active games, like racing or jumping. Or encourage your Aries toddler to use their imagination and walk like an animal: "fly" like a bird; gallop like a horse; leap like a frog.

Design a competitive game. If your little Aries is crossing the line, think of how you can flip the script and create a scenario in which good behavior leads to a mental win. After all, they're wired to strive to achieve in a major way and be awarded the grand prize. So whether they're refusing to nap or getting bored during a car ride, try a game, like a shapes pop quiz (name several objects, like the sun and a Hula-Hoop, and have them guess "circle!") or challenging them to name all the colors they see within a set time frame (maybe you set your phone timer for a minute) to redirect their attention and allow them to feel like they've come out on top.

WELLNESS-RELATED ACTIVITIES FOR YOUR MINI RAM

Take your little fire sign on a jog. Because they love speed, your tiny Aries will appreciate heading out into nature in a jogging stroller, enjoying the sights and sounds around them.

Do a quick-paced yoga sequence. To teach them that mindfulness and exercise can go hand in hand, encourage your Aries to join you in a fast-paced sun salutation sequence that perfectly blends both Mars and fire sign energy.

Give them a scalp massage. As the ruler of the head, your little Ram could benefit greatly from gentle, soothing, circular strokes on their head.

Teach them a body scan meditation. Arm your Aries with a technique for soothing stress and getting centered whenever their anger-prone Mars-ruled tendencies take hold. Coach them through lying down, taking several deep breaths, then thinking about how each body part—from their toes all the way to the crown of their head—feels. Make it even more appealing as a regularly scheduled activity by creating a special meditation chart for which your win-driven Ram can earn gold stars that go toward a reward.

Create a timed treasure hunt. Whether they're on a mission to track down their hidden toy truck or a particular block, you can tap into your Ram's love of competition and adventure by scouring—perhaps in a sandbox or their play space—on the clock, which will help burn off excess energy.

TAURUS

Your tiny Taurus's calm yet stubborn nature extends to their physical, mental, and emotional well-being. Those born under the fixed earth sign are tough, rarely griping about any kind of ailment. If they do end up feeling out of sorts, they might keep the stress to themselves in order to maintain their strong persona. This could mean that your baby Bull takes what appears to be a rough tumble during playtime and pops back up acting like nothing happened. Or they might be fighting off a cold yet remain surprisingly unfussy.

This tendency to not want to shed light on discomfort could extend to potty troubles, like struggling to pipe up when it's time to change their diaper or take a trip to the bathroom. For this reason, it can be helpful to gently remind your little Bull that it's OK to give voice to their needs.

You'll also want to take their acute attunement to all five senses into consideration. If they're overtired, try an infant massage using lavender-scented lotion or essential oil that appeals to their sense of smell. If they're not pleased with what you're serving for dinner—remember, they can be pretty obstinate—allow them a chance to touch or sniff the food being served.

And no matter what is irking your baby Bull, having a tried-and-true routine—their go-to snuggly lovey, soothing lullabies, and cuddle time with you—will help them feel more blissful and secure.

HOW TO MEET RESISTANCE FROM YOUR TAURUS

Your Taurus child is a fan of keeping the peace and pleasing you, but they're also apt to dig in their heels to maintain the status quo. This could make any moment that involves big change—like weaning them from breast milk to formula or moving from two naps a day down to one—especially challenging. Try these tricks for steering mini Bulls away from tantrums and troublesome moves while encouraging them to learn and grow.

Use a sticker chart. Even at their littlest, Taureans appreciate organizational systems. That's why you might want to consider a special chart or calendar that will allow your toddler Bull to track their progress by letting them add a sticker every time they've demonstrated the reward-worthy behavior, be that using the potty or putting away their toys. You could establish a rule that once they've gotten a certain number of stickers, they'll earn a reward like a trip to the playground (tapping into their earth sign nature) or a new art supply (making the most of their Venusian influence).

Give them options. When your little Bull is asserting their independence, as most toddlers do, they're looking for a way to be in control. On these occasions, set a boundary around their choices. If they're adamant about wearing the same outfit to school every day, offer them a couple of options and let them choose between the new ones; that way, they'll feel they've had their say.

Lean on crafts and coloring. Thanks to their ruler, beauty-loving Venus, your little Bull will quickly take to expressing themselves creatively. If you sense that they're acting out because they're bored or dealing with pent-up energy, give them crayons and blank paper and urge them to scribble out their feelings. Or consider a step-by-step art project, which taps into their interest in engaging with activities in a slow, steady, orderly way.

WELLNESS-RELATED ACTIVITIES FOR YOUR MINI BULL

Take tummy time outside. Whenever weather permits, your tiny Taurus will appreciate being surrounded by nature, even while developing crucial motor skills. Lay down a blanket in a patch of grass, set up a simple picnic, and work on building your Bull baby's core.

Wear your baby Bull on a stroll. Remember that your tiny Taurus likes to go slow. They'll love cozying up next to you while you traverse a peaceful park.

Don't be afraid to get dirty. Creating opportunities for your baby Taurus to play in sand (consider a trip to the beach) or dirt (think: gardening as a family) can be a wonderful way for your little earth sign to explore and get in touch with their element, which can be both mentally stimulating and calming.

Involve them in food prep. Because your mini Bull derives pleasure from experiences that involve their five senses, they'll love everything about eating. Take advantage of this and involve them in all the steps of meal prep. Pick out fruits and veggies together at the farmers market, talk about how you'll prepare them, then let them participate in an age-appropriate way—washing the produce, plating a dish, or bringing it to the table.

Strike a soothing yoga pose. During playtime, your small Bull might prefer low-key activities over fast-paced ones like joining you in a grounding yoga pose, such as Bitilasana, or Cow Pose, which can also help them channel the strength of their astrological symbol.

GEMINI

Raising a Gemini requires becoming familiar with their inquisitive, social, cerebral, and dualistic Mercury-fueled nature, which colors their overall well-being. For even the smallest Twins kid, the wheels are always turning as they aim to gather and share information with you, a sibling, a playmate, another caregiver—anyone, really. And spending all that time in their heads and striving to communicate and connect can lead to a restlessness that will have your spirited Gem flitting from one activity to the next, readily engaging with people and technology, and, at times, struggling to get centered, settled, and calm enough to sit still or catch some z's.

It follows that your little one might suffer from FOMO, wanting to play beyond their nap or bedtime. They can also tend to be on edge—sometimes because their little mind is racing, or given their tendency to learn about their environment through sound (a result of being ruled by the planet of communication), because they're sensitive to particular noises (like a car horn or a squeaky hinge).

Given the dualistic nature of Gemini, you might find that your little one can go from being calm to fussy, engaged to withdrawn, energetic to exhausted in the blink of an eye. This could make for a bit of whiplash when trying to tend to their needs, but thanks to your child's cerebral nature, a gloomy mood can often be rectified by an activity that engages them mentally like reading a favorite book or learning a simple breathing technique together.

Tapping into your Gemini's connection to the planet of communication is an essential key to helping them thrive. Urge them to talk about and show you what's bothering them, and you'll be on your way to supporting them effectively.

HOW TO MEET RESISTANCE FROM YOUR GEMINI

Your Twins kid loves social time and connecting with the people around them. Being confronted with quiet alone time could feel like a snooze fest to your Gemini, resulting in frustration and possibly a surprising spontaneous outburst. Some tips for combating boredom and focusing energy while helping your Twins child cultivate calm:

Encourage sensory play. Think of a device constantly bleeping, buzzing, and striving to notify you of a breaking news story or social media post. That energy is all Mercury, which you now know is Gemini's guiding light. So often, you'll realize that your Twins child needs some kind of mental stimulation—even when it's time to chill out. If they're getting into mischief as a result of being agitated or restless, try leaning into sensory play to help your little one focus their high mental energy on a task that's also helping improve their fine and gross motor skills and cognitive development. Consider listening to "sound tubes," which you can make at home. Take two or three paper towel rolls; insert some small items that make different noises, like beads or sand; and seal up the ends with duct tape. You can also bake bread or pastries with them. Working with a mound of dough can be a wonderful way for your child to get out of their head and into a tactile project.

Teach them the words to express their feelings. In a moment of frustration or acting out, remind your Gemini toddler that their superpower is communicating how they feel. Make up a memory game for learning all the words they can use to describe their feelings. (For example, you might make flash cards with different emojis that illustrate emotions, and your Gemini can earn points for every one they accurately label.) As they get older, journaling is an effective way for them to express themselves.

Have a Q and A session. Thanks to their information-gathering savvy, Geminis might grow up to be reporters, editors, or researchers. Tap into your little air sign's skill set by initiating a ritual you call "Q and A," "press conference," or "pop quiz," in which you ask them questions about their behavior, how they're feeling, and why they think they feel that way, all of which can boost your understanding of a given situation while amplifying their emotional intelligence.

WELLNESS-RELATED ACTIVITIES FOR YOUR LITTLE GEMINI

Do a breathing exercise. Teach your little one Bhramari, or "Bee Breath," a type of yogic breath control named for a black Indian bee. To do: Sit up straight and close your eyes. Put your index fingers on the tiny flap of cartilage between your ear and cheek. Breathe in. As you breathe out, make a humming sound (like a bee!) while lightly pressing the cartilage. Inhale again and repeat several times. This practice can help soothe a tiny Gemini.

Attend a festive get-together. Making time for your social Gemini to be around friends, loved ones, and—perhaps most important—their peers is sure to benefit their well-being.

"Travel" and chat. Being on the go is as centering for Geminis as sharing what's on their minds, so take them for a drive or a walk and ask them to describe everything they see, hear, and feel.

Massage their hands. Because Gemini rules the hands and fingers and often uses them to gesture when they're speaking, they might find a gentle hand massage especially satisfying.

Emphasize connection in the evening. Settling down during their pre-bedtime routine can feel more than boring to your high-energy Gemini—it might seem downright lonely. Incorporate socializing (like "inviting" their favorite toy or imaginary friend to join you for story time) or even a simple one-on-one discussion about their day into their winding-down time so they'll feel more prepared to doze off.

CANCER

Your Cancer baby is sensitive, emotional, sentimental, and intuitive, thanks to being ruled by the moon, and this disposition undoubtedly affects their overall well-being. The tiniest Crab feels with all of their gentle heart; craves snuggles and security more than the average kid; and is quick to find ways to take care of their nearest and dearest people (and animals!). The drawback of this tenderhearted vibe: Your Cancer child might be so in tune with their emotions that it can be exhausting at times.

That Cancerian sensitivity—and in turn, emotional fatigue—can result in your little Crab either figuratively grasping on to you with their little pincers even more tightly or withdrawing into their shell. Your little water sign will also be prone to tantrums, and as a strategic cardinal sign, they'll be one of the earliest masters of leaning on these displays to gain your sympathy and get their way.

You'll want to arm your little Crab with skills to take care of themselves mentally and emotionally, from cultivating a kid-friendly mindfulness practice to talking about healthy ways to manage big emotions (like going for a walk, throwing a ball in the backyard, or having a dance party).

Addressing a Crab's emotional needs also means empowering their go-getter streak. This could look like giving your Cancer baby plenty of space to explore and decide what they'd most like to do during playtime. As toddlers, they'll enjoy being involved in exciting brainstorming sessions (perhaps around what's for dinner).

Helping your Cancer thrive is all about holding them close while offering them plenty of chances to access the wide-eyed, ambitious side of themselves that'll fuel their independence.

HOW TO MEET RESISTANCE FROM YOUR CANCER

Your little Crab might struggle with their own independence—and act out when nudged to play alone—because they are so attached to you. Here are tips for addressing any growing pains while ensuring that your Crab feels heard, seen, and soothed:

Preempt separation anxiety with scheduled bonding time. All too often, your Crab will lose their cool simply because they want more cuddles and one-on-one time with you and other loved ones. Getting ahead of this could be as easy as setting aside designated times to connect. Take a daily walk with your sweet Crab—either in a carrier or stroller or, if they're able to walk, hand in hand. Weekend dance/breakfast-making parties with your funny Crab toddler can also make for heartwarming moments.

Teach them responsibility with tasks. When emotions seem to be running the show, help your Cancer toddler channel their energy into a responsibility-building chore like putting away their toys or assisting you in the kitchen. They have an instinct to want to take care of their home and their loved ones, so tasks like these can feel especially rewarding for them.

Be sure they have a calming "nest." If misbehavior stems from feeling overwhelmed, your sensitive Crab tot might need a time-out to rest and recharge; having a cozy space to do that in is a must. Be sure they have their favorite blanket, softest lovey, and maybe even a couple of family photos (particularly comforting to your Cancer) nearby.

WELLNESS-RELATED ACTIVITIES FOR YOUR LITTLE CANCER

Spend time near water. Just about every water sign kid will benefit from this, and go-getter cardinal Cancers will be particularly into energetic water or water-adjacent activities. For example, fly a kite at your nearest beach or lake or take them for swimming lessons.

Listen to meditative music. Playing tranquil meditation music (like Tycho or Liquid Mind) for your mini Crab could help calm their nerves, boost feelings of security, and possibly do wonders to alleviate their signature fussing and "crabbing," an expression my Cancer partner's late mom so perfectly used to describe his grousing as a baby.

Give them a chest and tummy massage. Tend to your baby Crab's ruling body parts with a gentle massage. Not only is it a lovely way to boost your connection, but it could also help to relieve congestion or achiness if your Cancer's contending with either.

Set up a giggle fit. Laughter is a stress-reliever for adults and little ones alike, and your funny little Crab will likely find a lot of comfort in humor throughout their life. For that reason, consider prioritizing activities or games that never cease to entertain them (like peekaboo or mimicking sounds).

Involve them in your own daily self-care practices. Whether you introduce them to your regular meditation routine, Pilates class, or aromatherapy bath, you'll model the importance of nurturing oneself—and what that can look like.

LEO

Born under the sun-ruled fixed fire sign Leo, your little one is bold, self-assured, driven, optimistic, and fun-loving—all traits that influence your Lion's well-being. Leo cubs have no problem zeroing in on what they want—be that their favorite bedtime story or plenty of playtime with their favorite light-up musical toy—then prowling after it with plenty of conviction. Like their regal feline symbol, little Leos are inherently proud, and they'll take great pride in pursuing their needs. The con here is that they may make risky moves to assert their independence.

Similarly, instead of acknowledging anything from a cut to fever, your dynamic little Lion might want to focus on continuing to charge after whatever is going on in front of them, especially if it's an activity they see as particularly fun. The playful, party-loving sign is apt to suffer FOMO, and their desire to be a part of anything exciting might cause them to push to stay up beyond their bedtime.

Additionally, your tiny Lion may not slow down long enough to tend to tough emotions. And when they do finally have to face anger or fear, they might display their feelings in a gasp-worthy, dramatic way.

Addressing your Lion's emotional needs—and, in turn, their physical well-being—involves fostering a sense of empowerment related to rest. Explain to them how low-key activities will help them recharge so they can continue having fun.

And prioritizing spiritedness is key. Playing their favorite music while you do your nightly bedtime routine or taking dance breaks on a family walk can keep your Lion engaged while teaching them that wellness activities can always be made lighthearted and entertaining.

Working with your Leo's sunniness, pride, and confidence is the key to promoting the kind of balance and flexibility that will help them feel their best.

HOW TO MEET RESISTANCE FROM YOUR LEO

Your fixed fire sign not only appreciates consistency and sticking to the routines, patterns, places, and experiences they know and enjoy but is also wired to be assertive about what they want and need. As helpful as it is to have a vocal, confident child, they are apt to get so attached to their likes and dislikes that they'll struggle with shifting gears and potentially act out when faced with change.

As the sun-ruled Lion of the zodiac, whose tendency is to be self-focused, your toddler might be prone to temper tantrums that stem from not being the center of the attention as well as bossiness, needing to be reminded more than the average kid that they are not, in fact, running the show 24/7. Some tips for nurturing and encouraging positive behavior in your feisty Lion:

Offer your Leo opportunities to feel powerful. On their worst day, mini Lions might struggle with being pushy and demanding, either of which stems from wanting to feel like they have control over any given situation. For that reason, it can help to give your Leo toddler chances to make big decisions, whether that's choosing which bath toys to play with or which shoes they'll wear to the park.

Teach them about empathy. Whether your little Leo is refusing to let another child use the slide at the playground or is demanding attention when the focus is on a sibling, you can ask them how their actions might make a playmate or relative feel. Helping them see the flip side of the situation can be valuable for developing emotional intelligence.

Make manners and etiquette fun. Because they're prone to veer into domineering behavior, your Leo may need extra coaching with language that goes hand in hand with graciousness. Use a sticker chart to track how many times your Lion toddler uses words like "please" and "thank you" when making requests, or plan an exciting activity—like heading to a neighborhood café where your luxury-loving Leo gets to order their own special drink—where you can practice regal (a wise way to spin it for your proud Leo!) etiquette.

WELLNESS-RELATED ACTIVITIES FOR YOUR LITTLE LEO

Dance, dance, dance. Whether you're working in the garden, hanging out after dinner, or entertaining their sibling, preempt boredom and promote physical activity by throwing on upbeat music and moving and grooving with your little Lion, who pretty much always wants—as fellow Leo Whitney Houston once sang—"to dance with somebody." Even on a road trip, they'll enjoy wiggling and shaking in their car seat, aka car dancing!

Caring for pets. Your bighearted Leo will be a natural when it comes to helping out with pet chores, like giving the dog a bath, brushing the kitty, or feeding the goldfish. These activities can promote empathy and compassion.

An upper back rub before bed. Because your Lion can hold tension in their upper back, they may find a massage or a back scratch of this ruling body part especially soothing.

Cozy aromatherapy. As a fire sign— one ruled by the sun, no less—your Leo might not be the biggest fan of cold, dreary weather. Even if they have a blast taking brisk walks through autumn leaves or playing in the snow, they'll enjoy getting toasty afterward even more. For that reason, consider incorporating comfy, warm scents (like a creamy vanilla or bright citrus) into bath time or in a home diffuser.

Healthy ways to manage fiery feelings. Encourage your Lion toddler to work through their most intense emotions by leaning on an activity that bolsters their self-expression, whether that's drawing a picture that represents the feeling or doing a visualization technique (perhaps you suggest that they imagine a color that makes them feel happy and secure, then think about breathing that color in).

VIRGO

As your little mutable earth sign grows and their thoughtful, health-conscious, and cerebral disposition becomes more and more apparent, you'll notice that it's clearly linked to their overall well-being. Sensitive, mercurial, and tactile Virgo babies tend to be more affected by little details like a room's temperature, a strong-scented candle, or a spicy food.

It bears noting that thanks to their ruler, Mercury, the planet of communication, Virgos have a tendency to overthink, which could cause your Maiden to have trouble winding down for a nap or bedtime or to worry about an ailment, fearing that it's worse than it actually is. And their desire to be useful and to please you can lead to prioritizing caring for others above themselves, which can take a toll on self-image. So it's important to acknowledge their efforts and encourage self-care first and foremost.

To tend to your Virgo's overall well-being, start with their busy brains, and lean into their affinity for routine. From practicing mindfulness out in nature (perhaps proposing that you watch the clouds move across the sky or listen to the birds chirping) to using a meditation app (like Headspace for Kids or Breathe, Think, Do with Sesame) together, strive to build consistent, calming rituals into your mutable earth sign's daily routine. After all, as the sign associated with the Sixth House of Wellness, Virgo loves effective tricks they can rely on.

Introducing your Virgo to self-soothing techniques early on will not only help them feel more centered mentally and physically but also lay the groundwork for habits they'll use for years to come.

HOW TO MEET RESISTANCE FROM YOUR VIRGO

As an earth sign, your pragmatic Virgo will follow the rules as long as they're presented with the why: *Put your toys away, so no one trips on them* and *Eating broccoli makes us strong and healthy*. Be prepared for pushback that stems from Virgo's characteristic overanalyzing and perfectionism, which fuel indecision. A few tips for empowering your Virgo:

Make step-by-step lists. Seeing small, manageable objectives written on a dry-erase board or even in pencil on a notepad can feel motivating to your Virgoan toddler.

Use calendars. If you're aiming to hit a longer-term goal—like no longer using a bottle or transitioning to a big-kid bed—track your Virgo's progress on a calendar; it's an especially empowering tool for your Virgo, who appreciates seeing how day-to-day accomplishments can add up to big change.

Turn story time into a win-win. Utilize your Virgo's adoration of the written word by reading books that involve a character learning any lesson or milestone you're actively working on. Whether you're helping your Mercury-ruled bookworm build courage, preempt nightmares, or get acclimated to the idea of a baby sibling, there's undoubtedly a title out there that explores that very topic, and Virgo will be enthused by the idea of following in a favorite character's footsteps.

WELLNESS-RELATED ACTIVITIES FOR YOUR MINI MAIDEN

Prioritize a.m. and p.m. routines. Your Maiden is eager to learn all about how to take care of themselves in those daily, Sixth House–style ways. In fact, while some children might need a bit of convincing to head upstairs to wind down for bed, a uniquely Virgoan trait is a love of feeling clean, so they'll usually happily comply when you say it's time for a bath or grooming.

Bring their favorite intellectual activities outside. Taking a blank pad and some crayons or your audiobook app to a serene park or even the backyard can be doubly soothing for a little Maiden. What a wonderful way to associate their favorite activities with an environment that can be emotionally grounding for them as an earth sign.

Offer them a comforting tummy massage. A belly rub will feel good to your Virgo baby, and it'll help move any trapped gas—which, as the ruler of the digestive system, your Maiden could be prone to.

Do this grounding yoga pose. Teach your cerebral Maiden Balasana, or Child's Pose. Show your child how to kneel with their knees hip-width apart, then lower their torso between their knees and rest it on the ground. They can then reach their arms out in front of them with their palms facing down. Their forehead should also touch the floor. Finally, they can wiggle their tush back toward their heels and take several deep breaths. This pose can serve as a wonderful way to simultaneously calm the mind and feel connected to the earth.

Garden together. Routines and acts of nurturing are both in your Virgo's wheelhouse, so they may very well have a green thumb. Whether they're roaming the house with a watering can or helping you pull up weeds, the to-dos of caring for plants benefit a Maiden toddler's mind and body. Plus: Growing anything you can later use in a recipe—from tomatoes to romaine or herbs—will strike your Virgo as exciting and rewarding, as "farm-to-table" is a concept earth signs embrace wholeheartedly.

LIBRA

Your cardinal air sign is fueled by beauty-loving, relationship-oriented Venus vibes, which go hand in hand with their physical, mental, and emotional well-being. Your Scales child is motivated to spend time around other people and participate in activities they find artistically appealing (like painting or dancing). But they're also one of the cardinal bunch, so they won't shy away from diving into uncharted terrain, whether that's trying the slide at a new playground or learning T-ball in the backyard. And they'll be happiest taking on a new challenge with a partner by their side, be that you or a playmate.

Your Libra baby might lack focus on a task like feeding or getting ready for bed when they sense there's an opportunity to connect with others. They are, after all, one of the signs most likely to suffer from major FOMO, so in those moments when they ditch the breast or bottle so they can make googly eyes at their aunt or throw a tantrum about having to take their evening bath when their sibling is still playing downstairs, you'll need to gently encourage them to get back on task. As they grow, sing the praises of sticking to healthy habits, even when it seems like there could be more fun to be had by socializing.

You'll want to be conscious of balance and harmony within your Libra's immediate environment. For instance, maybe you can show your Libra baby pretty photos from a recent trip to the beach while you wait in the pediatrician's office. Or your Libra toddler can listen to their favorite playlist while getting their first haircut or visiting the dentist. Showing them that they can lean on relaxing, beautiful art in any stress-spiking situation will offer your Libra a lifelong coping mechanism.

HOW TO MEET RESISTANCE FROM YOUR LIBRA

As a fan of all things easygoing and breezy, your cardinal air sign could get distracted, irritable, or even—gasp—act out as a result of having to do something that feels tedious, arduous, or uncomfortable. In their dream world, they would be able to rely on their natural amiability to get over any hurdle versus putting their nose to the grindstone, but of course, life is going to serve up a slew of occasions during which they'll have no choice but to do the latter. Tips for supporting your Libra during their tough moments:

Focus on self-love. Venusian energy helps us relate to one another, and it's what drives your little Libra. It's also what could cause them to put their bonds—and keeping the peace—above anything else, including their sense of self. Remind them that their relationship with themselves is the most important of all.

Be prepared to counter protests about "unfairness." Given how passionate your tiny Libra is about balance, serenity, and fairness, they might be quick to throw a fit over a situation being—in their eyes—anything but. "But that's not fair!" is something you'll hear from all the signs, sure, but it could come out of Libra's mouth more than most. The best way to handle this behavior: Try validating their feelings, showing them empathy by acknowledging that you often experience that emotion too, and urging them to focus on the aspects of the situation they can control.

Work on expressing anger. Because Libra's MO is to keep conversations conflict-free, light, and airy, their instinct is to tamp down any thoughts, opinions, or emotions they fear will spur rockiness. You can set a wonderful example for them by talking about—and, in turn, normalizing—feeling angry or sad. Then together you can try different ways to work through these less than harmonious emotions.

WELLNESS-RELATED ACTIVITIES FOR YOUR MINI SCALES

Use nature as a canvas. Urge your artistic little Libra to create their own masterpieces with anything they can get their hands on—leaves, branches, flowers, snow, dirt. Take photos of the final result so your child can look back on the beautiful work they produced.

Do a balance-building pose. Try Airplane Pose, or Dekasana, with your graceful, balance-focused air sign: Have them stand upright, their feet solid on the ground. Then they can slowly kick one leg back behind them while simultaneously bending their upper body forward. Encourage them to reach their arms back behind them as well, imitating wings. They can then work on staying balanced in the pose by picking a point or object on the ground to focus on. After several breaths, they can return their "flying" leg to the ground and try again on the other side.

Give them a lower back massage. Being that Libra rules this body part, your Scales baby will be all smiles when you offer up a gentle lower back massage, perhaps while they're being tucked in for a sweet night's sleep.

Pair them with a playmate. Libra will love doing anything active side by side or one-on-one with a family member or friend. Take your toddler out for a tricycle ride alongside their cousin or introduce your three-year-old to tennis.

Play parachute with friends. Any large swath of fabric like a bedsheet can transform into a magical parachute that your social air sign will be mesmerized by when you and another grown-up (or several) lift and float it up into the breeze. They and a friend or sibling or two can take turns racing to the other side before it falls back down.

SCORPIO

Given your Scorpio baby's intense, mysterious, powerful energy—owed to its co-rulers, action-oriented Mars and transformative Pluto—they can't help but be laser-focused on making fearless moves to pursue whatever their heart desires. Simultaneously, they're most content when they feel they're in control. This driving force can make for a determined child who wants to gain command of any challenge that's presented to them, whether that's rolling from their tummy to their back, getting accustomed to being worn in a baby carrier, or learning how to tread water during swim lessons as a toddler.

Fixed Scorpio's innate obstinacy can be a bit of a double-edged sword. It can help them hit milestones and stick to healthy habits but also cause them to dig in their heels and assert that they want just about anything their way—or not at all. Hold this in mind as you plan that trip to a new playground or begin teaching your Scorpion toddler how to brush their teeth. Given their co-ruler Pluto, which involves power and control, you'll find that they'll welcome new terrain more readily if they feel like they're getting to call the shots (at least to some extent; see page 129).

As they grow, you'll want to ensure that they have a comfortable, quiet, private space (ideally one that can be made dark and cool) to work through intense emotions, wind down, and recharge. This literal space goes hand in hand with giving them figurative space and respecting their need to share feelings in their own time, as this will also help them feel centered mentally, physically, and emotionally.

HOW TO MEET RESISTANCE FROM YOUR SCORPIO

When your little Scorpion encounters anything out of their comfort zone, they could react quite stubbornly. Whether you request that they put away their toys or propose going somewhere new, you could be met with a steely glare, an angry scowl, and/or deafening silence. Or if they feel overwhelmed by emotion, they could have a major meltdown that leaves your heart racing. Tips for supporting and nurturing your Scorpio when they refuse to budge:

Celebrate adventure. Scorpio's co-rulers—assertive Mars and regenerative Pluto—value action for the sake of transformation. Connect the dots for your Scorpion by explaining how getting out of their comfort zone and exploring the unknown can give them more knowledge, and the more we know, the more powerful we can be.

Talk about the consequences of their actions. As stubborn as a Scorp kid can be, they're also very methodical in how they think. Explaining that "Y" will lead to "Z" sounds simple, but it could be particularly effective when setting limits.

Build in ways for them to blow off steam. Because they're so private, your little Scorp is likely to let their biggest feelings brew and stew, raising the risk of an explosive tantrum—unless they have healthy outlets for working it all out. And given their Mars influence, being active can be especially therapeutic for your Scorpion. Show them that some of their favorite activities— doing an obstacle course in the backyard or going swimming—could all be wonderful ways to process anger or fear.

Applaud what you know are big leaps for them. Rewarding Scorpio for demonstrating adaptable behavior can encourage them to be more open-minded down the road.

WELLNESS-RELATED ACTIVITIES FOR YOUR MINI SCORPION

Bond near the water. Wear your little one as you walk on the beach or splash around in a backyard kiddie pool; spending quality time together near or in the water will benefit your fixed water sign's overall well-being.

Try Ananda Balasana, or Happy Baby Pose. This pose involves lying on your back with your feet in the air, holding the outside of the feet in your hands. Not only is this pose restorative but it can also release tension—and pent-up emotion—from the hips, which can be particularly beneficial for your deeply feeling but also quite private Scorp.

Give them a sinus massage—and use a humidifier. If your Scorpion is dealing with nasal congestion— which they may be more prone to than other children, as Scorpio rules the nose—you might offer delicate strokes between their eyebrows, the bridge of the nose, and above the sinus passages. You might also consider a cool mist humidifier

for your baby water sign's nursery, especially during dry winters.

Explore mindful movement. Talk about how we feel emotions in the body and encourage your Scorp toddler to show you where they feel excitement (maybe in their tummy) or where they feel anger (maybe in their temples). You might check out a book like *Listening to My Body* by Gabi Garcia to help them connect the dots between the physical sensations they experience and their feelings so they can get even more in tune with their needs and how to center themselves.

Go on scavenger hunts. Your Scorp is naturally investigative and has a penchant for mysteries, so age-appropriate, themed scavenger hunts can be mentally and physically stimulating for them. Try drawing five shapes on a piece of paper. Then challenge your toddler to locate an example of each one in a small space (the kitchen perhaps).

SAGITTARIUS

Your Sagittarius baby's daring, gregarious, optimistic energy is rooted in their ruling planet: fortunate, expansive Jupiter. The largest planet in our solar system, Jupiter amplifies everything it comes in contact with, promoting the belief that "More is better," which can often color Sag's overall well-being. They're highly motivated to be on the go and in the thick of any thrill they can find—or create—in an effort to explore, understand, learn, and grow. Plus, as a mutable sign, they're adaptable. This means they're one of the signs most likely to try anything new, which can be a boon for their health.

At the same time, they're pros at biting off more than they can chew—literally and figuratively. Your Archer can struggle to know their limits, which can result in bumps and bruises from daredevil tricks or pushing to stay up late because they want to spend more time "partying" with you or their older siblings. Any opportunity to have fun pretty much always beats whatever "makes sense" or is "good for them."

Support your little Archer's well-being by exposing them to various active learning experiences, like a dance class or soccer, a parent-and-child gym class, or a weekend getaway. Nurturing their well-being involves supporting their buoyant nature while simultaneously setting healthy boundaries to help them thrive.

HOW TO MEET RESISTANCE FROM YOUR SAGITTARIUS

Your Sag wants all the freedom in the world, and as a jovial, lively, upbeat little person, they can be incredibly entertaining or endearing while pushing for more of anything they enjoy, be that playtime, a snack, or maybe even an activity they're not quite old enough to do. Anytime they feel they're being held back from that free-spiritedness, you might face a tearful showdown. One of the best ways to care for their well-being—perhaps more so than for any other sign—is to set loving, healthy limits. This will benefit your restriction-averse, Jupiter-ruled child now and as they grow up and begin to set boundaries for themselves. Tips for supporting and nurturing your Sagittarius when they're pushing for more, more, more:

Strike a tone that's warm but definitive. Sag's playful ebullience can make it hard to put your foot down. But presenting and enforcing rules in a heartfelt but firm way is ultimately for their benefit.

Joke around. You can get pretty far with a challenging little Sag if you strive to make them laugh. Goofy, animated, physical comedy can be a particularly effective way to involve them in an activity they might initially have dismissed as dull.

Be direct. Even the smallest Sag values honesty above all else, so telling your toddler to stop jumping on the couch and not truthfully explaining the reason behind the rule—the fact that they could get hurt—might backfire. While you can't expect to rationalize with an exuberant toddler, you can explain in clear, direct terms why you need them to comply.

WELLNESS-RELATED ACTIVITIES FOR YOUR MINI SAGITTARIUS

Prioritize outdoor activities. Your Sag has an appetite for the great outdoors. Point out all the wildlife at a local park or try an age-appropriate archery set (quite on-brand for Sag). And whether you head to a park with a huge field and lay out a picnic blanket to practice tummy time with your Sag baby or take your Archer toddler to a spacious local playground, being in a large, open space will feel freeing and joyful for your mutable fire sign.

Practice mindfulness with a visualization technique. On days you can't make it outside—perhaps due to inclement weather or a multitude of must-dos at home—encourage your Archer to imagine they're watching the clouds or the birds or simply feeling the breeze, which will help them work on making the most of being in the moment—something that's particularly beneficial for an adventurer who often can't help but yearn to be somewhere more exciting.

Sprinkle a little magic into mundane activities. Infuse everyday routines with a little more fun and adventure. Perhaps you create a passport that they'll use to "travel" from dinner to bath time, or while waiting at the doctor's office, use a flash card set to learn about safari animals.

Try Warrior II, or Virabhadrasana II. This emboldening pose can help your Sag feel strong while stretching out and releasing a couple of their ruling body parts: the hips and thighs. To do: Stand upright, then step one leg behind you, keeping your heels aligned, and bending the front knee. Stretch your arms out to either side, and take a few deep breaths while looking past your fingertips. Then switch to the other side. (See Resources, page 347, for recommended sites.)

Combine creativity and activity. Whether you provide them with a huge blank canvas or a driveway, Sag will adore having a lot of room to make large-scale art. Encourage them to create something they can then use as part of a high-energy game, like a hopscotch course.

CAPRICORN

Your Capricorn baby's serious and collected energy stems from their ruling planet: taskmaster Saturn. The ringed planet's key purpose in astrology is to create and enforce boundaries, limitations, commitment, rules, and regulations in order to achieve goals, and this pragmatic, industrious perspective influences your little Sea Goat's well-being. They won't require much coaxing to eat their veggies or adhere to a schedule you or a caregiver sets for them, because they respect and find comfort in rules. But they're also industrious go-getters who are motivated to achieve, which can make it tough for them to embrace downtime.

Your mini Capricorn also aims to be seen as cool and calm even when they might not be feeling their best. The last thing in the world they want to appear is "weak," and society often sends the message that being in touch with your emotions—especially sadness and anger—is exactly that. But when pent up, Cap's emotions have to manifest somehow, and they might in the form of minor wellness woes, like a rash or a long-overdue cry. To support their mind, body, and heart, model emotional self-care and reframe downtime as empowering and integral to feeling your best inside and out.

HOW TO MEET RESISTANCE FROM YOUR CAPRICORN

Your Cap fancies themselves a little grown-up who is responsible and hardworking. And if they were born to be an authority figure, they certainly don't need *another* one telling them what to do! This is the thought that could be at the crux of clashes with your Sea Goat child. When the time comes for bed or getting buckled into their car seat to go on errands, you could be taken aback when they flat-out say "nah," completely chill and unbothered, as if they're your twenty-three-year-old sibling as opposed to your three-year-old child.

And as they grow and find themselves in more social situations, they'll tend to want to be in "charge" of their peers, implementing or attempting to enforce rules, which could lead to conflict. The key here: supporting their desire to lead while celebrating the joy of teamwork and being on the same page as their classmates and friends. Tips for tending to your Cap's emotional needs as they attempt to be in the driver's seat of any given situation:

Embrace your own authority. Sure, you don't want to be needlessly strict or harsh, but sometimes your C-suite exec in training will assume that if you're not putting your foot down on a rule, the power's all theirs. Instead, adopt a pragmatic Capricorn tone when they've pushed the limits. Direct, cool, and to-the-point ("It is now bedtime") should resonate.

Lighten things up. Because your mini Sea Goat takes nearly everything so seriously and fears being seen as foolish, you'll want to lean on humor when they've made a mistake. For example, say your little Cap spills their water all over the floor. They'll be upset and embarrassed. But you can make light of it—and put their mind at ease—by pretending to have a blast "going swimming" in the puddle. You can also remind them of that one time you spilled, and everything turned out OK, which also helps to normalize "oops" moments.

Offer specific opportunities for them to be in charge. Maybe they get to choose which family-friendly flick you'll watch together or which dinner veggie—avocado or sweet potato—you'll nosh on.

WELLNESS-RELATED ACTIVITIES FOR YOUR MINI CAPRICORN

Try Downward Dog, or Adho Mukha Shvanasana. This yoga pose is centering and energizing, and can help your little Sea Goat release pent-up frustrations, anger, or any other difficult emotion. Start out on all fours, aka Tabletop Pose, with hands slightly in front of shoulders, inhale and elevate hips back and up, keeping the feet parallel and relaxing the heels back. Encourage your Cap to ground the whole bottom of their feet and palms of their hands into the floor or mat while breathing in and out several times.

Take on outdoor projects. Your Cap innately adores being in nature and initiating a sweeping vision that will leave them feeling accomplished. Involve your Sea Goat in growing zinnias and cherry tomatoes or helping you decide which trail will be best for your weekend hike.

Go climbing. Like their symbol, your Cap will want to scale just about everything, even more than the average little one. Create safe ways for them to do this, from setting up a collapsible play tunnel in the living room to working on climbing staircases together. Gymnastics and tumble classes might also be a hit with your Sea Goat.

Try role-playing to boost emotional intelligence. While it can help to label emotions as you feel them in the moment, you can also make this lesson more of a challenge for your Cap to master. Make different faces and ask them to guess the emotion you're demonstrating, then have a conversation about when they've experienced that feeling and particular instances in which it might come up.

Model rest and breaks. You know how hard it can be to take a break from the daily grind yourself, so making a point to include unstructured playtime and restful moments in the day can be a winning way to show your assiduous cardinal earth sign how to best care for their whole self.

AQUARIUS

Your fixed air sign Aquarian baby's friendly, quirky, and spontaneous energy is informed by their ruling planet, electrifying Uranus. The planet of rebellion, which oversees sudden change, electricity, innovation, and brilliant breakthroughs, colors your Water Bearer's health and well-being. They'll be drawn to wellness tech, reaching for your smartwatch or taking note of how you blend up a green juice. This will very much be in keeping with their Uranian MO: Breaking new ground is thrilling and fun! It's for this same reason that they'll be especially enthralled by trips to a science museum or playing with cutting-edge toys, either of which could help them feel centered and tap into their unique sense of self.

Because your airy Aquarian toddler gravitates to all things technical and logical, they might come off as a bit detached and as though they're too cool for big feelings like sadness, anger, or mushiness. They would prefer to bond with you and their other loved ones—and, as they grow up, friends—on a mental level versus through an abundance of physical affection. But of course they'll be just as susceptible to waves of emotion as anyone else. And in the case of your Uranus-ruled child, those waves will look more like sudden, out-of-the-blue storms, complete with stunning lightning and thunder. That said, they'll benefit from pragmatic outlets for identifying and expressing their emotions (for example, family meetings or maybe a mood chart on which they can pinpoint their feelings with stickers).

HOW TO MEET RESISTANCE FROM YOUR AQUARIUS

With their disinterest in convention, penchant for science and fact-checking, and fixed nature, it's no surprise that your Aquarius loves to play the contrarian. For this reason, you may notice early on that your requests and suggestions are met with surprisingly obstinate responses. You'll say it's time to put the toys away, and you'll get a shrug, if that. You'll ask your Aquarius if they would like to help you with the laundry and get a hard "no thanks." They'll also find it fun and natural to argue with anything you've declared as a fact or a belief. "Why?" is basically a universal mantra for toddlers, but it's one your Water Bearer will passionately embrace for life—*and* they'll expect to be presented with all the footnotes. You'll wonder if you're raising a litigator or the next Marie Curie—and you might very well be. Tips for caring for your Aquarian's emotional needs while navigating their tendency to dig their heels in and come up with a counterargument for just about everything:

Strive to offer up rational explanations. "Because I said so" is likely not going to fly with your Water Bearer toddler. You'll have a better shot at getting them tucked in if you help them connect the dots—for example, noting that rest is good for their health, happiness, and energy.

Offer imaginative outlets for their stormiest emotions. If they've acted out—which, thanks to Uranus, may happen out of nowhere—you might steer them toward go-to practices, like their very own "breathing corner" or a box they can throw balls into to work through their frustration.

Meet them with warmth and empathy. If your Aquarius is beside themselves during a particularly shocking meltdown, do your best to stay centered, offering a hug or just taking their hands in yours in recognition of their emotional pain. As an aloof, intellectual air sign, your Water Bearer may not be the first to come running to you for soothing, but that doesn't mean they won't appreciate being met with heartfelt understanding. Plus, like all signs, they can benefit from seeing you model healthy self-regulation.

WELLNESS-RELATED ACTIVITIES FOR YOUR MINI AQUARIUS

Sit in Camel Pose, or Ustrasana.
This heart-opening pose may boost your Water Bearer's flexibility, which is a simple way to amplify emotional receptiveness and reduce stress. Sit on your knees then lean back toward your heels, putting your hands on the lower back or ankles. Then allow the head to fall back while you both open your chest and take several deep breaths.

Fly a kite or model airplane. Not only will your airy Aquarius love learning about the science of this outdoor pastime, but they'll benefit from simply being in the moment and enjoying the beauty and wonder of a sweet breeze.

Incorporate technology. Whether you watch a fun stretching session on YouTube, experiment with a meditation app, or simply set a timer on your iPad and see how many jumping jacks or somersaults you can do in that amount of time, your Water Bearer will likely be even more engaged in a mind-body routine that utilizes tech.

Sign up for play classes and events.
Associated with the Eleventh House of Friends, feeling like a part of a team is especially centering and stimulating for your Water Bearer, so consider prioritizing parent-and-child play classes or one-off events at a local kids' gym.

Get involved in climate action. Your Aquarius will never be too small to get fired up about a humanitarian cause. Involving them in composting or a tree planting event will benefit your Water Bearer's community-loving mind and spirit.

PISCES

Your Pisces baby's whimsical and sensitive nature is due to their ruling planet, mystical Neptune. The blue planet, named for the Roman god of the sea, rules spirituality, the subconscious, illusion, dreams, feelings, and inspiration. It's no wonder your sweet Fish is so easily swept up in their emotions. The key to their well-being is identifying and processing those emotions in an imaginative way.

Your Piscean toddler is incredibly creative; the more they can funnel their big feelings into imaginative outlets, the more centered—not to mention accomplished and vital—they'll feel. They are preoccupied with wanting to heal any living being, from a gloomy sibling to a nervous dog or wilted flower, which can often serve as a distraction from caring for themselves. And they struggle to know if they're maxed out emotionally or physically, because their intensely felt emotions have a tendency to manifest as bodily discomfort.

Supporting your Fish's overall well-being means meeting them with as much empathy as they're wired to give out to others. Validating their at times overwhelming emotions might seem like a no-brainer, but making a special point to do so consistently, in a way that makes your sensitive Fish feel seen and therefore more confident and grounded, will go far.

HOW TO MEET RESISTANCE FROM YOUR PISCES

Because they're usually so daydreamy and conflict-averse, it could be hard to imagine—at least when they're tiny—that your little Pisces would ever go to bat against you. But their emotions can get the best of your Fish, leading to a meltdown over a busy grocery store being just too darn stimulating or a showdown over having to hit pause on a make-believe and come to the dinner table. Preferring to stay in their dream world, Pisces is particularly apt to act out when they're faced with a harsh reality check. (Can you blame 'em?) Tips for nurturing Pisces's emotional well-being while helping them accept rules and real talk:

Be firm but gentle. Because your Fish has such a tender heart, it could be tempting to forgo putting your foot down when they've pushed too far. But they'll benefit just as much from boundaries as any other child. It might be best to adjust how you present a consequence. Maybe keep your tone on the softer, more even-keeled side.

Praise them for being direct and honest. All preschool-age children tell fibs. But as far as your Neptune-ruled child is concerned, they're offering you their own version of reality. Regardless of the spin, this is a no-go, and one of the best ways to nip this behavior in the bud is to dole out lots of encouragement and praise when they offer up the truth.

Get pragmatic. Because of how easy it is for your Fish to become overwhelmed, it might be best to lean on a practical fix, when they've pushed too far. Tell them exactly what the issue is ("You were frustrated so you threw the pillow at your sister"), then come up with a step-by-step solution ("First, we're going to figure out the best way to calm down, then we'll talk about what happened to make you so upset"). This "just-the-facts" approach should feel containing for your emotional Pisces while also laying the groundwork for them to problem-solve and self-soothe.

Try a time-off versus a time-out. A tip that applies to all signs but may be particularly wise to bear in mind with your Fish toddler: Time-outs or isolating your little one could perpetuate negative feelings that led to misbehavior in the first place. Instead, create a calming corner that's dedicated to working through big emotions. They'll especially benefit from an area where they can listen to relaxing music, play with sensory toys and art supplies, and be surrounded by watery elements (like a fish tank or ocean-inspired art).

WELLNESS-RELATED ACTIVITIES FOR YOUR MINI PISCES

Do Dragon Pose, or Anjaneyasana. This empowering yoga pose can help your mini Fish face their fears and get ready to take on the world. The pose involves your little one doing a low lunge with one leg behind them and the other bent in front of them. Have them sweep their arms up high to the sky then back behind them on the exhale, envisioning a powerful, fire-breathing dragon.

Set aside extra time for skin-on-skin bonding. Although every little one will benefit from snuggly time, your Fish, being a supersensitive lovebug, will thrive even more when they get regular doses of physical connectedness with you and your partner and/or other loved ones.

Blend bath time and make-believe. Being in the water and enjoying imaginative play while getting squeaky clean is an easy, lovely way to help a Pisces's tender heart get back to homeostasis no matter what they might be feeling.

Get active with animals. Take your loving Pisces to the aquarium or zoo or simply play in the backyard with your pup or indoors with your kitty. You'll notice that your Fish's intuitiveness extends to animals and pets, and spending time playing and caring for them can help them feel more grounded.

Meditate together. Your spiritually minded Pisces toddler will likely take to any mind-body practice, but breathing and meditation exercises are particularly useful tools for your deeply feeling Fish. Use an app like Smiling Mind with your preschool-age Pisces, or do a guided imagery meditation in which you challenge them to envision a place where they feel comfortable then ask questions about what they smell, taste, hear, and feel there.

PART 3

Parent & Child Relationships: Bonding with Your Growing Star

While getting to know your child through an astrological lens, you can't help but note similarities and differences. Maybe you're a Cancer raising a Pisces, and their sensitive heart and intensely empathic nature remind you of your own. Or you're a serious, quiet Capricorn striving to get on the same page as your supercommunicative and at times scattered Gemini. No matter your unique placements, learning more about yourself can result in better understanding your child and strengthening your inimitable bond.

Read on for how you'll connect and clash with your little star as well as the invaluable lessons you're bound to teach each other. And because knowing and caring for yourself can help you be even more receptive to your child's individuality and specific needs, you'll also find self-care tips for every parent's sign.

For the most nuanced portrait, be sure to look at both your own and your child's sun sign as well as other major placements—especially for the moon (the emotional compass) and Venus (the relationship ruler).

FIRE + CARDINAL + RAM

THE ARIES PARENT

The first sign of the zodiac, you're a dynamic, passionate, and competitive parent, fired up to take on whatever curveballs life—and raising your little one—has in store. You have a fun-loving, childlike energy and are all about playtime. Known for your daring, pioneering spirit, you'll be the first of your friends to try a new baby formula or expert-approved sleep training technique. True, you can be short-tempered, but your mood will dissipate quickly, and you'll be on to the next task.

Before you explore how you'll hit it off and experience challenges with each sign, consider how you can best fulfill your own needs, based on your placements. After all, caring for yourself goes hand in hand with caring for—and bonding with—your little one. Try these routines to nurture yourself:

BEST SELF-CARE ROUTINES FOR AN ARIES PARENT

- Go for a solo run. (Every parent needs a break from their kid on occasion, and you love to spend yours on the move!)
- Rock out to a playlist of your favorite songs from childhood to get in touch with your inner kid.
- Do a walking meditation—it will help you get centered while staying active.
- Play a round on a competitive game app (like Uno) with a friend.
- Tune in to—or better yet, head out to—a sporting event you love.

ARIES PARENT & LITTLE ARIES

Both born under the sign of the Ram, you and your child are passionate go-getters. You'll find that as your baby grows into a toddler and beyond, they'll have a keen sense of self and prioritize their independence—just like you. Your little one also mirrors back your impulsivity and disinterest in anything that prevents you from pushing forward at a lightning-fast pace, which could actually inspire you to slow down and do your best to be in the moment more. And because you've learned that it doesn't always pay to push to be number one, you're exceptionally well equipped to show your Ram the benefits of taking turns and holding space for others to shine.

YOU'LL CONNECT . . .

- **When playing to win.** Games or activities fuel your shared competitive spirit.

- **By getting outside.** Because you both adore getting active, take them with you for a run (using the chicest new jogging stroller) or try out a babywearing workout.

- **Through playful debate.** When you and your toddler are both trying to get your way—perhaps with the day's agenda or outfit—turn it into a game.

YOU'LL CLASH . . .

- **When their daring moves mirror your own.** Encourage them to explore while maintaining healthy boundaries.

- **When you're both committed to coming out on top.** You and your toddler may butt heads when neither will unclench their jaw.

- **If you're equally in the mood to go to bat.** Playful debate can quickly veer into butting heads for the sake of it, which could be wholly unproductive—and require a quick cool-off period for you both.

ARIES PARENT & LITTLE TAURUS

Fueled by go-getter Mars, you're action-oriented, while your Venus-ruled Bull is fine with simply being. That said, your little one can inspire you to be more present and mindful, while you'll show your tiny Taurus how moving at a speedier clip can be exciting and fulfilling.

YOU'LL CONNECT . . .

- **When you put your heads together to hit a milestone.** From walking without holding on to you to self-soothing after you drop them at day care, you two feel like any goal is achievable thanks to your enthusiasm and your Bull's resolve.

- **Through creative activities.** Think: finger painting or sensory play and games. As a cardinal sign, you enjoy making big-picture plans, while your little Taurus is ruled by artistic Venus, so they'll love putting their imagination to work to create something beautiful.

- **By spending time out in the world.** You love getting out of the house for brisk walks or impromptu drives, and your little earth sign enjoys being surrounded by nature, so choosing routes that allow your Taurus to gaze at trees and listen to birds can bring you closer.

YOU'LL CLASH . . .

- **When you both feel it's your way or no way.** Taurus's stubbornness squares off against your frequent refusal to back down for the sake of coming out on top.

- **When your paces are mismatched.** Your preference is to move at warp speed, while your baby embraces a glacial pace. This could result in a lesson on how to avoid losing your patience.

- **When you would rather keep it simple.** You tend to be no-frills, no-nonsense, while your little Bull wants to revel in—and might be particular about—life's creature comforts, like soft, fluffy blankets.

ARIES PARENT & LITTLE GEMINI

As a pair, you and your Twins baby are excitable, social, and eager to explore uncharted territory. By prioritizing new experiences and animated chatter, you'll find that there's much you can learn from each other.

YOU'LL CONNECT . . .

- **Through wordplay.** You both find the humor in the sounds of words, and your Gemini will crack up when you offer up silly language-based jokes, like "What is the cow's favorite rainy-day activity? Watching a mooo-vie!"

- **By socializing.** Be that during a family getaway where your little one can interact with cousins or in a parent-and-baby fitness class.

- **On an adventure.** Think: putting your teeny Gemini in a baby carrier and checking out all the sights and sounds of a buzzing farmers market together.

YOU'LL CLASH . . .

- **When it comes to sensory challenges.** Because you're so action-oriented, details can get lost in the shuffle. And as animated and curious as they are, they can be touchy about loud noises and strong scents and flavors. So it could be helpful to slow down and tune in to Gemini's sensitivities.

- **When you want to act, and they want to talk.** Ruled by Mars, you tend to be direct and to the point, because you'd rather move the ball forward than chitchat, yet your Mercury-ruled Gemini will often want

to have a discussion—or hear you explain a game plan. You can work to find a balance by striving to be more verbose while encouraging your Twins kid to turn their words into action.

- **When it comes to making decisions.** While you tend to make up your mind then instantly run with it, thanks to your cardinality, your mutable baby Gemini will be far more indecisive and require a bit of coaxing. In other words, they won't be quick about picking the shirt they want to wear—it'll be a conversation.

ARIES PARENT & LITTLE CANCER

While your nature is assertive and direct, your Crab's perspective can be intensely colored by their emotions. Your mini Cancer is a born nurturer, truly adoring and protective of those they love, which can inspire you to tap into your sentimental side. Meanwhile, you'll show them how to be more assertive when learning, playing, and pursuing their dreams.

YOU'LL CONNECT . . .

- **By taking on ambitious projects.** Whether you're watercoloring with your little Crab or involving them in a conversation about a family vacation, you'll enjoy working as a team.

- **When you're equally passionate about dreaming up a large-scale undertaking.** As big-picture thinkers, you share the experience of feeling that fire in your belly to tackle a major goal.

- **By diving right in.** You might be the one to make the game plan, but your baby Crab will be right there by your side figuring out how to support you and help move the ball forward.

YOU'LL CLASH . . .

- **If you're confused by their sensitivity and moods.** At times, you might not understand why your little Cancer is acting so reserved or fussy when a particular moment calls for showing enthusiasm and having fun. True to their symbol, the crustacean, they can retreat into their shell when they're feeling, well, crabby. This just means your Crab needs a little extra time doing whatever soothes them the most, whether that's snuggling with a favorite lovey or with you.

- **When they spend more time feeling than acting.** Whether you're heading out to the park or plowing from one playtime activity to the next, you're often ready to go yesterday, while your sensitive Crab could use a little more time to feel a situation out. Making room for them to acknowledge an emotion can be hugely beneficial.

- **When your desire for space conflicts with their desire to be attached 24/7.** You're naturally independent, and they're born to cling (hey, even baby crabs have pincers!).

ARIES PARENT & LITTLE LEO

Your Leo's loyal, energetic, and spotlight-loving nature is brilliantly apparent. They can't help but warm up the room with their inner light, courtesy of their ruler, the sun. As a fellow fire sign, you're very much in sync in terms of sharing a high-energy approach to life and loving each other with a great deal of verve. And although you have so many similarities in how you tackle life, there's a lot you can learn from each other.

YOU'LL CONNECT . . .

- **When you're equally vivacious and competitive.** At your parent-and-baby music class, your shared joie de vivre can't help but capture classmates' attention, and whenever you pair up to win a game, you mean business.

- **When you admire your Leo's charm.** Because you can be more brash, you'll admire your little Lion's ability to endear themselves to just about anyone.

- **When your Leo is impressed by your assertive attitude.** Although you're both action-oriented, you're more apt to dive right in, which can be exciting to your slightly more cautious Lion.

YOU'LL CLASH . . .

- **When you both want to be the boss.** You'll say it's time for a meal, a bath, or bed, but your tiny Lion begs to differ. Cue the power struggles.

- **If it's hard to get your little Lion to move on to the next task at hand.** Given their fixed nature, and your innate speediness, you could be ready to forge ahead with a new activity, or to leave the house to make an appointment on time, before your mini Leo has had a chance to fully absorb what is on the horizon.

- **When you're both being dramatic.** The flip side of being equally passionate is being equally loud and proud, which can cause some fireworks.

ARIES PARENT & LITTLE VIRGO

Your little Maiden is frequently interested in helping you, as being of service is their greatest badge of honor for a Virgo. By pairing your initiative and inner fire with your mini Virgo's diligence and attention to the rules, steps, and specifics, you can make magic.

YOU'LL CONNECT . . .

- **When you work in tandem.** You're a natural leader and manager, and your Virgo is eager to have a blueprint to follow. For instance, when you propose an organizational system for their playroom, they'll find a way to take it to the next level, like setting up special boxes for each type of toy. And whether you're blowing and chasing bubbles in the backyard or crafting a suncatcher together, your little one will want to follow your lead to a T.

- **When you appreciate each other's strengths.** Your little Maiden can teach you to be more attentive to the details of everyday life, while you can show them how to be more adventurous.

- **When you inspire your Virgo to dive right in.** As a mutable—and occasionally indecisive—sign, your Maiden is slower to act, but they'll be inspired by your self-starter approach.

YOU'LL CLASH . . .

- **When you're all about the big picture, and they're focused on the details.** You might raise your eyebrows over their tendency to be especially particular (some might say picky) about their favorite foods, clothes, and even the books they want to read at bedtime.

- **When you don't beat around the bush, and they're feeling sensitive.** Your default is bold and loud, and your baby Maiden can be soft-spoken, reserved, and delicate about certain words or volumes, so at times, it could be best to strike a more soothing tone.

- **When you prefer different paces.** You often follow your gut when taking action, but your tiny Maiden is wired to gather all the information available before moving ahead.

ARIES PARENT & LITTLE LIBRA

Your Ram is the opposite sign of Libra's Scales, so it might feel like you're two sides of the same coin. Your communication style is direct and to the point, whereas your mini Libra prefers diplomacy. You enjoy sparring and swiftness, while they're interested in keeping the peace and floating through life at whatever pace feels the most harmonious. As they grow up, your tiny, Venus-ruled Libra will show you how to prize beauty and balance above speed and the end game, while you can show them how to use their airy talents to turn a glowing ember of an idea into a full-blown flame.

YOU'LL CONNECT . . .

- **When you explore.** You will both love visiting new places and being around other parents and kids, whether at a parent-and-baby yoga class or at a local playground.

- **When you tell stories.** Although you might see the world through different lenses at times, you are both adventurous. Libra will love hearing about all your experiences out in the world, especially those involving other people and social situations.

- **When you can learn from each other.** When your baby Libra is being flighty, you can model more decisive thinking. And they'll show you how to adopt a more diplomatic tone.

YOU'LL CLASH . . .

- **When your Libra wants to take their time.** Your baby is a social air sign, which could mean they want extra time to play at the park while you're ready to pick up dinner.

- **When your excitability conflicts with their need for calm.** Tiny Libras can be sensitive to big, loud noises and experiences they feel are too intense, abrupt, or aggressive, as their number one goal is to create a sense of harmony.

- **When you define success differently.** For you, winning means being declared the victor of any game, competition, or sport, while mini Libra is more interested in winning people over with their innate charm.

ARIES PARENT & LITTLE SCORPIO

You and your Scorpio share a ruling planet: go-getter Mars. But your tiny Scorpion is also co-ruled by powerful Pluto, which can make them equally interested in moving the ball forward, like you, and in maintaining a sense of control. And their fixed nature can also make it tough for them to switch gears, which you excel at. By blending your ability to initiate with your baby Scorpio's laser-focused follow-through, you can take on anything as a team.

YOU'LL CONNECT . . .

- **Through physical play.** Whether you get into a tickle fight or head to a tumbling class, your shared Mars influence can help you bond in this dynamic way.

- **When you take on the unknown.** Little Scorpions are detectives, and you adore adventure, so exploring any uncharted territory—be that a scavenger hunt or road trips to Grandma and Grandpa's—can bring you together as a team.

- **When you love intensely.** Thanks to your fieriness, your mini Scorpion's Plutonian vibes, and the way assertive Mars colors both of your perspectives, neither of you is satisfied with doing anything halfway. And when it comes to showing how much you care for each other, you're equally passionate.

YOU'LL CLASH . . .

- **When they're driven by emotion and you're driven by action.** Not only is your mini Scorpion pretty much always in their feelings, but they'll keep it to themselves, which can strike you as fussy or unproductive.

- **When you're being equally strong-willed.** Whether they're refusing to eat what you've offered or to accept a substitute bath toy when their favorite has gone missing, your tiny Scorpion is one to dig their heels in, and you also want to have the final say. This can set up an opportunity to work on compromises.

- **When your independent nature conflicts with their desire to be closely connected.** Baby Scorpios crave a lot of cozy, emotionally intimate time with you—and might get jealous if they feel that your focus is elsewhere.

ARIES PARENT & LITTLE SAGITTARIUS

You and your baby Archer have a similar enthusiasm for life. Both fire signs, you're action-oriented, adventure-loving movers and shakers. While you want to push on from one activity, game, or accomplishment to the next, your Sag is more driven to be in the moment, absorbing everything around them for the sake of understanding. Still, your shared optimism makes bonding easy.

YOU'LL CONNECT . . .

- **When you're similarly fun-loving.** Ruled by jovial Jupiter, your mini Sagittarius is often the life of the party, which dovetails with your childlike, playful disposition. Whether at a family barbecue or at the pediatrician's office, people will perceive you as an entertaining pair.

- **When you're charging into the unknown.** Your wide-eyed, go-getter nature complements your little Archer's desire to understand the world around them. When you initiate a plan, they'll be quick to get on board.

- **When you're equally goofy.** Cue lots of silliness, giggles, and liveliness. It just happens very naturally between you.

YOU'LL CLASH . . .

- **When you would rather stick to a tried-and-true experience and your Sagittarius is pushing for an eye-opening one.** You like to keep certain routines (like family dinners) straightforward, but your little Sag is most stimulated by whatever's new and different. For example, they might ask to play a game you've never heard of, which could nudge you out of your comfort zone.

- **When you want to win, and they want to learn.** Your Archer's number one goal is to soak up knowledge, so they might not be as interested in winning a game as they are in coming away from it feeling like they had a new experience.

- **When their straightforwardness catches you off guard.** From the time your little one starts to talk, they'll tell it like it is. This might make you laugh but also bristle, if you happen to be the target of their surprisingly bold commentary.

ARIES PARENT & LITTLE CAPRICORN

Your Capricorn takes everything seriously. Although you are both invested in action and achievement, your little Goat prefers to think everything through before moving forward—and once they're ready to go, they'll do it in a methodical way, thanks to the influence of their ruling planet, taskmaster Saturn. They're also wise beyond their years and could sometimes seem like a mini parent themselves. The more open you are to learning from each other, the more harmony and joy will flow between you.

YOU'LL CONNECT . . .

- **As a formidable team.** While you're a master of initiating, they can teach you about the ability to persevere. If you get the ball rolling on an herb garden, their interest in regularly watering each plant will make for a successful result.

- **When you bond over leadership.** Though your style is feverish while your little Goat is more strategic, you admire each other's take-charge natures, courtesy of your shared cardinal element.

- **When you set an ambitious goal.** Neither of you will shy away from a major undertaking.

YOU'LL CLASH . . .

- **When your mini Goat doesn't express the same level of enthusiasm as you.** When you're pumped about something, you're open about it. But when your little Goat is pleased—with a special birthday gift, for example—they'll be much more reserved, potentially giving you pause.

- **When your little Cap is a rule follower, and you're a rule breaker.** Your tiny Goat naturally has a lot of respect for authority. You, on the contrary, prefer to either be the authority or challenge whoever is. This could work when you want them to follow your lead, but be tougher when a toddler Goat notices that you're straying from what they believe is a hard and fast must-do, whether that's bundling up when it's chilly out or washing your hands after outdoor play.

- **When you're jumping from one project to the next, and your Capricorn is stuck due to perfectionism.** You will wrap up a chore or project and not look back. But your baby Goat is interested in accomplishing one task at a time, and if they haven't done it to the level they know they can, they could get gloomy. Acknowledge their feelings while encouraging them to think about the big picture.

ARIES PARENT & LITTLE AQUARIUS

You'll appreciate your baby Aquarian's quirkiness, and they'll adore your nonstop energy. However, despite the fact that your tiny Water Bearer is an open-minded air sign, they're also the fixed one of the bunch, so once you initiate a game plan, they'll require a bit of extra coaxing to switch it up. In general, their inventive, silly, social disposition inspires you, and your adventurous nature thrills them.

YOU'LL CONNECT . . .

- **When you come up with innovative ideas and make them happen.** You can propose a fun, educational project (like baking or making slime) that captures both of your imaginations, and your little fixed air sign will be beyond thrilled to follow through.

- **Over your shared curiosity.** Science-minded Aquarians are forever gathering information and questioning what they've learned, and you'll enjoy making exciting discoveries together.

- **When you're independent, and they're individualistic.** You can appreciate each other's passion for being authentically yourselves. Celebrating this, perhaps by creating your own sport or making up funny lyrics to a song, is a way you can naturally bond.

YOU'LL CLASH . . .

- **If your mini Aquarius's originality catches you off guard.** They march so much to the beat of their own drum and are so future-minded—taking immediately to any kind of new technology they're presented with that even you have yet to master—that you may feel like you have to play catch-up.

- **When you set rules, and they rebel.** Although all toddlers go through the "I want to do it myself!" phase, most are simply asking to be given a chance. On the other hand, your baby Water Bearer will be more likely to think—and possibly even defiantly say—"I do what I want!" conveying their intention to march to the beat of their own drum, whether you like it or not. Chalk this up to their ruler, rebellious Uranus.

- **When you're thinking about what's best for you two while they're thinking about everyone else.** If you have to leave a playdate early to get your Aquarius to bed on time, your humanitarian air sign could be concerned that they're leaving playmates hanging in the middle of a game.

ARIES PARENT & LITTLE PISCES

Your little Fish is very loving and feels everything deeply. Their sensitivity can be particularly challenging for you given your direct, super-speedy nature. You'll revel in how much they adore you, but as they grow, you could struggle with the fact that their dreamy, wishy-washy nature is very different from your independent, action-oriented wiring. The best way forward involves braving their watery world of feelings—and in turn, showing your mini Fish how lighting and nurturing their inner flame will boost their self-confidence and sufficiency.

YOU'LL CONNECT . . .

- **When they show you how to tap into your intuition.** While you tend to be consumed mostly by the concrete aspects of everyday life, your baby Fish is much more internally focused— even a little psychic. Embracing this can lead to magic.

- **When you dream big.** The best way for your Fish to process their emotions is through a creative outlet. You'll be able to initiate an exciting way for them to do this—from coloring together to asserting that your backyard is a magical kingdom to set up make-believe play.

- **When you give your little Fish tools for making their wishes real.** It's easy for your Pisces to spend lots of time letting their imagination run wild, but you'll show them how to take action. Whether they say they're going to be a doctor or a unicorn when they grow up, your playful, ambitious spirit will kick into gear and help them run with it.

YOU'LL CLASH . . .

- **When you're fired up about an activity but your Fish is unsure.** Your little Fish will struggle to commit to a plan— whether that's to blow bubbles or play in the kiddie pool—but you can coach them through being more decisive.

- **When your straightforward tone is perceived as abrasive.** Take special care to use a more gentle tone to appeal to your baby Pisces, who will deeply feel every layer of communication.

- **When your impulsivity is at odds with their sensitivity.** Mini Fish often need a lot of time to process a situation emotionally, given their delicate hearts, so slowing your roll can be helpful.

THE TAURUS PARENT

Born with your sun or other placements in the fixed earth sign, you're a grounded, pragmatic, reliable, and comfort-loving parent, determined to take slow, steady steps on just about any must-do. Whether you're working on getting your baby to latch or contending with a toddler temper tantrum, you take most challenges in stride and commit to following through. More adventurous friends might not get it when you shrug off trying trendy new baby gear in lieu of something more traditional, but they'll be impressed by your ability to stick to a go-to game plan, whether that's a tried-and-true lullaby or a beloved park for leisurely strolls. And when you're caring for yourself—so that you can care for others—you do best when you prioritize activities that bring you pleasure, thanks to your ruler, Venus, the planet of love, beauty, and values. Try these routines to nurture yourself:

BEST SELF-CARE ROUTINES FOR A TAURUS PARENT

- Listen to a playlist of your favorite power ballads.
- Experiment with aromatherapy—maybe even making a signature scent for your home or to add to personal care products.
- Have a wine and cheese picnic at your favorite park—or even just in the backyard—with a dear friend.
- Spend extra time wandering around a farmers market, perusing the freshest produce and handmade soaps.
- Treat yourself to a cozy new throw.

TAURUS PARENT & LITTLE ARIES

You and your Ram child move through life at different paces. They're a little speed demon, and you can be as unhurried as a sloth. But as they grow, they can teach you the merits of picking up the pace, while you can show them how to be in the moment.

YOU'LL CONNECT . . .

- **When you're expressing yourselves through a creative outlet.** You're equally empowered to channel your unique voice into an artistic project.

- **By tackling puzzles.** You both appreciate being challenged to play any kind of brain game.

- **Through outdoor activities.** Your Ram will get active anywhere, but they feel especially free outdoors, and being in nature feeds your spirit.

YOU'LL CLASH . . .

- **When you both refuse to budge.** Your baby wants to be number one, and you can struggle with adaptability, so it can help for you to both work on embracing a nuanced, open-minded point of view.

- **When they're moving at lightning speed.** Your little Aries takes everything—from crawling to toddling— daredevil fast, which can cause you to lose your cool.

- **If they're bored.** Your Aries often prefers to be on the go while you'd rather chill, which means you'll have to work to find common ground.

TAURUS PARENT & LITTLE TAURUS

A pleasure-seeking, slow-paced duo of Bulls, you and your little one are as grounded as you are hardheaded at times, so you could butt heads the most in moments when neither of you is willing to budge. Still, your heartfelt loyalty to your bond—and desire to choose snuggles over scuffles—will usually win the day.

YOU'LL CONNECT . . .

- **Through gift-giving.** Whether you create art for each other or make a delicious weekend breakfast together, you'll show your love through tangible things.

- **By taking it slow.** You both live for restful, cozy moments (think: babywearing, feeding, or snuggling up on a quiet weekend).

- **When you're enjoying being in the moment outdoors.** You'll find tons of joy from being surrounded by nature.

YOU'LL CLASH . . .

- **When either of you digs your heels in.** You share the tendency to do this, and every time is a lesson—for you both—in being a bit more open to change.

- **If either of you shuts down emotionally.** Though you both have long fuses, you're just as susceptible to getting upset as anyone, and when you do, your first instinct is to project eerily cool radio silence versus talk it out.

- **If either of you pushes the other's most sensitive buttons.** As two of the same sign, you're intimately familiar with each other's innermost triggers. And out of respect, you'll rarely go there—but if either does, watch out.

TAURUS PARENT & LITTLE GEMINI

Your curious little one, influenced by the Twins, needs to be on the go and soaking up info to feel at peace, while you'd prefer to move through life at a leisurely pace, focused on what's right in front of you. But you both understand the importance of infusing every day with lots of pleasure, so you'll enjoy plenty of playful, fun-loving moments together.

YOU'LL CONNECT . . .

- **By blending emotions and creativity.** When you put words to your most heartfelt emotions and get creative (consider singing or using poetry), your Mercury-ruled little one will be elated.

- **By spending time with loved ones.** You pour energy into your closest bonds, and your little Gemini adores any opportunity to socialize.

- **When playing brain games.** This can be wonderful common ground as you can always appreciate a challenge, and your Twins tot craves intellectual stimulation.

YOU'LL CLASH . . .

- **When your love of what's tried-and-true clashes with their need to experiment.** You'd prefer to stick to what you know, and your Gemini is wired to seek out anything shiny and new.

- **When pragmatism feels like a buzzkill.** Play beats rationality for your Twins kiddo, so you'll want to find a way to make the practical approach a little more fun.

- **If your paces are out of sync.** On days when you need to chill and they're especially frisky, it'll help to have go-to independent play activities up your sleeve.

TAURUS PARENT & LITTLE CANCER

You and your tiny Crab find joy and security in an abundance of family time, coziness, and warm, fuzzy displays of affection. The key difference: While you approach any bumps in the road pragmatically, your Crab can't help but follow their heart and intuition. Nonetheless, you'll find that it's easy to trade skill sets.

YOU'LL CONNECT . . .

- **Whenever you have a chance to cuddle up.** You adore being comfy, and your Cancer will jump at any chance to be close to you—ideally while snuggling up in the softest blanket you can find.

- **Through emotionally expressive art.** Think: singing a pop ballad in the car or using finger paint to depict feelings.

- **When you're getting sentimental.** You both love making and reliving memories, particularly those involving loved ones and your roots.

YOU'LL CLASH . . .

- **When they retreat emotionally.** There may not be a logical explanation for why your little Crab is withdrawing, but given your rational, practical nature, you can help them put words to their big feelings.

- **When they're spontaneously bossy.** Crabs are softies, but they're also ambitious, so having opportunities to hone their leadership skills can preempt acting out.

- **If your practical take is perceived as too harsh.** Your little Cancer is a sensitive soul who will respond best when you strike a gentle parenting tone.

TAURUS PARENT & LITTLE LEO

Both fixed signs, you and your Lion share a steadfast determination to follow through on any game plan. But while you prefer to take a slow, controlled, practical route, your charismatic, sunny baby believes they can charm their way to the finish line. You'll be as frequently impressed as you are left shaking your head by this.

YOU'LL CONNECT . . .

- **By putting on a show.** You like setting the stage for imaginative play, and they love to be the star.

- **When you're tackling a challenge as a team.** When you take on any milestone together—be it learning how to walk or sorting shapes and colors—you're unstoppable.

- **By spending time in a beautiful, elegant space.** Your shared love of all things luxe is a case for making sure your Lion's nursery is as gorgeous as can be (see page 60 for design ideas).

YOU'LL CLASH . . .

- **When your Lion's domineering side comes out.** Your Leo might act like they're the authority figure in the house, and you'll have to remind them that's not the case.

- **If you're both being rigid.** Your Lion may mirror your fixed, obstinate tendencies back to you in a big way, inspiring you to be more open-minded.

- **When your priorities conflict.** Moments in which you want to check to-dos off your list but your Lion is engaging in theatrics might drive you a bit bonkers.

TAURUS PARENT & LITTLE VIRGO

As two earth signs who are grounded and practical, you and your Virgo child both prefer the rational approach and aim to be of service to others. You can help your Virgo get out of their head in order to tune in to all their senses and teach them how to stand strong, while your Mercury-ruled, mutable Virgo could inspire you to be more adaptable and curious.

YOU'LL CONNECT . . .

- **When completing a task one step at a time.** Creating and following a logical plan, ideally turned into a visual list, is motivating for you both.

- **Through acts of service.** Think: making breakfast for loved ones or sorting the recycling together.

- **When spending time in nature.** Because you're both earth signs, dedicated downtime in the backyard or a nature preserve can't help but have a centering effect for you both. And if you're able to be safely barefoot, all the better, as that'll help you feel especially connected to the earth.

YOU'LL CLASH . . .

- **If you're glossing over a detail Virgo's focused on.** Whether their bedroom door wasn't cracked open just the right amount at bedtime or you reached for a different scent of soap from what they're used to, your Maiden is hyperaware of specifics that you're not as quick to key into. But noticing and tending to these details can make a world of difference for your Virgo.

- **When you're in the moment, and they're overthinking.** You tend to have an easy time staying in the present, but they can be worried or fussy because they're concerned about the immediate past or future. In these moments, extra communication could be required.

- **If you're frustrated by their indecisiveness.** You make choices and stick with them, while your Virgo struggles with that. Thankfully, you can show them the way—with confidence.

TAURUS PARENT & LITTLE LIBRA

Both ruled by sweet Venus, you share an eye for beauty and art. But while your little one is head over heels for being social, you're more of a homebody. Libras tend to flit from one thing to the next, while you stick to what you know. That said, making room to see the world through each other's eyes will broaden both of your horizons.

YOU'LL CONNECT . . .

- **When surrounded by beauty.** You and your Libra adore all things aesthetically pleasing, and will love taking art classes or even trips to the florist.

- **By having heart-to-hearts.** Sharing Venusian rulership means you're equally in touch with your emotions and eager to tell each other about them.

- **Through your sense of style.** You both enjoy expressing yourselves visually, whether it's through decor or clothes.

YOU'LL CLASH . . .

- **When they leave loose ends dangling.** Your little cardinal air sign starts big projects but might get distracted before finishing them, whereas one of your greatest strengths is your determination and follow-through—which will ideally rub off on your Scales child as you regularly model it for them.

- **If you struggle to switch things up.** Your penchant for anything tried-and-true can feel snoozy to your airy child, so flexibility can go far.

- **When they want to weigh all the sides of a decision.** Incredibly concerned with balance, your Libra prefers to consider all sides of any given strategy, while you tend to make up your mind and stick to it. You can inspire them to stand their ground, while they can show you how to consider more angles.

TAURUS PARENT & LITTLE SCORPIO

You and your fixed water sign might be opposites, but similarly determined, you see eye to eye on how you tackle any challenge and need to accept any change at your own, often slow pace. Still, your Scorpion feels everything in an intense, passionate, sometimes fixated way, while you let tough emotions roll past like a storm. Given the ratio of common ground to key differences, you're almost like two puzzle pieces meant to fit together in order to learn and grow.

YOU'LL CONNECT . . .

- **By completing challenging projects.** Both you and your Scorp take pride in getting to the finish line on any endeavor.

- **When spending quality time with loved ones at home.** You both thrive when you're somewhere familiar and comfortable and surrounded by your support network.

- **By enjoying your favorite foods.** Because you're both fixed signs who usually stick to what you like at all costs, once either of you finds a treat you're into, it's probably time to stockpile.

YOU'LL CLASH . . .

- **When you both struggle to adapt.** If neither of you is willing to embrace change, you could find yourselves feeling quite stuck and frustrated.

- **When your Scorp's emotions overwhelm you both.** Your innate pragmatism might make it hard for you to relate to your water baby's need to get swept away in the deep end of their feelings.

- **If either of you could use more time to yourself.** As strong as the love is between you two, you're equally passionate about your privacy and space.

TAURUS PARENT & LITTLE SAGITTARIUS

You and your Sag have very different points of view to offer each other. While you prioritize familiarity, which heightens your sense of comfort and security, your fiery, knowledge-craving Archer child will dream of adventuring and globe-trotting. They can inspire you to act more boldly, while you will show them how relaxing it can be to slow down from time to time.

YOU'LL CONNECT . . .

- **Through hands-on learning.** You soak up the world around you with every fiber of your being, and your little Archer is big on experiences, so you'll both love any opportunity to discover by doing.

- **By taking trips as a family.** Visiting Grandma's lake house or going to an amusement park—a blend of tradition and travel elates you both.

- **By being silly.** You're pretty good at being a goofball, and your Sag loves to laugh and be entertained.

YOU'LL CLASH . . .

- **When your version of comfort is Sag's idea of being confined.** You'll want to make plenty of room for them to explore. On occasion, you'll realize that sacrificing predictability and pragmatism is worth it for your little Sag's joy.

- **When Sag strikes out against boundaries.** Ruled by Jupiter, your Archer will love to push past any guardrails you've set up for their safety and security, which will test your patience.

- **When your desire for harmony conflicts with their attachment to speaking the truth.** Ruled by diplomatic Venus, you're likely to subscribe to the philosophy that if you have nothing nice to say, it's best to say nothing at all, whereas your proudly unfiltered Sag often can't help but blurt out an honest take.

TAURUS PARENT & LITTLE CAPRICORN

As two earth signs, you and your Capricorn are frequently in sync. You're both down-to-earth, hardworking, and goal-oriented, and you know how to keep calm and carry on. You admire your Goat's precociousness, and as they grow up, they'll be impressed with your follow-through. You can teach them how to relax, and they'll inspire you to reach for the stars.

YOU'LL CONNECT . . .

- **By making any ambitious plan.** You both take slow, steady action toward any intention, so you'll enjoy tracking progress together (think: using a visual chart).

- **When you're prioritizing productivity.** Because you value each other's commitment to hard work and tackling everyday tasks, you can accomplish even more as a team.

- **By making each other handmade gifts.** You and your Cap both express affection in tactile ways, so you can safely assume that plenty of crafts are in your future.

YOU'LL CLASH . . .

- **When your Cap thinks they're the adult.** Though you'd prefer to do whatever is needed to keep the peace, you'll have to assert your authority to remind them who's really in charge.

- **If your Goat needs to be challenged more.** Although you might prefer to stick to that same game or park, your Goat must feel like they're working toward taking anything—yes, even playtime—to the next level.

- **When relaxation is called for.** You're both so driven, especially when you're together, that you might forget to take a break and end up feeling cranky.

TAURUS PARENT & LITTLE AQUARIUS

As two of the fixed signs, you and your Water Bearer are both dedicated to seeing a particular action plan through. But you have different ideas about how to get to the finish line. Your little Aquarius prefers to take the most unexpected route, which can feel at odds with your desire to follow the already paved path. Being open to each other's point of view can make you feel unstoppable—and supported.

YOU'LL CONNECT . . .

- **By nurturing mutual friendships.** Your Water Bearer is a social butterfly, and you'll love cultivating a close inner circle of their playmates' parents.

- **When you surprise each other.** You'll be endlessly impressed by the brilliant, out-of-the-box ideas your little one comes up with. And they'll appreciate how you're everyone's rock.

- **Through self-awareness.** Finding the humor in your similar stubbornness can lead to lots of laughter.

YOU'LL CLASH . . .

- **When routine feels too stale to Aquarius.** Ruled by game-changer Uranus, your Water Bearer will often push to innovate and shake up any established plan.

- **If your Water Bearer shifts into contrarian mode.** They'll often argue and throw a fit just for the sake of doing something differently. Consider throwing your hands up and letting them give their way a shot.

- **When you both dig your heels in.** Seeing just how stubborn and black-and-white your Aquarius child can be could inspire you to be less so.

TAURUS PARENT & LITTLE PISCES

You and your empathic little Fish will find joy in taking it easy and letting your imaginations wander. You might be caught off guard by their sensitivity, while they might be thrown by your practicality. But you can show them how to work through their deeply felt emotions in a productive way, while they'll encourage you to open your heart and mind to the magical and unknown.

YOU'LL CONNECT . . .

- **By talking through big feelings.** You believe in taking concrete steps to tackle a challenge, so when your Pisces is working through difficult emotions, you can help them simplify and verbalize.

- **When you're tender with each other's hearts.** You provide your Fish with a sense of safety and security, and you'll feel like they truly see and understand what's in your heart.

- **By managing stress through art.** When life gets busy, you'll enjoy taking a step back from your routine to finger paint or play instruments together.

YOU'LL CLASH . . .

- **If your sweet Fish gets inexplicably tearful or withdraws.** You might realize that some moments don't call for talking or an action plan—just let them know you're there for them instead.

- **When you're thinking practically, and they're in the clouds.** You might have to put rationality on the back burner when their imagination is running wild.

- **If you get impatient with their indecisiveness.** From meals to milestones, you might need to do some hand-holding to help them stick to a plan and to their choices.

AIR + MUTABLE + TWINS

THE GEMINI PARENT

With your sun or other placements in the mutable air sign, you're a communicative, curious, and easily adaptable parent, eager to connect with others to trade notes and always talking to your little one, likely even before they came into the world. Ruled by Mercury, you're on a perpetual mission to gather information and share it with others, so it's comforting to be constantly in touch—via social media or a group text—with other parents who've got your back. The playful, lighthearted moments of raising your baby come naturally to you, as you'll have an inquisitive, childlike spirit throughout your life. Because you're so accustomed to—and, to be fair, tend to love—going nonstop, you might not even realize that you've run yourself ragged. But when stress catches up with you, talking it out and prioritizing social moments helps, thanks to your ruling planet, buzzy Mercury. Try these routines to nurture yourself:

BEST SELF-CARE ROUTINES FOR A GEMINI PARENT

- Freewrite in a journal.
- Play a vocab-testing game like Wordle or solve the *New York Times* crossword puzzle.
- Trade funny memes back and forth with friends in your group text.
- Research and plan your next road trip.
- Read, even for a few minutes, which can offer the perfect blend of relaxation and stimulation for your Mercury-ruled brain.

GEMINI PARENT & LITTLE ARIES

You and your Ram child are both fired up to see and experience the world around you. However, while your priority is to explore through communication, your Aries wants to take quick and bold action. You can teach them to weigh their options before plowing ahead, and they can help you use your copious thoughts and ideas to fuel concrete, decisive steps.

YOU'LL CONNECT . . .

- **By burning off all that energy you share.** You'll adore bonding through active playtime, like a parent-and-baby dance class.

- **When you're out and about.** Whether you're babywearing your Aries at a friend's barbecue or heading out with a jogging stroller, being out in the world thrills you both.

- **By blending wordplay and physical humor.** You're a pro at finding the comedy in language, and your Aries gets a kick out of slapstick, so fusing the two (think: physically acting out new words like "escalator" or "giraffe") can make for hilarity.

YOU'LL CLASH . . .

- **When you're immersed in communication, and they're acting out.** Of course it'll be when you're on a FaceTime call that your Mars-ruled Aries tot gets a little too physically wild, making you feel like you need eyes in the back of your head.

- **If they opt to lash out physically.** Whether your aggressive fire sign is thrashing around at the top of the stairs while suffering FOMO at bedtime or getting too rough and boisterous with a sibling, you'll want to encourage them to express their anger in a more verbal way— something you're a pro at, given your Mercury influence.

- **If their impatience flares up.** Your Aries's attention span will be tested by too much talking and too little action.

GEMINI PARENT & LITTLE TAURUS

Unhurried, steady, and prioritizing comfort and pleasure above just about everything else, your little Bull will teach you how to slow down and soak up information about the world around you by using all of your senses. Meanwhile, you can teach your Taurus how to put their experience into words. When it's tough to get them to budge—literally and figuratively—and join you when you're on the go, patience and a willingness to be still can be your most useful tools.

YOU'LL CONNECT . . .

- **By talking through practical lessons.** From numbers to making their bed, your Taurus wants to understand the rational application of anything they're learning about, and who better to explain it than a supercommunicator like you?

- **By blending art and socializing.** Because your baby is ruled by Venus, they will value making—and maintaining—social connections as much as you. One of the ways you will both enjoy nurturing those bonds is through artistic activities, like making a collage or stringing beads alongside playmates.

- **When you join forces to make pretty music.** Ruled by Mercury, you're a whiz at coming up with fun or heartfelt lyrics while your artistic, Venus-ruled tot will love banging on a xylophone or drums, or shaking maracas.

YOU'LL CLASH . . .

- **When your little Bull struggles to try something new.** You live for experimentation, and they'd prefer to stick to what they know they already like, so perseverance is integral when introducing them to, well, just about anything.

- **If you lose focus.** Taurus is slow to lose their cool, but they could be frustrated if your attention is scattered while they're homed in on one specific activity.

- **When your airiness is at odds with their need for security.** Sometimes you'll be ready to move on to the next thing when your Bull is craving more snuggles and together time.

GEMINI PARENT & LITTLE GEMINI

As two dualistic Twins people, you and your Gemini each have two sides of your personality; are endlessly curious, social, and on the go; and most enjoy connecting through language. You'll mirror each other in a way that makes you feel seen and understood. The primary issue will be deciding who gets to talk when—and honing your listening skills along the way.

YOU'LL CONNECT . . .

- **Through animated conversation and debate.** Even when your Twins baby is tiny and preverbal, you'll feel like you're constantly connecting on a mental level.

- **When you're digging up information.** From educational moments to travel experiences and everyday conversations, you're both eager to learn and share what you've learned.

- **Through wordplay.** Making each other giggle endlessly by experimenting with language is your specialty.

YOU'LL CLASH . . .

- **If indecision leads to irritation.** When neither of you is willing to commit to an action plan, you could find yourself gridlocked, and you both loathe feeling stuck.

- **If you struggle to communicate.** You both have a ton to say—and feel it's important to express your emotions verbally—so taking turns will be integral to smooth sailing.

- **If one of you is feeling more outgoing when the other is more reserved.** Your two sides won't always be in sync, and that's OK.

GEMINI PARENT & LITTLE CANCER

Deeply sensitive, your sweet Crab intuits and feels as much as you think and speak. This could lead to an intellectual versus emotional disconnect at times, but with a little extra TLC, they can teach you how to tune in to your heart and let it lead the way as much as your mind, and you can teach them how to find the best language to express their feelings.

YOU'LL CONNECT . . .

- **When you both share what's in your heart.** Your loving Crab will be over the moon to hear how you feel, as you'll articulate it with just the right words.

- **Through lively family bonding sessions.** Not only is it a fun social opportunity for you, but Cancer feels especially supported when surrounded by loved ones.

- **By blending socializing with traditions.** Your sentimental Cancer will have a soft spot for holiday rituals, which can easily be shared with your wide circle of friends and neighbors.

YOU'LL CLASH . . .

- **When your Crab's emotions are beyond words.** When their feelings take over, it might be best to give them a bit of space to retreat into their shell versus pushing for a conversation.

- **If you both retreat at the same time.** If they're in their shell when you're similarly withdrawing from a heavy moment, you might both end up feeling lonely.

- **When you have different emotional needs.** If one of you is feeling blue, your default is to talk it out, but sometimes your little Crab just needs more cozy snuggle time with you.

GEMINI PARENT & LITTLE LEO

Your sweet, sunny Lion baby is just as playful as you, and you're both passionate about making exploration and fun a priority. But while you might love to read and talk, your action-oriented Leo would prefer to get a move on. You can teach them to gather and share information, and they'll inspire you to be optimistic, bold, and confident.

YOU'LL CONNECT . . .

- **Through whimsical, fun-loving experiences.** You're both capable of upbeat, wide-eyed wonder, so the moments in which you can tap into that are the ones that'll bring you closest

- **By getting creative.** You and your little Lion are naturals when it comes to artistic self-expression, whether that's drawing self-portraits or making funny collages from pictures in the many magazines and periodicals most Geminis have lying around.

- **In any opportunity to celebrate.** You adore connecting with others, and your little Lion will relish the chance to potentially be the center of attention.

YOU'LL CLASH . . .

- **When your Lion's domineering side comes out.** Talking it out just won't do when they're roaring up a storm. It might be best to let them have their moment and cool off before leaning into your supercommunicating skills to create a teachable moment.

- **If their fixed nature feels stifling to you.** Your Lion prefers to stick to what they know they like, while you'd rather see where the moment takes you. You might have to nudge them out of their comfort zone—and respect their need to go with the familiar option on occasion.

- **When you crave different types of affection.** While you tend to express your emotions in an intellectual, verbal way, your Leo prefers to give and receive love in an action-oriented way (like with lots of big hugs or a surprise trip to the beach).

GEMINI PARENT & LITTLE VIRGO

As two Mercury-ruled people, you and your cerebral Maiden are natural communicators. Buzzy, engaging conversations come naturally to you. But while you cast a wide net when information-gathering, your Virgo is more detail-oriented. They might also shy away from the crowded spaces and high-energy activities that you adore. By honoring their analytical perspective and desire to be of service, you'll find that it's easier to relate to your Virgo.

YOU'LL CONNECT . . .

- **When "investigating."** You're both natural-born researchers who will stop at nothing to gather information—whether it's on a zoo animal or the specifics of an at-home science project on a rainy Sunday.

- **Through intimate social moments.** Your Virgo may prefer engaging with smaller groups than you, but in those groups, their inner, Mercury-ruled uber-communicator will come out, reminding you of yourself.

- **By playing word games.** You both enjoy—and have a knack for—communication and language, so you'll both find games that tap into that skill especially fun.

YOU'LL CLASH . . .

- **When you don't take notice of your Virgo's preferences.** Whether your Maiden has decided that a particular blanket's too scratchy or that the only fruit they like are apples, they'll be upset if you haven't keyed into those details.

- **When you aren't seeing eye to eye during an educational moment.** You believe in learning for the sake of it, whereas your Virgo toddler will want to understand the reason behind any lesson and to know how it could help them or someone else.

- **If either of you gets nitpicky.** As two very perceptive, investigative people, you might find that in especially challenging moments, you're tempted to point out each other's weaknesses, which can cause mutual crankiness.

GEMINI PARENT & LITTLE LIBRA

As two air signs, you and your Libra will find an easygoing harmony based on your mutual love of socializing. You're both happiest when you're around others. You also both appreciate being able to weigh all your options, whether in the grocery store aisle or when deciding what activity to do next. Your Libra's need for balance and serenity is uniquely their own, though, so you'll want to learn more about—and engage with—that as your relationship grows.

YOU'LL CONNECT . . .

- **Through double playdates.** There's no such thing as a crowd to you, but your Libra prefers to engage with others one-on-one, so you may make some of the sweetest memories when you two hang out with your bestie and their little one.

- **By researching then creating a beautiful project.** From crafting to cooking, your research skills and Libra's artistic eye make you a power duo when it comes to making anything eye-catching.

- **When you're flitting from one to-do to the next.** Whether you're running errands or visiting friends, you both love being on the go.

YOU'LL CLASH . . .

- **If your pace feels too frenetic to Libra.** They might be as airy as you, but your balance-loving Libra generally prefers not to rush.

- **If indecision makes you both antsy—and cranky.** You'll both have moments when it feels impossible to take a stand or stick with a game plan, and this will be especially the case when you're together; to circumvent a stalemate, someone will have to make a definitive choice.

- **When you speak different love languages.** It'll be important to not only say but show how you feel with your Scales child, who appreciates flowery affection, including aesthetically-appealing gifts (like a stylish new outfit) and sweet lullabies.

GEMINI PARENT & LITTLE SCORPIO

You and your Scorpion see the world through very different lenses, which can be exciting albeit challenging at times. While you're lighthearted and lightning-paced, they feel everything intensely and take their time. You love to juggle, and they're laser-focused. You'll connect best when you remain open to seeing the world from each other's vantage points.

YOU'LL CONNECT . . .

- **Through brain games and puzzles.** Both you and your Scorpio are thrilled by the opportunity to gather information, connect the dots, and reach the finish line on a competitive challenge.

- **When you're having a spirited debate.** Your Scorp will be quick to dig their heels in, and you'll be eager to explain why they might want to consider alternatives, which could lead to an energetic back-and-forth.

- **When you talk about your feelings.** Your Scorpion will be reserved about expressing emotions, but you can show them how healthy it is to verbalize what's in their heart.

YOU'LL CLASH . . .

- **When you want to communicate and your Scorpio needs privacy.** You'll want to be thoughtful about being social at times and in places that Scorp sees as sacred. Even replying to a text while they're getting tucked into bed could feel invasive. And as your secretive water sign grows, they'll be quite passionate about being asked for consent.

- **When your mutability conflicts with their fixed nature.** Whether you want to jet from one activity to the next or are advocating going swimming at a different community pool than usual, your Scorp will easily get stuck on their go-to.

- **If your Scorp needs more of your undivided attention.** You're a multitasking wizard and it can be hard for you to zero in on only one thing, but there will be times your Scorpion needs you to do just that.

GEMINI PARENT & LITTLE SAGITTARIUS

You and your adventurous Archer may be opposites, but you're more like two sides of the same coin. Both endlessly curious and hungry for new experiences, you're an unstoppable, excitable duo. You might just have to acclimate yourself to the unfiltered, passionate way your little Sag delivers their fiery opinions.

YOU'LL CONNECT . . .

- **By getting out of your comfort zone.** From exploring new parks to discovering exciting flavors, you'll love being on the go and broadening your horizons together.

- **Anytime you're having an educational moment.** Sagittarius's Ninth House also oversees soaking up knowledge, while your Third House is communication and learning, so you both adore filling your brains up with an array of facts and ideas—simply for the sake of knowing more.

- **By traveling.** You'll be psyched to realize that even as a tiny one, your Sag is as pumped as you are to jump in the car, on the train, or even onto a flight to soak up new sights.

YOU'LL CLASH . . .

- **When your airiness conflicts with their intensity.** Your Sag might not understand why you're not as fired up and opinionated as they are, and you might not relate to their dramatic view. But there's always room to be impressed by each other's perspectives.

- **When your Sag needs more space.** Your free-spirited Archer needs plenty of room to breathe (physically and mentally), so you'll want to avoid a cluttered nursery or overly busy schedule.

- **If they're thinking big picture and you're in the weeds.** For example, you'll want to spin potty-training as "the ultimate big-kid challenge" your Jupiter-ruled baby gets to conquer versus trying to use a super-organized sticker chart they'll see as a snooze fest.

GEMINI PARENT & LITTLE CAPRICORN

While your MO is to learn and communicate—the quicker, the better—your Capricorn's is to work hard to succeed and be recognized, no matter how long it takes. Despite your different energies and paces, you're driven to get on the same page. Your Goat might be confused by your innate need to multitask and scatter your energy, and you won't get why they're so serious and pragmatic—especially when they're so young. But you'll bond the most when you appreciate their old soul and use your information-gathering skills to support their goals.

YOU'LL CONNECT . . .

- **By finding playful solutions to big-picture goals.** You can infuse any undertaking with a lighthearted perspective, and believe it or not, your driven Goat might inspire you to be more ambitious.

- **Whenever you put in hard work that can't help but earn recognition.** Think baking up a storm for a family gathering or creating an impressive look for their preschool costume contest.

- **Through heartwarming traditions.** You both appreciate marking special occasions with loved ones in a time-honored way.

YOU'LL CLASH . . .

- **When your pace feels too frenzied for your Cap.** Even when they're tiny, your Goat will value being "in control" at all times, which means that being nudged into your signature busy bee mode could result in overwhelm and frustration.

- **If you can't see eye to eye on how to follow the rules.** Whether you're making up a new route to get home or a different way of tackling a bedtime routine, your Saturnian, rules-and-regulations-loving kid will push back.

- **If you want to socialize when your Cap needs peace and quiet.** Your Goat is more reserved than you and requires more downtime than you might realize.

GEMINI PARENT & LITTLE AQUARIUS

You and your forward-thinking Water Bearer enjoy feeling involved in a community, connecting with other people, and gathering information to launch your latest invention or imaginative game plan. But while you and your Aquarius are equally airy, you'll be reminded of their fixed nature when they're particularly contrarian and stubborn, presenting you with an opportunity to encourage more flexibility. Meanwhile, they can teach you how to commit to a particular path.

YOU'LL CONNECT . . .

- **Through group activities with plenty of parents and playmates.** You agree that more is always merrier.

- **By brainstorming.** Your mental energy is equally high, so together, you can invent your very own games, routines, pastimes—even language.

- **Whenever you can turn plans into action.** Your innovative Water Bearer will appreciate when you tap your research skills to help them turn even their quirkiest vision into reality.

YOU'LL CLASH . . .

- **When your Water Bearer's fixed nature conflicts with your mutable one.** They tend to be susceptible to some rather black-and-white thinking, which can feel very much at odds with your preference to consider all the options.

- **If you lack focus.** Your Aquarius could get frustrated if you're struggling to hunker down on a plan you've landed on.

- **If your Aquarius decides that they're in charge.** As open-minded and free-spirited as the Water Bearer might be, they'll also have their domineering moments, in which you'll want to gently remind them who's running the show.

GEMINI PARENT & LITTLE PISCES

Similarly adaptable, you and your Fish move through the world with different priorities. They're in their emotions as much as you're in your head. That said, they'll inspire you to embrace your imagination and your feelings, and you can help them explore and talk through what's in their heart.

YOU'LL CONNECT . . .

- **By talking about dreams.** Ask your little Fish lots of questions about their most recent daydream or big-picture wish, and you'll spur a colorful, entertaining back-and-forth.

- **When you get curious about spiritual pursuits.** Even as a little one, your Fish is drawn to the ethereal, magical, and otherworldly themes in books and movies, which you can find intriguing too.

- **When you're swept up in an artistic project.** Being creative and self-expressive comes naturally to you both in your own ways.

YOU'LL CLASH . . .

- **If you get stuck in a cycle of miscommunication.** There will be moments in which you think you're being super clear about what you mean, yet something will get lost in translation with your dreamy Fish, so practicing patience is key.

- **If your pace feels too hectic to your sensitive Fish.** Sometimes empathic Pisceans' senses get overwhelmed, and they need to center themselves in a quiet space away from the hustle and bustle you're often caught up in.

- **If you're leaning too heavily on rational versus intuitive thought.** The latter is Pisces's language, while the former can feel foreign and frustrating to them.

THE CANCER PARENT

With your sun or other placements in the cardinal water sign, you're maternal, family-oriented, intuitive, and sentimental. At the same time, you're a go-getter who thinks in terms of sweeping, ambitious visions. Innately nurturing, you pour your whole heart into anything you do with your child and likely grew up imagining what kind of parent you'd be. Friends, loved ones, and your child are sure to find your signature goofy sense of humor endearing, and because you're as entertaining as you are comforting to others, your nearest and dearest lean on you quite a bit. It could be a struggle to care for yourself as well as you care for others, but you'll be at your happiest and most vital when you do. When you're overwhelmed, you often retreat into your shell to process your emotions, recharge, and tune in to your inner voice, given your ruler, the intuitive moon. You also find it centering to prioritize quality time with family. Try these routines to nurture yourself:

BEST SELF-CARE ROUTINES FOR A CANCER PARENT

- Spend time in or near water, like going for a run by your favorite neighborhood lake.
- Browse a vintage clothing store or antique shop for your next nostalgic find.
- Scroll through photos and videos of cherished memories with your little one and other loved ones.
- Take special care preparing your go-to comfort food.
- Devote extra time to playing with the family pet.

CANCER PARENT & LITTLE ARIES

You and your Ram child are both initiators who prefer to think in terms of the big picture and love diving into projects. But your Aries plows into everything quickly and with unparalleled fervor, which can have you a bit freaked out about their safety. You'll also want to bear in mind that they show affection in a fiery, playful, action-oriented way versus your more snuggly, deeply feeling, intuitive approach.

YOU'LL CONNECT . . .

- **Through coming up with big, ambitious plans.** Think: talking about what your Aries wants to be when they grow up or what you're going to do on your next vacation.

- **Through active playtime.** Aries's athleticism is pretty off the charts, and you'll enjoy making time to throw a ball or play a game of tag.

- **By slowing down.** After you've sped up to keep up with your Ram, you can show them the joy of slowing down for a meditative walk or heartfelt cuddle session.

YOU'LL CLASH . . .

- **If what you've said seems to go in one ear and out the other.** Action-oriented Aries is often so distracted by needing to *do* that they don't hear you; you can work with them on reframing listening as an action—and a valuable one at that.

- **If your love languages conflict.** You may want to show you care through snuggles and sweet words, but your Aries might prefer to bond with you by telling jokes, engaging in spirited game play, or running outside.

- **When their impulsivity feels too risky to you.** You often need to check in with your heart and intuition before making a move, but your Aries child dives right in. The solution: Set the guardrails, then let them do their bold, daring thing.

CANCER PARENT & LITTLE TAURUS

You and your sweet little Bull have a lot in common, from enjoying a slower-paced life to reveling in cuddle time, family time, and of course mealtimes. You might be challenged by their stubbornness but see it as a chance to nurture and coax them into learning and growing.

YOU'LL CONNECT . . .

- **Through lots of snuggle time.** You're equally happy to show how much you care through cozy, skin-on-skin moments.

- **By pouring your emotions into a creative outlet.** Artistic pursuits come naturally to you as a water sign, and the same can be said for your Venus-ruled baby.

- **By preparing and enjoying meals.** When your Taurus is tiny, feedings might be among your favorite moments together, and as they get older, you'll find that time in the kitchen is particularly joy-filled and memorable.

YOU'LL CLASH . . .

- **When your Taurus gets a bit stuck.** They'll want to rely on the two crayons they know while you'll want to encourage them to try the whole box, but they might need a bit more time to warm up to that idea.

- **If you're struggling to help your Bull rely on their intuition over their head.** You might get frustrated if they're not as comfy letting their heart guide the way as you are, but modeling that for them can do wonders.

- **When you start projects and have difficulty with follow-through, or they struggle to get started in the first place.** If you can initiate, then support their ability to take the reins, you'll reach the finish line.

CANCER PARENT & LITTLE GEMINI

Your on-the-go Twins tyke is super cerebral—always gathering and sharing information—while you're fueled by emotion, which can create some rockiness at times. But you can also show them how to get in touch with and verbalize their feelings, while they can open your eyes to moving through life in a more excitable, communicative way.

YOU'LL CONNECT . . .

- **When you talk about your feelings.** Gemini loves learning new ways to think and use language, while you'll be elated to help them foster their emotional intelligence.

- **When you're enjoying high-energy activities with loved ones.** You both enjoy the warm feeling of making memories with family, especially if you're having dynamic fun (think: playing in a bounce house or at a nearby playground).

- **By celebrating.** From birthdays to the winter holidays, you love traditions, and your social Gemini adores any excuse to get festive and be around as many people as possible.

YOU'LL CLASH . . .

- **When your energies are mismatched.** Sometimes you'll need alone time, and your Gemini is as chatty as ever; these moments could show your Twins kiddo that quiet, centering activities can be fun and fulfilling.

- **If you get aloof at the same time.** You both handle emotionally heavy moments by pulling away, but you'll want to emphasize the importance of coming back together once you've found your inner calm.

- **If you're struggling to understand how the other expresses affection.** While you're inclined to show you care through physical touch and gifts, your Twins baby will default to sounds, warm words, and animated body language.

CANCER PARENT & LITTLE CANCER

You and your little Crab are two deeply feeling, intuitive, sentimental—and OK, occasionally moody—peas in a pod. You want to nurture and be nurtured in the same deeply feeling, intuitive way and equally value snuggles, hugs, and time with each other and your whole family. And when those tough moods strike, you'll know better than anyone how to give your Cancer the right combo of space and sweet guidance and support.

YOU'LL CONNECT . . .

- **Through plenty of heartfelt cuddles.** From skin-on-skin when they're tiny to post-nightmare soothing sessions, you and your Crab both find a lot of comfort in latching on to each other to show your love.

- **By spending time in the kitchen.** As two foodies, you'll enjoy whisking and kneading up a storm together.

- **By making then reminiscing about sweet moments you've** shared with each other and your family. You never have to worry you're being overly sentimental with your little Crab, who will always be just as gleeful to take a walk down memory lane.

YOU'LL CLASH . . .

- **If your Crab needs more space.** When your Cancer toddler is struggling with a big emotion and isn't interested in talking about it just yet, you'll want to give them a bit more time in their shell.

- **When one or both of you are feeling crabby.** Sometimes you'll just have to acknowledge that you're swimming in some uncomfortable emotions, but you have each other to make it through.

- **If your Cancer starts scheming their way out of bedtime or any other plan they don't want to adhere to.** You can see right through any manipulative tactic—and you'll also know how to shut it down as gently as possible.

CANCER PARENT & LITTLE LEO

You and your Lion child are equally creative and demonstrative when it comes to sharing what's in your big hearts and showering each other in a lot of warm, sunny love. You'll be reminded of their fixed nature when they dig their heels in on occasion, and should your fiery Leo start fancying themselves the one in charge, you'll aim to foster their leadership abilities while setting and holding healthy boundaries.

YOU'LL CONNECT . . .

- **Through showy displays of affection.** Leo's as adoring as they want to be adored while you're endlessly dedicated and nurturing, so you innately light each other up.

- **Whenever you document your adventures.** Because you're so sentimental, you love having any kind of record of a heartwarming moment to look back on, and your Lion enjoys being in the spotlight, so you'll rarely have to question if they're up for that family photo or social media video.

- **When you support their big, bold dreams.** Your Leo is shooting for the stars, and you're happy to cheer them on however you can.

YOU'LL CLASH . . .

- **When your Lion attempts to step into an authoritative role.** They might need a gentle reminder that although you're a softie, you're still the one who calls the shots.

- **When your Leo wants to be social, and you'd rather stay in.** While you're happiest at home and surrounded by loved ones, your outgoing, party animal Lion wants to make an impression on friends and strangers alike, so be sure to split time between your homey sanctuary and anywhere they can command the spotlight.

- **When their action-oriented temperament conflicts with your sentimentality.** You'll notice, especially as they grow up, that your little Lion is eager to feel like they're moving forward no matter what, and you're more nostalgic. For example, they might scrunch their nose at that box of holiday decorations you've carried around from home to home, because they'd rather make or buy new ones.

CANCER PARENT & LITTLE VIRGO

You and your earthy little Maiden are both nurturing, sensitive, and dedicated to being helpful to the ones you love. But while you lead with your heart, your Virgo leads with their head. In turn, your sweet Virgo might worry sometimes unnecessarily. You'll teach them to trust their feelings and find tools that help them be more centered, while they'll teach you new ways to communicate and get organized.

YOU'LL CONNECT . . .

- **Through caring for others.** Whether by grooming your pup or making breakfast for your partner together, you both find a lot of pleasure in nurturing each other and beloved family members.

- **Through caring for yourselves.** Your Virgo will be very interested in caring for their health and well-being from the time they're tiny (eager to eat the veggies you offer that will make their body healthy and happy), and you've always had high emotional intelligence, so you can easily trade notes on the best emotionally and physically grounding practices, whether those are baths or mindfulness routines.

- **Through everyday tasks around your home.** You both love to feel like you're contributing to not only your family's list of to-dos but also the coziness of your shared space.

YOU'LL CLASH . . .

- **If you find yourselves speaking two different languages.** At times, Virgo's cerebral, Mercury-ruled nature could conflict with your far more emotional, moon-ruled one. They'll want to stick to the facts—and details—while you'll want to open their eyes to subtext and so much more.

- **If your Maiden gets picky.** You could find yourself feeling sensitive and bruised by their seemingly critical nature, but these moments are opportunities to consider how they might simply be flexing their analytical muscle.

- **When they're overthinking.** While you might be confused by just how in the weeds your Virgo is getting, you can help them take a step back and think about any situation in a way that doesn't feel so overwhelming.

CANCER PARENT & LITTLE LIBRA

You and your Scales child, born under cardinal signs, are both drawn to anything and everything beautiful, adore lighthearted playtime together, and aim to make the world a sweeter, more loving place. You'll find that as an air sign, your Libra is in their head more than in their feelings, so quite often, nurturing your bond will be about bridging the gap between the intellectual and emotional—and getting out of your comfort zone as a homebody, since your Libra is quite the social butterfly. You can also help them be more decisive, while they can inspire you to share what's in your heart.

YOU'LL CONNECT . . .

- **By beautifying.** Your aim is to make spaces, especially around the home, cozier and more welcoming, while theirs is to add aesthetic touches that promote balance. That said, they'll love helping you pick out a new throw or the perfect color paint for their big-kid room.

- **When you balance comfy, homey activities with more social ones.** You crave the former while they need the latter more, but enjoying both together brings you closer.

- **When you're initiating as a team.** As two cardinal signs, you can easily set your sights on a big goal (think: organizing a messy playroom) and dive in boldly.

YOU'LL CLASH . . .

- **If your Libra needs a greater sense of serenity in a given moment.** Your Scales baby avoids conflict at all costs. But because you're so in touch with your emotions and intuition, you know that not all moments can be peaceful, so you'll want to present that reality to your sensitive Libra as delicately as possible.

- **When your Scales child is leading with their head versus heart.** It could be tough for you to understand their point of view at times, but they might also inspire you to try a more mental versus emotional perspective on for size.

- **When you're both in go-getter mode but not on the same page.** Although sharing the same quality can be helpful, there will be moments in which you both want to take on a big project but will need to put in a little bit of work to make sure your visions align.

CANCER PARENT & LITTLE SCORPIO

As two water signs, you and your Scorpion are equally intuitive, comfortable exploring deep emotions, and never hesitate to put each other and your family first. You could be challenged by the fact that as a fixed sign, Scorpio is resistant to embracing uncharted terrain, which you're generally up for. But you're also able to offer them a lovely sense of security that makes it easier to be open to anything new.

YOU'LL CONNECT . . .

- **By blending creativity with family traditions.** Whether you're brainstorming themes for your annual Halloween celebration with your spookiness-loving Scorpio or preparing a beloved family recipe together, your sentimentality complements their admiration for ritual.

- **When you're sharing what's in your hearts.** Neither of you shies away from swimming in the deep end of emotion. Although your Scorpio is generally quiet and private, they'll find it easy to open up to you.

- **When you set out to hit a milestone.** From potty-training to reading lessons, you and your Scorp are so in sync that it's easy for you to co-create a plan that'll get you across the finish line.

YOU'LL CLASH . . .

- **When your Scorp gets sneaky.** Your Scorpion can be even more scheming than you at times, which could make you laugh but may also reflect on how you're setting and maintaining their boundaries.

- **If you want to forge ahead and your Scorpion is slow to budge.** When your Scorp's fixed nature kicks in and conflicts with your cardinal one, you'll want to remind them that striving to be more adaptable and open-minded can help them feel empowered.

- **If your Scorpio needs more privacy.** You can feel so close and connected that you could be caught off guard when your little Scorpion goes radio silent, but you can rest assured they'll share what's up when they're ready.

CANCER PARENT & LITTLE SAGITTARIUS

You and your Archer can learn a lot from each other, as you bring two very different perspectives and sets of priorities to the table. Your fiery baby's mission in life is to explore while you're happiest nesting at home. But whether through food or storytelling, there are many ways to bring eye-opening experiences that will appeal to your Sag into your cozy place. And you'll find that your Archer challenges and inspires you to embrace your inner adventurer as well.

YOU'LL CONNECT . . .

- **By soaking up lots of knowledge about the world through books and movies.** You can offer your Sag plenty of globally inspired lessons from the comfort of your home.

- **When you try new flavors.** As a foodie, you can more than appreciate your Archer child's interest in learning through their taste buds.

- **When you initiate an adventure you and Sag are equally excited about.** Tap into your ability to map out a bold game plan— whether you're going to Grandma's for the weekend or meeting up with friends at the playground—and you'll thrill your little Archer.

YOU'LL CLASH . . .

- **When you're feeling out of sync emotionally.** Even the littlest Sag has the ability to blurt out unfiltered truth bombs that could wound you more than you expected.

- **When your definition of comfort conflicts with theirs.** Although it might seem counterintuitive, giving them more room to do their own thing is actually what will help them feel the most secure.

- **When your Sag needs more physical space too.** Because you love your home, it can be challenging for you to understand why your Archer is bored or frustrated by playing in the same spot at home. But your freedom-loving kid gets claustrophobic, preferring to get out and spend time somewhere big and open where they can run, jump, and spread their wings.

CANCER PARENT & LITTLE CAPRICORN

You and your baby Sea Goat may be opposites, but you're also both initiative-taking cardinal signs, which offers you plenty of room to teach each other. While you're keen to dive into exploring your emotions and intuition, your Capricorn leads with a reserved, controlled demeanor. You can show them that getting in touch with their feelings can be healing and therapeutic, while they'll never cease to impress you with their work ethic.

YOU'LL CONNECT . . .

- **By recognizing how you feel, then coming up with a step-by-step action plan.** Cap might shy away from big emotions, but you can give them the language to label them, then, together, you can figure out the best, most grounded way to work through them.

- **When you're equally dedicated to crossing the finish line.** Whether you're working on a craft or tackling chores with your Sea Goat toddler, you'll motivate each other to dive into and complete the task at hand, no matter how long it might take.

- **By cheering on each other's hard work.** Not only will you be your Sea Goat's greatest cheerleader but they'll be yours in return.

YOU'LL CLASH . . .

- **When your Sea Goat is acting too cool for emotions.** There will be times they won't get why you're so mushy or sensitive, and you won't get why they're so standoffish, so you'll have to practice accepting where you both are in that moment.

- **When you're both fired up—about conflicting plans.** If you have your heart set on forging ahead on an agenda that is at odds with the one your Sea Goat has already landed on for themselves, sparks could fly.

- **If you're having trouble understanding how the other shows affection.** Your Cap might show they love you by pitching in on chores or wanting to accompany you on a walk to reach your daily steps goal versus requesting one of those snuggle sessions you've been craving.

CANCER PARENT & LITTLE AQUARIUS

In some ways, you and your Water Bearer are quite different. Even when they're tiny, their aloofness could feel foreign as you prefer to be close physically and emotionally. But you'll also find that your nurturing nature and their humanitarian one offers overlap, and the amount of compassion you share is unsurpassed.

YOU'LL CONNECT . . .

- **By helping others.** Both you and your Aquarius feel it's important to care for people and animals in need. You'll find that they're naturals at pitching in on any kind of volunteer opportunity.

- **By talking about feelings in an objective way.** You're not one to intellectualize your emotions, but your airy child can show you how to take a step back and consider a situation from an external point of view.

- **When you celebrate differences.** In your nurturing Cancerian way, you can gently remind your Water Bearer how everyone's a little quirky in their own way—a philosophy they hold dear—which can bring you even closer.

YOU'LL CLASH . . .

- **When their intellectual approach conflicts with your emotional one.** You could find that your social Aquarius will be most interested in talking about how they feel versus showing you through hugs and kisses.

- **If their fixed nature feels limiting to you.** As forward-thinking, progressive, and tech-savvy as your little Water Bearer might be from a very young age, they'll also struggle with black-and-white thinking (a signature fixed sign trait) that could frustrate you as you urge them to get out of their comfort zone.

- **When you're not sure how to respond to their contrarianism.** "No" or "I don't believe you" could be common phrases you hear from your Aquarius kid, both of which might baffle you when you're simply trying to give them a bath or teach them how to brush their teeth. Your best bet: leaning on your keen sense of humor.

CANCER PARENT & LITTLE PISCES

As two heartfelt, sensitive water signs, you and your Fish baby feel like you're very much in sync. As the cardinal one of the aquatic bunch, you're happy to show your sensitive Pisces how to pinpoint a big dream and take action to make it their reality. And as the mutable one, your wise-beyond-their-years—possibly even slightly psychic—Fish can show you how to be even more adaptable and open to the ebb and flow of life.

YOU'LL CONNECT . . .

- **By opening up to each other on a deep emotional level.** Even without words, you and your Fish will get what the other is feeling and, in turn, needs.

- **Through time in or near the water.** Being in your element feels therapeutic and bond-bolstering for you both.

- **When you're blending imagination and sentimentality, which you and your Fish have in spades.** Neptune rules film, so your little one will enjoy starring in a video that you'll both be eager to look back on in a week, a month, or years from now.

YOU'LL CLASH . . .

- **When your Fish is lacking motivation.** You know what it's like to be swimming in big feelings, but you don't often let it deter you from forging ahead. That's not always the case for your extra-sensitive Pisces, who might also need extra TLC and patience at times.

- **When you want to take action, and your Fish wants to dream.** You might both be guided by intuition, but you tend to be more pragmatic than your Pisces. When they're lost in the clouds, you can show them the benefit of a game plan.

- **When you're up for more time spent with loved ones than your sensitive Fish.** Because they tend to pick up all the energy around them, they can get overwhelmed and withdraw. Although this might be initially frustrating, because you'd prefer family time be harmonious for everyone, you'll learn to meet these moments with plenty of compassion.

FIRE + FIXED + LION

THE LEO PARENT

With your sun or other placements in the fixed fire sign, you're driven, charismatic, sunny, fun-loving, and self-assured, as well as action-oriented and occasionally willful. Ruled by the vitality-bringing sun and as the sign connected to the Fifth House of Self-Expression—which also oversees fun and romance—you're creative and forthcoming about your feelings. You shower your child and loved ones with radiant, all-encompassing love, intent on modeling an unflinching brand of confidence that you hope will help them feel equally empowered in the world. You enjoy soaking up the spotlight, often regaling others with entertaining stories and happily jumping in front of the camera with your baby to document all the milestones. As your little one grows, no matter their sign, they'll be inspired by your signature positive, proactive perspective. Motivated to accomplish lofty goals as much as you are to prioritize pleasure, you take on a lot, especially for those you love. But you also innately understand the value of tending to your own needs. Try these routines to nurture yourself:

BEST SELF-CARE ROUTINES FOR A LEO PARENT

- Have an impromptu dance party to your favorite '80s pop or EDM playlist.
- Meet up with friends for a beach day or get-together at your go-to restaurant.
- Take a hot yoga class.
- Treat yourself to a bouquet of your favorite flowers.

LEO PARENT & LITTLE ARIES

As two fire signs, you and your tiny Ram are passionate, independent, and action-oriented. Because your Aries—the firstborn of the zodiac—is intent on being number one, and you also fancy yourself the top royal of the jungle, you can anticipate fiery power struggles. But at the core of your bond is a shared ability to move through the world in a bold, take-charge way. Your Ram inspires you to jump-start just about anything as a cardinal sign, and as a fixed sign, you can model and guide them with the follow-through.

YOU'LL CONNECT . . .

- **When you're getting fired up and funny.** From getting your Ram baby to crack up when you make funny faces to singing a favorite song at the top of your lungs, you'll find it thrilling to channel your inner flame into entertaining each other.

- **By asserting yourselves.** You'll be delighted to see your little Ram piping up about their wants and needs in a direct, confident way—much like you.

- **When you're cheering each other on.** You each want to see the other win, and you'll both show how you feel confidently, enthusiastically, and loudly.

YOU'LL CLASH . . .

- **When you're both determined to be in charge.** You'll inevitably have differing ideas about how a particular routine or activity is supposed to go, and your Ram will thoroughly believe that they should get their way, so allowing them opportunities to feel like the boss can be helpful.

- **If you're struggling to take a risk and try something new.** As a fixed sign, you know what works for you and your baby, but your Ram will be happiest when they feel like they're getting their fill of bold exploration, even if that's just switching up the scenery when you go for walks.

- **When tempers flare.** For two fire signs, even a minor dustup could quickly lead to blazing blowups and a display of big emotions. But take heart: You both do everything fast—including make up.

LEO PARENT & LITTLE TAURUS

As two fixed signs, you and your baby Bull are both persistent and capable of making decisions and holding tight to them (for better or worse). As a fire sign, you tend to move more quickly than your Taurus, whose slow, plodding, steady approach can feel exasperating to you at times. But you're both bighearted and soak up the world around you with all of your senses. Your Bull's love feels grounding to you, and yours inspires them to reach for the stars.

YOU'LL CONNECT . . .

- **By creating something beautiful.** You can help your Venus-ruled Taurus express themselves with a range of colorful mediums, whether that's painting, sculpting, or singing.

- **When you're eyeing a concrete goal.** Once you're both clear on what you want to achieve, very little will stand in your way.

- **By spending time somewhere serene.** You're both supersensitive to your surroundings, preferring them to be as comfortable as possible.

YOU'LL CLASH . . .

- **Should stubbornness reign supreme.** When either of you has decided on a particular approach, you are apt to dig your heels in and fail to budge altogether. By modeling open-mindedness and adaptability, you can avoid getting stuck at a dead end.

- **If you're running at two different paces.** Your Bull likes to take their sweet time, and while you're not the speediest sign (ahem, hey, Aries), you do prefer to plow forward decisively. That said, your Bull can help you embrace the pleasures of slowing down.

- **When your priorities aren't in sync.** You could feel like your parent-child dynamic is thrown for a loop in the moments when your Taurus is in a pragmatic headspace, preferring to take a nap or eat, while you're interested in putting fun first.

LEO PARENT & LITTLE GEMINI

Your chatty, fun-loving Gemini baby is as upbeat and curious as you, and you're both apt to put lighthearted playfulness above anything else. But while you'd rather take steps toward making any proposed plan a reality, your Twins tyke would often prefer to think, talk, read about it, then discuss it some more. While you can show them how to channel their mental energy into confident action, your airy and adaptable child will show you the value of gathering all the info and changing course midstream.

YOU'LL CONNECT . . .

- **When you find the fun in everyday aspects of life.** You'll love making up songs together on a drive or bird-watching in the backyard.

- **By making up your own inventive craft project.** You love to lead the charge, and your cerebral, creative Gemini will adore the opportunity to experiment.

- **Whenever you can throw a party or host a get-together.** You and your Twins child enjoy being around people—especially for a cheerful occasion.

YOU'LL CLASH . . .

- **When fixed aspects of your personality conflict with their mutable ones.** You'd rather stick to what's tried-and-true, while your Twins baby thrives on switching things up as much as possible, so you might find that you're more inclined to go with the flow to suit their temperament. You can also show them how empowering it can be to take a stand—and find pleasure joining them in exploring various options.

- **If their mental energy is off the charts.** It can be tough for your Gemini to slow their many excitable thoughts— even in moments when you've explained it's time to wind down. This might be an opportunity to practice mindfulness together.

- **When you show and they tell.** You can't help but shower your little Gemini in warm hugs and surprise gifts, but their love language tends to be more verbal than action-oriented, so know that all those giggles, boisterous noises and, later, chattiness show how much they care.

LEO PARENT & LITTLE CANCER

You and your Crab are both eager to show each other how much you care. One point of contention: While their cardinal nature makes them eager to initiate new projects, you might prefer to stick with the path well-trodden. But in general, you'll find that because you're both so bighearted and dedicated to nurturing your bond, lots of sweet, loving, and playful energy flows easily between you.

YOU'LL CONNECT . . .

- **By being demonstrative.** You and your little Crab are equally committed to sharing how much you care in a big, showy way.

- **By taking lots of photos and videos.** You love being the center of attention, and your Crab's super sentimental about capturing heartfelt moments, so you'll rarely suffer for a lack of social media posts or family photo albums.

- **When you dream big.** You love to see your Cancer assert their desires, sweeping ideas, and goals, then pour their whole heart into them—just like you.

YOU'LL CLASH . . .

- **Whenever your Crab's sensitivity conflicts with your direct communication style.** Your "roar" can feel too harsh at times to your delicate Cancer baby, so you might find it more effective to motivate them through upbeat cheerleading.

- **If you have a specific game plan in mind, and your Crab needs to go with the flow.** Your Cancer might need to do things in their own time, based on their emotions.

- **If you want to connect but your Crab needs to go into their shell.** You might not understand their instinct to pull away, preferring to talk through big emotions, but they'll often need to be in their feelings for a bit before they can fully address them.

LEO PARENT & LITTLE LEO

As two sun-ruled Lions, you and your cub share a particularly radiant, warm, sweet, and loyal love. You'll be proud of your Lion's confidence and drive and see your own optimism in their bright smile and cheerful disposition. The main conflict will be when there's a dispute over who's the true royal of your mini jungle.

YOU'LL CONNECT . . .

- **By getting dramatic.** Whether they're on the fly or well-thought-out, you'll always be putting on shows together. Sharing the spotlight brings you joy.

- **When showering each other in big displays of affection.** Like you, your Lion can't help but be effusive and demonstrative.

- **Through playful creativity.** You'll find that you're even more in touch with your innate flair for the artistic and inner child as a result of being inspired by your baby.

YOU'LL CLASH . . .

- **When your fixed natures collide.** If you both have set ideas about how a particular activity or moment should play out, and neither is willing to budge, you'll find yourselves at a particularly heated standstill.

- **If either of you is too proud to admit you were wrong.** It can be tough for a regal Lion of any age to say they messed up, but you'll want to show your cub how it's done, so they have an easier time with it.

- **When you can't decide who's in charge.** Your Lion might understand fully that you're calling the shots but do their best to find a way to assert their own power, something you'll want to foster in a productive way by giving them plenty of their own territory over which to rule, whether that's letting them pick out a playlist of lullabies or choose their favorite snack from a selection.

LEO PARENT & LITTLE VIRGO

You and your little Maiden could be a force to be reckoned with as a duo. Although they might be quieter and more detail-oriented while you're more assertive and action-focused, they'll be excited to follow your lead and pitch in on any endeavor you've proposed. Honoring their sensitivities can preempt fussiness, and you'll show them the ropes of spontaneity and embracing life with gusto.

YOU'LL CONNECT . . .

- **Through planning ahead.** Your Maiden is happiest when they're following a fairly predictable routine, and although you enjoy being spontaneous, you'll find comfort in more regularity.

- **When you come up with an exciting game plan and go over all the details with your Virgo.** They'll eagerly support your big idea.

- **By being expressive and affectionate.** Even from the time they're tiny, your Maiden will be aware of even the slightest sounds, words, and gestures you'll rely on to shower them with love.

YOU'LL CLASH . . .

- **If Virgo needs to be comforted in a specific way that you wouldn't have thought of.** They might be quite particular, preferring that you use a lavender lotion versus chamomile or wanting to be swaddled in a blanket that's a bit more well-loved and worn-in than a new one.

- **Whenever Virgo believes they know better than you.** You have one smarty-pants, curious, and aware kid on your hands, and they know it—and, in turn, might second-guess your judgment.

- **When your paces and modalities conflict.** Mutable Virgo's indecisiveness might slow you down at times, so you might want to consider reframing those instances as opportunities to take a breath.

LEO PARENT & LITTLE LIBRA

You and your sweet Scales child are both on a mission to bring lots of beauty, joy, and light into the world. You'll be enamored with their desire to keep the peace and willingness to be up for just about any adventure. Your greatest challenge will be to understand their need to consider all sides of any proposal, which can make it tough for them to make up their minds. But in turn, your Libra baby will teach you how to bring more balance into your perspective as you model confident decision-making.

YOU'LL CONNECT . . .

- **By admiring anything and everything beautiful.** From stunning sunsets to glimmery snowflakes, you and your Libra little one will be equally mesmerized by prettiness everywhere you go together.

- **Through creating visual art.** As you and your Libra possess a particular love of visual and performance art, you'll bond by painting, coloring, or creating eye-catching costumes you can then wear while putting on a show for other family members.

- **When you're jointly charming friends or loved ones.** You were both born to be social butterflies.

YOU'LL CLASH . . .

- **When Libra struggles with indecision.** Noticing that your Scales child is comforted by weighing all the options will help you be more patient.

- **If you're digging your heels in when they want to try something new.** You might find that you're more willing to be open-minded and experimental for your curious airy baby.

- **In moments when your Libra gets too passive for your liking.** You're forever aiming to raise an empowered, strong, and independent child. And they will be—in their own, diplomatic, balance-loving way.

LEO PARENT & LITTLE SCORPIO

As two fixed signs, you and your Scorpion are equally dynamic, self-possessed, and determined to hit whatever finish line you've set your sights on. That said, moments in which you're both immovable can lead to friction but can also serve as opportunities to work on being more flexible. You'll admire how in touch with their emotions your fixed water kid is, and they'll love soaking up your abundant sunshine.

YOU'LL CONNECT . . .

- **When you're both working toward the same endgame.** When you and your Scorp jointly decide to hit a particular goal, you'll be unstoppable.

- **By exploring everyday magic.** From seeing brightly hued blooms pop up everywhere in the spring to coming up with spooky costumes (on Halloween or really any time of year), you and your Scorpio love to be enchanted.

- **Whenever you're fired up.** You'll notice fairly early on that you and your Scorpio are similarly passionate, and you'll enjoy supporting your baby's interests and introducing them to yours.

YOU'LL CLASH . . .

- **When your Scorpio keeps their feelings under wraps.** Even as a little one, your Scorpion will tend to be private, quiet, and mysterious, which can feel quite foreign to you. Over time, you'll know when they might need a bit of prodding to open up and when they just need their own space.

- **When your Scorpio's overwhelmed by their deepest emotions.** You'll wish every moment could be sunny and breezy, but the fact is that you're raising a water baby who feels intensely.

- **If neither of you can agree who's in charge.** Power struggles may be unavoidable, but they'll at least be educational moments for you and your little one.

LEO PARENT & LITTLE SAGITTARIUS

You and your fellow action-oriented, adventurous fire sign baby can tackle just about anything you set your minds on. You also find each other fun to be around. You'll notice that your Archer is as opinionated as you are—or perhaps even more—so you'll want to be prepared to negotiate and hash out any disagreement before it has a chance to build to an inferno.

YOU'LL CONNECT . . .

- **Through humor.** Well before the moment in which your Archer is toddling around in a particularly entertaining way or you're making the goofiest faces at them, you'll both specialize in sending each other into a flurry of side-splitting giggles.

- **When you're taking spontaneous action.** As soon as you land on any game plan—even if it's completely spur-of-the-moment—you'll plow forward as a dynamic team.

- **When you're living life at full blast.** From turning an afternoon at the park into a memorable adventure to throwing the ultimate toddler birthday bash, you and your Sag baby never fail to make fun a priority. No surprise you're the parent-child duo everyone wants to book a playdate with.

YOU'LL CLASH . . .

- **When your Sag struggles with boundaries.** You're OK with a bit of limit-pushing for the sake of having a good time, but your Jupiterian child won't be a fan of limits, period, which could present you with a chance to reinforce healthy boundaries.

- **If you find it tough to teach your Archer how to be tactful.** Your enthusiastic, preverbal Sag baby might bang on their high chair or screech loudly and out of the blue to get their point across, no matter what else is going on. And as a toddler, they'll blurt out whatever they're thinking—even more than the average child—which might frustrate you as a proponent of diplomacy, but you might also be amused by how unfiltered they can be.

- **If Sag isn't satisfied with the status quo.** As a fixed sign, you're a creature of habit, but your mini Archer is on a perpetual mission to explore and discover anything and everything outside of the norm. That said, you'll want to consider putting the familiar aside to satiate their wanderlust.

LEO PARENT & LITTLE CAPRICORN

Though you might not initially see your own disposition reflected in your reserved, serious Sea Goat, you and your cardinal earth sign are actually quite similar in terms of what you're striving for. You both want to be respected and admired for your achievements. Your Cap prefers to move slowly but steadily toward any goal, which can feel at odds with your dynamic pace. They'll teach you about the beauty of taking your time, while you'll show them how to be comfier with their inner fire.

YOU'LL CONNECT . . .

- **When you strive for recognition.** Whether you're teaming up to prep a delicious meal for loved ones or to win a game, you'll enjoy working together to earn a round of applause for your efforts.

- **By being ambitious.** As a fire sign, you're action-oriented, and your ruler, the sun, makes you especially confident, so when your serious Cap toddler asks questions about school or says they can't wait to learn how to ride a big-kid bike, you'll be impressed and excited by their drive.

- **As you foster their leadership skills.** You might just be the perfect role model to show your Cap how to take the reins of any undertaking in a positive, upbeat way.

YOU'LL CLASH . . .

- **When your Cap's seriousness and your playfulness conflict.** At times you might wish your Sea Goat were having more fun, but they might feel best by meeting their responsibilities like devoting extra time to putting their toys away just so.

- **If you're hoping they'll love the spotlight as much as you.** Cap wants solid recognition for their efforts, but they'd prefer to focus on their work versus being the center of attention. This isn't to say they won't enjoy dance recitals or singing in their preschool concert, but they'll prefer to be acknowledged for the effort they made versus for entertaining others.

- **If your Sea Goat thinks they're the grown-up in the room.** Your wise-beyond-their-years cardinal earth sign might amuse—and also challenge—you by assuming they're wise enough to be their own authority.

LEO PARENT & LITTLE AQUARIUS

You and your Water Bearer may be opposites, but as two fixed signs, you're both deeply committed to showing each other that you care. Your rebellious Aquarian takes pride in being a contrarian, and they could strike you as unnecessarily difficult at times. But you each have plenty to teach the other. Their desire to be a part of a communal effort is infectious, and your upbeat perspective could inspire them as well.

YOU'LL CONNECT . . .

- **By socializing with a group.** You and your Aquarian are equally talented at making friends and enjoy being a part of any team effort.

- **When you're giving back.** Your Aquarian toddler will want to get involved in charity efforts, which you're happy to lead the charge on.

- **Through meaningful, intellectual conversations.** Your Water Bearer will ask why more than the average toddler, and they genuinely want to know the answers, which you can offer in a warm, entertaining way.

YOU'LL CLASH . . .

- **Should obstinacy take over.** Because you and your baby are both fixed signs, you'll both be learning how to be more flexible.

- **If you're missing the big picture.** You'll be urging them to think about their self-interest, but more often than not, they want to do what's best for the collective—even if that's currently just their entire tumbling or music class. For example, if they're gifted a new instrument, they may feel wrong keeping it to themselves and possibly ask if they can leave it in the classroom for everyone to use.

- **When Aquarius says no . . .** for the sake of saying no. As a fellow fixed sign, you understand how resolute your Water Bearer may be, but ruled by the upbeat sun, you're interested in keeping things copacetic while they're naturally contrarian. Though you might be initially frustrated by their antagonism, you'll admire your Aquarius for taking a stance but encourage them to think about the root of their rebuttal.

LEO PARENT & LITTLE PISCES

You and your Fish baby might not share an element or quality, so you may feel like you're speaking different languages at times, but your hearts are invested in learning to be fluent. In tune with their emotions and with their head in the clouds, your Pisces child is a dreamer and a romantic like you. You can teach them how to act on their most artistic ideas, and they'll show you the beauty of being in the moment versus perpetually forging ahead.

YOU'LL CONNECT . . .

- **Through hands-on creativity.** You'll love using your imaginations to create something tangible together, whether that's a whimsical watercolor or an animal puppet made from a brown lunch bag.

- **By escaping reality.** You might like to take a time-out from the regular grind to spend a day at the nearest beach or playground.

- **Through performance.** Your imaginative Pisces will gravitate to theater, poetry, or dance, all art forms you're similarly drawn to.

YOU'LL CLASH . . .

- **If you struggle to understand their passive approach.** Your mutable water sign is not exactly action-oriented, preferring to let life happen and go with the flow, which could actually be an interesting perspective for you to observe and adopt yourself on occasion.

- **When your Fish isn't feeling so sunny.** You pride yourself on the ability to light up a room and make everyone smile—especially your little one. But when overwhelmed by emotions, your sensitive Pisces might not be as receptive as you'd like, challenging you to contemplate how best to comfort them.

- **If you'd prefer to stick to a set plan, and your Pisces needs something different.** Though you might have scheduled a class or a pediatrician appointment, there could be days when plans have to shift to honor your Fish's changeable emotions.

EARTH + MUTABLE + MAIDEN

THE VIRGO PARENT

With your sun or other placements in the mutable earth sign, you're analytical, health-conscious, thoughtful, sensitive, and service-oriented as well as research-savvy and adept at communication. You take great pride in your ability to identify and tend to your baby's needs while always remaining vigilant about what could be coming down the pike, gathering all the details of every parenting stage and potential or current challenge. Should your friends need a recommendation on the best stroller, formula, or parent-and-baby yoga class, you're at the ready with fully fleshed-out tips. As a child, you were a bookworm who delighted in making up stories of your own, so you'll hope your little one takes to reading and writing as much as you did. As the sign associated with the Sixth House of Wellness, you see the beauty in caring for others in small, simple ways. In fact, you can be so invested in this type of care that looking out for yourself and managing your stress—usually stemming from Mercury-fueled overthinking—lands on the back burner. Try these routines to nurture yourself:

BEST SELF-CARE ROUTINES FOR A VIRGO PARENT

- Browse a local bookstore.
- Take a mentally and physically soothing restorative yoga class.
- Pick out and bring home a new plant.
- Take your favorite journal to the park and spend time writing in nature.
- Cook up a healthy recipe using seasonal produce.

VIRGO PARENT & LITTLE ARIES

Your Ram baby is as focused on taking action as you are on gathering all the details before taking action. You'll be on a forever mission to show your little one the merits of looking—and then looking again—before leaping, concerned that all their fiery risk-taking will result in trouble. They'll show you the merits of being a bit more daring, while you'll prove that there's merit to embracing a diligent approach.

YOU'LL CONNECT . . .

- **When you applaud what the other brings to the table.** Your little one will inspire you to be bolder, while you encourage them to key into specifics.

- **When you work together to check tasks off your list.** If you lay out exactly what you need done—which is, of course, a specialty of yours—your cardinal fire sign dynamo will be eager to dive in.

- **By tackling a big-picture endeavor.** You'll note that presenting your Ram with a challenge you might fear is overwhelming actually motivates them, and that, in turn, will fire you up.

YOU'LL CLASH . . .

- **If you're zeroed in on details, and they want to focus on the big picture.** Your little visionary may inspire you to get out of the weeds.

- **When they're direct, and you're feeling a bit delicate.** Your Ram kid will often just do what they want or say what they think. For someone who tends to overthink before making a move, this could feel jarring.

- **If you're moving at conflicting paces.** You want to take your time to plan ahead and then make sure any chore or task is completed just so, and your Aries prefers spontaneity and moving lightning fast.

VIRGO PARENT & LITTLE TAURUS

As two earth signs, you'll find that you're both innately grounded, pragmatic, analytical, and organized, especially as your Bull grows up. You both appreciate rational thought and find spending time outdoors particularly therapeutic. Your little one is the fixed earth sign, however, so when you do butt heads, it could stem from the fact that they're struggling with inflexibility. But because you're so tuned in to their specific needs, you'll solve that with a little extra snuggle time or anything else that offers them a sense of security, gently guiding them toward embracing change.

YOU'LL CONNECT . . .

- **By slowing down.** You tend to move at a quicker, more mercurial speed than your Bull, but when your detail-oriented lens meets their pleasure-loving perspective, you can be even more in the moment.

- **When you work toward a big-picture goal over time.** You're all about planning ahead, and your little Bull can teach you what true determination looks like.

- **Through your love of organization.** You'll find that your Bull is as enamored with—and motivated by—charts, journals, and spreadsheets as you are.

YOU'LL CLASH . . .

- **When you're shifting gears, and they're stuck.** Given your Taurus's fixed energy, any miniscule diversion from an original, expected plan could trigger a tantrum. Meanwhile, as a mutable sign, you find it easier to go with the flow and adapt. Modeling this ability for your Bull can help them get comfier with transitions.

- **If the ways in which you show you care are out of sync.** You tend to say how you feel and demonstrate it through acts of service (like neatly organizing your Bull's wardrobe) whereas your Taurus prefers to show and receive love in more physical ways, like enjoying a sweet snack or cuddling up in a soft blanket together.

- **If you're in your head and they're in the moment.** Although your Mercury-fueled analytical take will be appreciated by your pleasure-seeking, Venus-ruled Bull, they might prefer to hit pause on thinking in order to simply be, a state that can be challenging—but also potentially therapeutic—for you.

VIRGO PARENT & LITTLE GEMINI

You and your fellow mutable, Mercury-ruled baby are two supercommunicators who will rarely run out of ideas to trade back and forth. Even when your Twins kid is tiny, they'll be sharing their thoughts with facial expressions, gestures, and, ultimately, language, and you'll be excited to pick up on every detail they want to share. Your main challenge will be understanding and embracing the airy—and sometimes frenetic—way your Gemini moves through the world. When you do, you'll learn the beauty of occasionally swapping lists and plans for simply seeing what the world serves up.

YOU'LL CONNECT . . .

- **Through the written word.** You and your Gemini child adore expressing yourselves through writing, so as they grow, you'll trade sweet notes and word art.

- **By having animated conversations.** Even before your Twins baby is able to string together a full sentence, you'll feel like you're enjoying witty repartee through facial expressions and gestures galore.

- **Through creative and communicative group activities.** Think: story time or music class at your town's recreation department.

YOU'LL CLASH . . .

- **When you're focused on the details and they're more scattered with their approach.** Your Twins tyke isn't particular at all about the info they're taking in. They'll skip around in a book, or start listening to a song and switch halfway through. This can feel a bit foreign to you, but it can also teach you how to move through life in a lighter, airier way.

- **When you're struggling to be quite as adaptable as your Gemini.** Virgo may be mutable, but once you've come up with a thoroughly researched approach, you'd like to see it through, but you'll learn how to adjust when your Twins baby changes course midstream.

- **When you're both being finicky.** You can both be highly particular in your own ways—for example, you can be picky about certain foods while your Gemini might despise wearing certain fabrics—so struggling to find common ground could lead to the occasional conflict.

VIRGO PARENT & LITTLE CANCER

You and your baby Crab are one tenderhearted team. You're both inherently nurturing and find it incredibly fulfilling—and even fun—to care for those you love. It's true that you're as practical as your Cancer is deeply feeling, but you're equally sensitive in your own way. They'll bring out your intuitive side, and you'll inspire them to lean into their inner go-getter.

YOU'LL CONNECT . . .

- **By nurturing everyone in your orbit.** You and your Crab will enjoy joining forces to care for loved ones, pets, neighbors, and friends.

- **When you practice self-care.** Because you and your Cancer can't help but pour a lot of energy into supporting others, you'll want to model healthy ways you can give back to yourselves, whether that's by taking an aromatherapy bath or winding down with a kid-friendly meditation routine.

- **When you check off family to-dos.** You and your Crab are equally driven to tend to your home. They'll be a quick study when it comes to helping you with laundry or food prep.

YOU'LL CLASH . . .

- **When you're in a cerebral place, and they're in their feelings.** At times, your analytical, Mercury-ruled disposition might be at odds with their sensitive, moon-ruled temperament, which can open your eyes to seeing life through a less logical but more emotional lens.

- **If you're hemming and hawing, and they're ready to go.** As a mutable sign, you might struggle to figure out the best way to spend a Saturday afternoon, and as a cardinal one, they'll just want to get a move on.

- **When you go down the rabbit hole.** When you're so heavily focused on minutiae—because you're doing your best to pinpoint the ideal snack/activity/safety protocol for your little one—your Crab might just need you to keep it sweet and simple.

VIRGO PARENT & LITTLE LEO

Your fiery Lion might be louder, more assertive, and more action-oriented than you, but by pairing your pragmatism with their dynamism, you'll move mountains together. You'll be impressed with the leadership skills and sunny optimism your Leo baby exhibits right out of the gate. They'll inspire you to step into your power, and by teaching them how to organize their big ideas and plan ahead, you can help them hit all their lofty goals.

YOU'LL CONNECT . . .

- **By making a plan and taking bold action.** Once you've researched and mapped out your route, your Lion will bring a ton of enthusiasm to fuel any team effort.

- **Through dreaming big.** Your Lion will innately believe that anything is possible—and they'll know that's the case because you're forever in their corner.

- **By hitting pause on what makes sense and embracing whatever feels right.** Your playful Lion will inspire you to tap into your most carefree and fun side.

YOU'LL CLASH . . .

- **If you're in the weeds when your Lion just wants to see what happens.** Your fixed fire sign child is innately spontaneous and will prove to you that not every moment needs to be planned ahead of time.

- **When your Lion acts like they're running the whole jungle.** Even the youngest Leo will offer glimpses of that rare, impressively take-charge Leonine energy that's apparent in leaders like Barack Obama and Jennifer Lopez. But never forget that you share astro qualities with none other than Beyoncé.

- **When you're moving at different speeds.** While you're determined to gather all the information on any given subject, your Lion might already be four steps ahead of you.

VIRGO PARENT & LITTLE VIRGO

You and your Maiden baby share a deep love of gathering and sharing information in an effort to be of service to others. With shared placements in the mutable earth sign, you can easily work together to make detailed plans and check them off one by one. Your little one will want to help you as much as you want to guide and support them. Meanwhile, you'll have insight on what's really driving any picky behavior: that tendency to overthink you know all too well. But by holding space for your little one to share and work through any roadblock, you're sure to foster their confidence.

YOU'LL CONNECT . . .

- **Through learning all the specifics of anything that intrigues you.** Whether you're doing a science experiment or researching a mythical creature mentioned in a book, you'll love adding to your mental databases.

- **By sharing your favorites.** *High Fidelity's* Rob Gordon, with all of his "Top 5" lists, was most likely a Virgo. From the best local sightseeing spots to all-time beloved pop music acts, you know what's best, and you'll love to share what you know with your mini Maiden.

- **Through healthy habits.** From taking the dog for a walk to experimenting with different types of fruit purees, you and your Virgo baby find joy in everyday wellness routines.

YOU'LL CLASH . . .

- **When you're not sure how to address a particular sensitivity.** Because you can relate and are so committed to soothing your Virgo baby, you could find yourself frustrated if you're not able to find a solution stat.

- **Should nitpicking reach a fever pitch.** When your Maiden huffs and puffs about minutiae, you might be inspired to rein in your own hyper-focused and sometimes critical take.

- **If your Maiden's worries set off your own anxieties.** This could lead to nothing more than a vicious cycle, so slowing down and sticking with what you know will benefit your own headspace—and model a healthy approach for your baby to boot.

VIRGO PARENT & LITTLE LIBRA

You and your Scales baby can absolutely agree that the world could be kinder and more balanced. While you contribute to this goal by doing research and getting organized, your Libra little one aims to bring more beauty and harmony wherever they go. You can both be indecisive, but as a cardinal sign, your Libra may surprise—and inspire—you with their go-getter disposition and artistic lens.

YOU'LL CONNECT . . .

- **By countering chaos.** When you set up a new organizational system in your Libra toddler's room, they'll complete it with a flower or pretty picture.

- **When you're making new friends.** Your communication skills and even the littlest Libra's ability to be a social butterfly make you magnets for forging new connections at the park, the playground, or preschool.

- **When you're problem-solving.** You're both especially capable of analyzing all sides of an issue to pinpoint a solution.

YOU'LL CLASH . . .

- **When Libra's airiness conflicts with your pragmatism.** Although your mutability makes you almost like an air sign at times, your changeable Libra will challenge you to let go of logic and thoroughly researched plans in order to be in the moment.

- **If you're ready to take action but your Scales child is still in debate mode.** It can be tough for Libra to move from weighing their options to actually making a decision, so you'll want to do your best to slow your Mercury-ruled pace to support their process.

- **When your perfectionism clashes with their artistic sensibilities.** While ensuring that everything has its proper place and is neat and tidy might feel like the epitome of harmony to you, your Venus-ruled baby might need to make a mess with finger paints or put their toys in a spot that doesn't quite make sense to you because they're flexing their artistic muscle.

VIRGO PARENT & LITTLE SCORPIO

While you're comfiest dealing with the nuts and bolts of everyday life, your mysterious Scorpion is deep in the depths of emotion from the get-go, which—to be fair—might be intimidating at times. But your devotion and love overrules everything else. You'll model a pragmatic point of view that they'll find grounding, and they'll teach you how to tackle anything you set your mind on.

YOU'LL CONNECT . . .

- **Through taking a daunting challenge one step at a time.** You're happy to get into the weeds to make sure a plan you've created is followed to a T, and anything your fixed water sign starts, they'll want to see through. Together, you can make magic.

- **When your intuition is particularly high.** As a water sign, your Scorpio's ability to tune in to their gut is especially strong. And when you can hit pause on your nonstop thoughts and get in sync with your own intuition, you'll find that it's easier to get on the same page as your Scorp.

- **By showering each other with loving gestures.** Your Scorp is sure to appreciate your thoughtfulness, while the intensity with which they show their attachment mesmerizes you.

YOU'LL CLASH . . .

- **When your fixed water sign baby's obstinacy throws you for a loop.** Given your adaptable nature, you could be unfamiliar with the black-and-white way your Scorpio sees the world. On the other hand, their steadfastness will be downright impressive.

- **If your high mental energy is at odds with their intense emotional vibe.** You tend to be in your head as much as they're guided by their heart, so there will be times when you'll want to put whatever is "rational" aside in order to meet them where they are—which is, most likely, in their feelings.

- **When they're seeking power as you seek perfectionism.** While you're busy gathering information, your dynamic Scorp is looking for opportunities to take the lead—and test the guardrails you've oh so logically and carefully put in place.

VIRGO PARENT & LITTLE SAGITTARIUS

You and your free-spirited Archer have much wisdom you can impart to each other. While your day-to-day hustle brings you a sense of comfort, your Sagittarius baby is a fiery creature of spontaneity, on a mission to go big versus get into the nitty-gritty details. While you aim to show them that details are the building blocks with which they'll build their bold dreams, they'll encourage you to cast an even wider net on your own mission to learn and grow.

YOU'LL CONNECT . . .

- **When you're fired up to learn.** You and your Archer are both passionate, lifelong students, and when you're in sync on what you want to learn, you'll soak up everything there is to know.

- **By making colorful connections.** Your Sag will hit it off with joyful, bold, spirited playmates like them, and in turn, you could click with parents or other people you wouldn't meet otherwise.

- **By turning must-dos into an adventure.** By applying your creativity to make regularly scheduled tasks and errands seem like an exciting undertaking, your mutable fire sign will get their exploration fix.

YOU'LL CLASH . . .

- **When your Sag toddler blurts out exactly what they're thinking—even if it hurts.** You'll quickly learn that your Archer is even more unfiltered than the average tot. Should their blunt take sting, instead of bristling, remember it's a side effect of their mission to seek and share the truth.

- **If your fiery baby wants to focus on the big picture, and you're in the weeds.** It can be a challenge to get your Archer to focus on—or care about—the specifics you feel are the foundation of any activity, but you might be surprised to find that should your Sag inspire you to let go of minutiae, it'll be a relief.

- **When your Sag gets bored.** You could find yourself spinning your wheels to entertain your Archer, but it's OK to keep it simple, as they'll be impressively capable of amusing themselves.

VIRGO PARENT & LITTLE CAPRICORN

As two earth signs, you and your Sea Goat have an easy time seeing eye to eye. Equally pragmatic, grounded, and goal-oriented, you'll tend to move through life in a similar way. You'll get a kick out of noticing that your Saturnian tot is an old soul—at times, seemingly even wiser than you. And they'll appreciate your sensitivity and ability to talk through just about anything, as they might struggle to verbalize what's in their hearts.

YOU'LL CONNECT . . .

- **When you map out an ambitious game plan.** You'll both be motivated by creating a step-by-step plan that requires putting in steady work.

- **Through achieving everyday successes.** Whether you're making incremental progress on a milestone together or tackling chores around the house, you'll bond by cheering each other's practical accomplishments.

- **When you honor your emotions.** By framing the concept in a grounded way, you'll show your little Sea Goat that there's not only no shame in acknowledging your emotions but

that it's also healthy and important to work through them.

YOU'LL CLASH . . .

- **If either of you is struggling to take a break.** You'll notice that, like you, your Sea Goat has a tough time slowing down and resting—and failing to do so can leave you both resentful and cranky.

- **When your Cap surprises you with their seriousness.** You may have researched all the best activities for a rainy Sunday, but your Sea Goat tot would rather perfect their potty training or clean up their play space. While you admire their work

ethic, you'll also want to do what you can to promote fun.

- **When your Sea Goat needs to feel like they've reached the top of a mountain.** You want your baby to hit milestones to learn and grow, but they want to feel like they've achieved something and are worthy of recognition. While this might feel a bit unfamiliar to you at first, it simply means adapting the language you use when applauding their efforts and results. (This might sound like, "Yes, you walked across the room all by yourself! Amazing job!" versus a more straightforward "You did it!")

PARENT & CHILD RELATIONSHIPS: BONDING WITH YOUR GROWING STAR 259

VIRGO PARENT & LITTLE AQUARIUS

You and your Water Bearer share a similarly intense curiosity about the world. But while you tend to wait until you've gathered all the data to come to a conclusion, your strong-willed, often contrarian fixed air sign will often decide on whatever is simply the opposite of the status quo, which could be befuddling to you. But this just means you'll be on a perpetually entertaining mission to learn more about your independent-spirited, slightly quirky Water Bearer, and as brilliant as they may be, they'll still look to you for your down-to-earth perspective.

YOU'LL CONNECT . . .

- **By blending playtime and technology.** Uranus (which rules Aquarius) oversees electricity, and Mercury (the ruler of Virgo) is the planet of technology, so you're both not only comfortable with but also especially engaged by high-tech activities and games.

- **Whenever a logical perspective is called for.** Friends and family members can rely on you and, as they grow, your Aquarius for a rational take.

- **Through charitable activities.** From a young age, your Water Bearer will be motivated to give back to their community, something that, as a service-oriented Virgo, you can certainly relate to.

YOU'LL CLASH . . .

- **If you're unsure of how to respond to their contrarian retorts.** Even after you've put a ton of energy into their dinner, outfit, or bedtime routine, your Aquarius toddler might say no simply for the sake of saying it, which could require getting creative (see page 177).

- **When your Aquarius is stuck in a black-and-white perspective.** Despite being so forward-thinking and airy, your Water Bearer will struggle to adapt, which could prove frustrating at times, but luckily, this is something you have no problem modeling for them.

- **When you express your emotions differently.** Your Aquarius tot can be pretty aloof while you're more of a sensitive softie, so you might need to do a bit of translating between your love languages.

VIRGO PARENT & LITTLE PISCES

You and your little Fish share a deep sense of empathy, but as astrological opposites, you'll also feel like you can offer each other what the other lacks. Dreamy, whimsical, and often caught up in emotions over logic, your Pisces baby will help you get out of your head and swept up in your imagination, while you'll model the benefits of zeroing in on details, organizing, and planning ahead.

YOU'LL CONNECT . . .

- **By blending learning and make-believe.** No matter what skill you're working on, you'll enjoy coming up with educational games and activities that allow your Neptunian baby's imagination to run wild while locking in must-knows.

- **When caring for others.** You and your Fish both have empathic hearts and a desire to lend a shoulder to anyone who's struggling.

- **When you show up for each other emotionally.** You offer your Pisces a sense of grounding, and they'll respond to you with gentleness and warmth.

YOU'LL CLASH . . .

- **When you have a plan, and your little Fish has other ideas.** In moments when they're not interested in dealing with a particularly logical task because they're off in dreamland, you might need to get creative to engage them.

- **If you find yourselves at a dead end due to indecision.** Although you're very adaptable, you'll have moments when you both feel unclear about how to proceed, which could inspire you to be more resolute in the interest of modeling that for your Fish.

- **If your rational thinking clashes with their imaginative lens.** You'll want to bridge the gap between whatever makes sense to you and what feels right to your Pisces.

AIR + CARDINAL + SCALES

THE LIBRA PARENT

You're a balance-seeking, diplomatic, partnership-oriented social butterfly who tends to shy away from conflict at all costs. You excel at bringing beauty and harmony into any space and calming your little one with an exceptionally calm, heartfelt tone, even in the midst of their crimson-faced meltdowns. You're also known for being the ultimate host, thriving on opportunities to connect with your social network and plan picture-perfect events. You take pride in applying your artistic eye to curating enviably pretty spaces for your baby. As your little one grows, no matter their sign, they'll appreciate the peacefulness you instill in their world. When you're feeling in need of more balance, you'll find comfort in tending to your one-on-one bonds and enjoying art, like dance, thanks to your ruler, Venus, the planet of beauty and relationships. Try these routines to nurture yourself:

BEST SELF-CARE ROUTINES FOR A LIBRA PARENT

- Catch up with your best friend at your favorite café.
- See a concert or dance performance.
- Spend a bit of extra time on your skin care or beauty routine.
- Practice Tai Chi, which appeals to your peaceful, balance-seeking nature.
- Listen to music with inspiring, romantic lyrics, like tracks by John Legend or Alicia Keys.

LIBRA PARENT & LITTLE ARIES

As opposite signs, you and your tiny Ram can teach each other all about the perspective the other lacks. Your Aries, as the firstborn of the zodiac, tends toward self-focus, while you're geared to partner up. They're a fiery, direct go-getter, while you're a diplomatic peacemaker. As your Mars-ruled Aries grows up, they'll show you the joys of being more independent and passionate, while you'll show them how to infuse their fast-paced, fiery path in life with a sweet dose of beauty and balance.

YOU'LL CONNECT . . .

- **On an adventure.** As two initiative-taking cardinal signs, you relish being out in the world and have an appetite for exploring.

- **When you share the details of everyday experiences.** You're sure to listen with rapt attention to your Aries toddler's tale—and likely reenactment—of their thrilling playdate.

- **By seeing the world through each other's eyes.** As opposite signs, you'll be impressed by your Aries's bold approach, and they'll be fascinated by your peacemaking abilities.

YOU'LL CLASH . . .

- **If they want to make a big move, but you want to think it through.** You tend to deliberate and weigh—Scales-style—all your options, while Aries is wired to act, then muse about what they've just done. You may get nervous about their impulsiveness, and they might not understand why you're dragging your feet.

- **When you need tranquility, and they're especially fired-up.** Tiny Rams are balls of nonstop energy, and you're on a constant mission to keep everything perfectly in balance, but you'll need to put that aside at times to make space for your Aries to be their wild, frenetic selves.

- **When you're not seeing eye to eye on how you define success.** If your Ram decides to do anything, they want their efforts to result in being considered number one, while you'd prefer to make friends. If you model this for your Aries, they may be inspired to adopt a less competitive tone—while inspiring you to more fervently pursue big-picture goals.

LIBRA PARENT & LITTLE TAURUS

Because you and your sweet baby Bull share the same planetary ruler, beauty-loving Venus, you equally adore all things aesthetically pleasing, serene, and artistic. But while you're happiest when your calendar is brimming with social engagements, your Taurus feels most at peace when they're cozied up in their tranquil domestic bubble. And while your airiness means you're up for switching gears at a moment's notice, your little Bull is a fan of routine. But ultimately, the abundance of warm, fuzzy love between you can fuel your ability to learn from each other.

YOU'LL CONNECT . . .

- **By appreciating anything visually stimulating.** You're both inspired to bring more beauty into the world, whether through art or planting and nurturing a flower garden.

- **When opening up about your purest emotions.** As Venus-ruled people, you're equally adept at telling each other what's in your hearts.

- **By fostering your personal style.** Because you're both drawn to creative pursuits, you'll love helping each other curate everything from eye-catching playroom details to winning wardrobes.

YOU'LL CLASH . . .

- **When your Bull struggles to go with the flow.** Your airiness and initiative are qualities your steady and occasionally obstinate Taurus baby lacks, so opening their minds to a new game plan might require an extra dose of your signature Libran patience.

- **When you're having trouble taking a stand.** Making a choice and sticking with it over and over—and over—again is how your Bull moves through life, so they might get (just ever so slightly) fussy if you're being indecisive in your signature Libran way.

- **If your paces aren't quite in sync.** As a cardinal sign, you're generally happy to dive right into exciting new undertakings, but bear in mind that more often than not, your Bull needs to go at their own—often quite slow, by your measure—pace.

LIBRA PARENT & LITTLE GEMINI

Because you're both air signs, you and your Twins baby share a natural serenity that stems from your love of socializing with others—friends, loved ones, or new connections. You also appreciate the opportunity to choose from a range of activities and flit from one to the next. But you'll still have plenty to learn from each other. For instance, while you're perpetually on a mission to cultivate peacefulness (like ensuring that a room is neat and tidy, and looks like it could be in a magazine), your sprite-like Gemini tyke is fine with creating a bit of chaos (tearing through toys and books and art supplies) in an effort to gather new information.

YOU'LL CONNECT . . .

- **Through playdates.** Plan get-togethers with your friends and their babies. Your Gemini will almost always be up for a routine hang with one of their pint-size buddies.

- **By researching a creative project.** Your Gemini will enjoy watching you pore through books or websites to find the perfect artistic project that you can then dive into together.

- **When you're on the move.** Your perpetually airy, on-the-go paces are so much in sync, you'll often bond by keeping busy.

YOU'LL CLASH . . .

- **If your Gemini's frenetic energy feels slightly overwhelming for you.** Your Mercury-ruled Twins toddler can't help but be drawn to multitasking—maybe playing a game and eating a snack and petting the family dog, all at once—but you may want to encourage them to focus on one activity at a time as that feels more centered and calm.

- **When you're both struggling to make a choice and stick to it.** Shared indecisiveness could lead to a standstill at times, which could be frustrating for you both.

- **If you're showing affection in different ways.** Although you'd prefer to show your sweet Twins baby you care through cuddles and harmonious lullabies, they're more apt to say what they feel or simply initiate a lengthy chat about a topic they're excited about.

LIBRA PARENT & LITTLE CANCER

You and your baby Crab both believe the world could always use more love and beauty. As cardinal signs, you two will rarely hesitate to dive headfirst into a project that intrigues you and will usually find it easy to enjoy imaginative, fun-loving playtime as a pair. However, you tend to be more intellectually fueled than your deeply emotional, sensitive water sign child. And while you'd almost always prefer to be out and about, socializing with anyone and everyone, your Crab is more of a homebody. While you can show them the joys of coming out of their shell, they'll show you how to take a stand and get comfier swimming in your emotions.

YOU'LL CONNECT . . .

- **When you're making your space cozier and more welcoming.** You both have an innate ability to put others at ease, especially by setting a nurturing tone wherever you are—but especially in your home.

- **When you strike a balance between staying home and socializing.** Your Crab could help you feel more satisfied staying in and snuggling up on the couch, while you'll inspire them to get out and make new friends.

- **When you're taking on a big-picture goal.** Because you're both cardinal signs, you can set a bold intention, then jump right in to make it happen.

YOU'LL CLASH . . .

- **If you need serenity, and your Crab needs to express tough emotions.** Although your Cancer may express big emotions in moments you had hoped would remain harmonious (like during a family photo shoot), you'll learn how much they need you to hold space for them to be tearful, angry, or just plain moody at times.

- **When you're both initiating—in conflicting ways.** Although you're both cardinal sign go-getters, there will be times during which you have very different ideas about what you want to accomplish, and you'll need to work to find common ground.

- **If your rational take conflicts with their heartfelt one.** As an air sign, you tend to problem-solve in a more intellectual way while, as a water sign, they'll lead with their emotions. Ultimately, you'll want to bring both perspectives to the table.

LIBRA PARENT & LITTLE LEO

You and your charismatic Lion baby are equally charged up to infuse luminosity into every space you enter. Like you, they naturally connect with and charm anyone. In fact, you'll find that you're even more effective in doing this when you're together. While there will be times when you're not quite sure how to manage their over-the-top fieriness and occasional obstinacy, they'll inspire you to own your voice and passions, while you'll show them how to take a step back and weigh their options a bit more before taking action.

YOU'LL CONNECT . . .

- **Through your love of romantic moments.** Whether you're taking in a field of flowers or feeling warm and fuzzy when you see loved ones embrace, you'll both be awestruck by the heartfelt elements of everyday life.

- **When you're pouring your energy into an imaginative project.** Your artistic eye and your tiny Lion's knack for self-expression combine to make you a power pair when taking on any creative endeavor.

- **When you're spending time with friends.** As two social butterflies, you and your Lion make it a priority to nurture relationships.

YOU'LL CLASH . . .

- **When your Lion wants to move too quickly for your liking.** You prefer to think through both sides of any given situation before making a move, but your tiny Leo is so action-oriented that they might take off without much forethought.

- **If Leo struggles with adaptability.** Your light, breezy perspective might not be shared by your fiery and fixed baby, which will require extra patience and understanding on your part.

- **When your disdain for conflict is at odds with their flair for the dramatic.** You'd like to avoid making a scene at all costs, but your Lion will do whatever it takes to ensure that the spotlight shines on them—even if that means throwing a temper tantrum in what feels like the most inopportune place.

LIBRA PARENT & LITTLE VIRGO

You and your baby Maiden are in sync when it comes to doing everything you can to meet others with kindness and a soothing energy. But while you tend to do this by focusing on how you can add beauty and serenity to interactions and environments you're in, your Virgo little one will be on a constant mission to gather information that might prove helpful to others. Your airiness and their mutability also mean you might both take some time to make up your minds, but you'll be impressed with just how observant and thorough your Virgo is along the way.

YOU'LL CONNECT . . .

- **By organizing even the wildest mess.** You understand why your cerebral, detail-oriented little one needs to have their space organized in a particular way, and you'll work together to make that space not only neat, tidy, and peaceful but pretty too.

- **When you're connecting with others.** Your Maiden's communication skills and the fact that you're such a people person combine to make you a pair to make a playdate with.

- **When you're in fix-it mode.** You and your Virgo are naturals at meeting any challenge with an analytical, can-do mentality.

YOU'LL CLASH . . .

- **When your changeability conflicts with their rationality.** You're often breezing from one thing to the next simply to see what happens, while your little Virgo will need at least a brief explanation behind why they're moving from point A to point B.

- **If your desire to cater to everyone's preferences doesn't make sense to Virgo.** Should a disagreement break out among loved ones or friends, your Maiden's default mode is to be pragmatic versus diplomatic, so they might not understand your initial instinct to attempt to neutralize conflicts versus address them head-on.

- **When your experimentation isn't in sync with their perfectionism.** You take chances and go with the flow if only for the sake of creating something beautiful (perhaps trying your hand at crochet or pour paint for the first time to make a gift for a friend who's expecting), while your Virgo would prefer to stick to what they believe will result in a flawless result—which is just one of many ways you can learn by seeing the world through each other's eyes.

LIBRA PARENT & LITTLE LIBRA

You and your fellow Libra might just be the most social, peacemaking duo around. With a shared love of art, desire to connect with and entertain others, and penchant for prioritizing balance, diplomacy, and justice above all else, you'll feel an innate sense of harmony with your mini you. Your main challenge will be creating space for difficult emotions and disagreements when they do arise, because you're both apt to brush them under the rug, which, if done repeatedly, could lead to passive-aggressiveness.

YOU'LL CONNECT . . .

- **Through art.** Both you and your Scales baby adore creating and appreciating anything that could be perceived as beautiful, so you'll forever be making up sweet melodies, enjoying paintings at a local museum, or tackling an eye-catching craft together.

- **When you're spending time with your social circle.** Making and nurturing friendships comes naturally to you both and very much feels like a priority.

- **By weighing all the angles of any given conundrum.** When you're problem-solving, you and your mini Libra will see eye to eye on giving enough airtime to (at least) two different sides of the story.

YOU'LL CLASH . . .

- **If you've been avoiding a necessary confrontation.** As admirable as it may be for you both to perpetually strive for harmony, you realize that you don't want your Libra little one to repress challenging emotions for the sake of keeping the peace. Instead, you'll be inspired to urge them to acknowledge and work through their feelings sooner versus later, which can preempt even bigger, more painful meltdowns down the road.

- **If you want to initiate two very different projects or tasks.** This could be a moment of cardinality overload if you're both attempting to dive into an undertaking but are on different pages in terms of what you want to accomplish.

- **When neither is willing to take a stand.** An abundance of wishy-washiness could fuel frustration.

LIBRA PARENT & LITTLE SCORPIO

You and your baby Scorpion can't help but be mesmerized by each other, given how very different you are. While you're generally invested in keeping the vibe of social interactions light and sweet, your tiny Scorp prefers intensity and dealing with deep-rooted emotions. And while you're airy and adaptable, your Scorp sets their sights on what they want to do and often commits to it with an all-or-nothing point of view. But you're both invested in relationships, especially the one you share, so you'll put in any work required to find common ground.

YOU'LL CONNECT . . .

- **When you prioritize one-on-one time.** Scorp will be head over heels for any opportunity to feel more connected with you, and bonding as a pair is your specialty.

- **By tapping into emotions for creative projects.** Your perceptive water baby will inspire and challenge you to get in touch with your deepest feelings, and together, you can channel them into painting, dancing, singing, or any artistic outlet that strikes your fancy.

- **When you let your ambition fly.** You share an ability to dream big and a desire to accomplish what you've decided you're going to achieve. And as a fixed sign, your Scorpio can show you a thing or two about resolve.

YOU'LL CLASH . . .

- **If you're flitting from one thing to the next, and your Scorp is digging their heels in.** You often want to switch up your approach simply because it feels right in the moment, but your Scorpio prefers to stick to any strategy they've gotten accustomed to. That said, you'll want to consider whether a change you had in mind is necessary, and if so, hold space for them to get comfortable with it before plowing forward.

- **When you're confused by their secretiveness.** While you're generally pretty open about what's on your mind and in your heart, your Scorpio baby is more reserved. Although you might want to talk intense feelings through, it's best to give them space to come to you in their own time.

- **When they struggle with not having control.** Wired to hold the reins in any given situation, your Scorp little one may find it challenging to let go. Thankfully, this is something you can easily model for them.

LIBRA PARENT & LITTLE SAGITTARIUS

Because you both have a love of being out in the world, learning, connecting, and shining light on what's just and true, you and your Archer baby will share an easygoing dynamic. You appreciate their buoyant, jovial nature, while they're impressed with how you bring so much light and harmony to the table. On the flip side, you might be stunned by their fiery directness. You'll aim to show them the benefits of diplomacy, but they'd prefer to deliver the truth. In this way, you'll often be striving to learn each other's language.

YOU'LL CONNECT . . .

- **When you're in adventure mode.** Your airiness fuels your comfort with being up for anything, and your little Sag is wired to seek out eye-opening experiences at every turn, so together, you'll gleefully check out all kinds of uncharted terrain.

- **By being around lots of exciting people.** Hosting is your jam, and your entertaining little Sag will love being the center of attention at any event or impromptu get-together you're sure to make memorable for everyone in attendance.

- **When you put fun first.** Whether you're on a family vacation or engaging in imaginative play at home, you and your Archer are both big fans of hitting pause on chores in order to relax, celebrate, and enjoy the moment.

YOU'LL CLASH . . .

- **If your Sag's allegiance to the truth is at odds with your need to keep the peace.** Your fiery baby loves blurting out the facts more than the average toddler—even if it's uncomfortable—and this will conflict with your preference for diplomacy, but you'll still appreciate their unfiltered, bold voice.

- **If your big-picture plan feels too constricting to your free-spirited Sag.** You may have an exciting vision in mind, but they might shut it down—swiftly, vocally, and bluntly—because it doesn't resonate with what's in their heart.

- **When your shared adaptability leads you to a standstill.** Sag's mutability and your airy indecisiveness could make it tough for you to know how to proceed toward a given endgame, causing occasional impatience and irritation.

LIBRA PARENT & LITTLE CAPRICORN

You and your industrious Sea Goat are two natural go-getters, which makes it easy to brainstorm big ideas and dive right into bold undertakings together. But you might be surprised by just how serious, traditional, and wise beyond their years your Cap is. You'll be inspired by your Cap's mission to work hard to achieve whatever they've set their sights on but also wonder if perhaps they should be having more fun, especially as a little one. Noticing that industriousness is as important to them as harmony is to you and will foster mutual respect, admiration, and understanding.

YOU'LL CONNECT . . .

- **By dreaming up ambitious undertakings.** Both you and your little Cap are ready to initiate bold game plans, so you're sure to approach any undertaking—whether that's coaching them on taking their first steps or preparing for preschool—with an enterprising attitude.

- **When you're cheering each other on.** Your Cap will appreciate watching you follow your heart, while you'll champion their relentless drive.

- **By embracing the power of teamwork.** Celebrating the power of partnership with your Cap will show them that even if they can pursue their goals solo, they could be even more effective when they pair up with you or a friend.

YOU'LL CLASH . . .

- **When you set the stage for fun, and they're focused on getting results.** While your little Cap may be taking something like a tumbling activity quite seriously, you'll simply hope they're having a good time.

- **In moments when your Cap's serious pragmatism conflicts with your airiness.** Once they've set their sights on a goal, your Sea Goat wants to move slowly but surely toward the finish line, so they may struggle to understand—and exhibit impatience with—the way you take action in a less linear fashion.

- **If they're less interested than you are in being social.** To you, it's second nature to be nurturing your connections, but your Sea Goat is simply more reserved and, in moments when you're entertaining or on FaceTime, needs more quiet time than you may initially realize.

LIBRA PARENT & LITTLE AQUARIUS

As two air signs, you and your Water Bearer baby are both at your happiest when you're surrounded by lots of people, ideally those with whom you can have mentally stimulating interactions. You strive to connect with others one-on-one, while your tiny Aquarius is a bigger fan of groups, teams, and community, but you can both easily adapt to each other's ideal social scenario. But you might struggle to understand your Aquarian's stubbornness, black-and-white thinking, and contrarian streak, and they might not get your desire to steer clear of conflict, but your shared curiosity ensures that you'll figure it out.

YOU'LL CONNECT . . .

- **By socializing with others in groups large and small.** You and your Aquarius are two of the most social signs, and it'll show whether you're at a playdate, the playground, or the grocery store, easily making new friends and nurturing ongoing relationships as a power pair.

- **When you're learning.** Your patient, calm teaching style will be soothing and supportive to your Water Bearer, and their innate curiosity elates you.

- **When you care for your community.** Deeply invested in working toward the greater good, even from the time they're tiny, your Water Bearer will love joining you in volunteer efforts that you also happen to appreciate as opportunities to nurture your social life.

YOU'LL CLASH . . .

- **When your Water Bearer is being a contrarian, and you're being a peacemaker.** Your Aquarius is wired to strike out against anything conventional, even if that means rocking the boat in moments when you're doing everything in your power to keep the waters placid. Meet their skepticism with a sense of humor.

- **If your Aquarius finds art less fulfilling than you.** While you prefer to learn about art and romantic subjects, your Water Bearer is drawn to STEM topics that resonate with their rational mindset.

- **If your paces are out of sync.** As a cardinal sign, you might be ready to kick-start an ambitious project, but your fixed air sign baby will need a little more time and prodding to wrap their heads around switching up what they were already engaged in.

LIBRA PARENT & LITTLE PISCES

You and your baby Fish share the ability to see the world through rose-colored glasses. Your prioritization of beauty and balance can be especially soothing for your tiny Pisces, who's quite sensitive to their surroundings and equally conflict-averse. You can also show them how to take the initiative, as they'll tend to be more inclined to see where life takes them as opposed to going after what they want. But as an intuitive, deeply feeling water sign, they'll also teach you how to get more in touch with your spiritual side, embrace escapism, and find magic and romance in everyday moments.

YOU'LL CONNECT . . .

- **Through your mutual love of performance art.** Acting, listening to or playing music, or dancing can be powerful ways for your Fish to work through big emotions, and as a Venus-ruled person, you're similarly captivated by visual art.

- **By keeping the peace.** You and your Fish will go to great lengths to avoid confrontations. And your sweet Pisces will admire how easily you can smooth over any tense situation.

- **By romanticizing simple details.** You both find the pleasure and beauty in anything from a balmy springtime breeze to faint violet and rose-colored streaks strewn throughout a twilight sky.

YOU'LL CLASH . . .

- **When you want to act boldly, and your Fish is dragging.** While you can model initiative and leadership for your Pisces, they're simply more passive, which could be challenging as well as intriguing to you.

- **When you're thinking, and they're feeling.** As an air sign, you lead with mental energy, while whatever is in your Pisces's heart will rule the day, so creating and holding space for that is integral to your bond.

- **If you're hoping to be social and they'd prefer quiet time.** Your empathic baby Pisces can't help but pick up on everyone's energy, so being around a lot of people, especially if they're loud, can overwhelm their senses, causing them to withdraw, which could be at odds with your desire to host a lively party or a playdate. A possible compromise: encouraging them to try spending a limited amount of time around others before enjoying a snuggle session.

THE SCORPIO PARENT

You're a self-motivated, magnetic, private, family-oriented, and passionate parent who's deeply in touch with your heart and spirituality. Depending on where in your natal chart Scorpio falls, others may see you as commanding and perhaps even a bit intimidating. For example, if it's your rising sign, this is definitely the case, whereas if it's your moon, only your closest loved ones may see that side of your personality. Endlessly loyal to the people you love, you're likely friends with people you've known since you were a child yourself, and you'll lean on each other for advice. While you may struggle with vulnerability, because you don't want to appear weak, remember that feeling deeply and viscerally is a strength when it comes to being acutely attuned to your little one's needs. Ruled by action-oriented Mars and powerful Pluto, you often push through exhaustion and stress in order to be strong for others. Try these routines to nurture yourself:

BEST SELF-CARE ROUTINES FOR A SCORPIO PARENT

- Meditate or practice deep breathing while listening to rain or ocean sounds.
- Pour out your heart to your partner or a trusted loved one.
- Take a sweaty spin class.
- Stream a crime docuseries you've had queued up—or watched over and over again.
- Practice tapping into your intuitive and psychic abilities. (You might enjoy reading *Moving Beyond: Access Your Intuition, Psychic Ability and Spirit Connection* by Fleur Leussink, a world-famous medium.)

SCORPIO PARENT & LITTLE ARIES

You'll notice quickly that you and your passionate Ram both enjoy pinpointing a goal and beelining in whichever direction will make it a reality. This is because you share a ruling planet: the planet of action, Mars. However, as a fire sign, your Aries is more of a daredevil and initiator than you, diving headfirst into anything that intrigues them. You prefer to take your time, calculating a game plan and sticking to whatever's worked for you in the past. You'll model endurance and commitment for your fiery kid, and they'll inspire you to—at least occasionally—more readily act on a whim.

YOU'LL CONNECT . . .

- **Through physical playtime.** Because action-oriented Mars guides both of your energies, you'll have the most fun together when you're moving your bodies, from running to tumbling and splashing around in a pool.

- **By exploring.** Your baby Ram is quite the adventurer, and you're innately investigative, so from scavenger hunts to museum trips, you'll enjoy broadening your horizons together.

- **When you show how much you care.** Being ruled by Mars means you both move passionately through life—and your relationships. That said, you and your Ram show your love for each other in a fiery, assertive way.

YOU'LL CLASH . . .

- **When you're feeling moody—and they just want to get a move on.** Aries is driven to act versus feel, so moments in which you're consumed by your emotions will present an opportunity to discuss and teach them about the importance of acknowledging and moving through whatever's in your heart.

- **If you're both digging your heels in.** Your little Aries might not be one of the fixed signs, but when they've made up their mind to win at something, they can be as relentless as you are laser-focused on your goals. If you have different aims, you may experience some headbutting with your Ram.

- **When you want to hold on tightly, and they need their independence.** As a deeply feeling water sign, you crave lots of closeness with your little one, but your free-spirited Ram will likely need a good deal of space to run wild—figuratively and literally.

SCORPIO PARENT & LITTLE TAURUS

You and your baby Bull may be opposites, but you still have plenty in common. You both adore staying close to home, cozying up with each other, and once either of you have committed to an objective, you'll be equally unwavering in your approach. You'll even move toward what you want to achieve similarly, taking your sweet time. But while your emotions are intense and lingering, thanks to your ruling planets, Mars and Pluto, your Venus-ruled child has a long fuse, remaining unperturbed in moments that would likely trigger meltdowns in other children. They can inspire you to embrace a more chill approach, and you'll show them how to tap into their passion.

YOU'LL CONNECT . . .

- **By successfully completing any task, big or small.** Whether you set out to tackle an art project, household chore, or game, you and your baby Bull are an unstoppable team.

- **When you're bonding with family.** You and your tiny Taurus are at your most fulfilled when you have plenty of quality time with loved ones in a tranquil domestic bubble.

- **By discovering new recipes.** When either of you finds a flavor, a product, or a type of food you enjoy, you adore it with your whole heart, and you'll appreciate searching for and concocting those favorites as a duo.

YOU'LL CLASH . . .

- **When you both have trouble going with the flow.** Because you're both fixed signs who struggle with black-and-white thinking and being stubborn, you might set a rule or plan an activity only to find that your little Taurus responds by refusing to budge. It's possible that seeing this familiar trait reflected back to you might inspire you to become a bit more open-minded.

- **If your emotional perspective conflicts with their practical one.** Your Taurus often sees the world through a rational lens, while you're more in tune with your intuition. But instead of holding you up, this difference could create learning opportunities for you both.

- **When either of you needs space but has trouble expressing it.** Because you both value strong attachment, it could be tough to recognize when you're craving solo time.

SCORPIO PARENT & LITTLE GEMINI

Because you and your Twins baby see the world in different ways, you could find each other quite curious at times—and confusing at others. While your emotions run deep, your tiny Gemini is more mentally charged. They'd prefer to multitask, while you concentrate on a to-do with laser focus. But you share an intense inquisitiveness about the world around you. By keeping that attitude in mind when it comes to each other and what makes you tick, you'll find that there's so much you can learn.

YOU'LL CONNECT . . .

- **When you're piecing together a puzzle (literally or figuratively).** You'll teach your breezy Gemini to follow through, and they'll be thrilled by the mental exercise.

- **By having a lively conversation.** Your communication styles may differ, but your passion and your Twins baby's love of language can combine to make for lots of fun volleying of big ideas.

- **When you open up about how you feel.** You can teach your Gemini to tune in to their heart over their head, and they'll inspire you with how adept they are at self-expression.

YOU'LL CLASH . . .

- **If you want to lie low and your Gemini is eager to connect with others.** Your tendency to be more private and reserved could conflict with your Twins baby's desire to mix and mingle—but these moments may also present a chance to get out of your comfort zone.

- **When you're focused on a task at hand, and they're onto the next thing.** Once you're invested in a project or chore, it can be tough for you to switch gears, but your mutable Twins baby switches gears constantly. Together, you can work to strike a happy balance between obstinacy and capriciousness.

- **When you're trying to show you care.** You might hope to have your Gemini's undivided attention in the midst of bonding moments, and they might be looking for more lighthearted playfulness from you.

SCORPIO PARENT & LITTLE CANCER

As a water sign duo, you and your baby Crab are both family-oriented and in touch with your emotions. However, while you're a bit slower to embrace anything new or different, given your fixed quality, your tiny Cancer, as a cardinal sign, is a go-getter and occasional risk-taker who comes up with sweeping, big-picture plans and dives into them without hemming and hawing. They'll inspire you to be more open to change and to take action more quickly, while you'll model follow-through and fearlessness.

YOU'LL CONNECT . . .

- **When you tap into your creativity as a family.** Whether you're drumming up a summer vacation plan, a Halloween costume theme, or a beloved meal on a random weeknight, your love of tradition and their innate sentimentality will shine.

- **When you're talking about big feelings.** As a perceptive water sign yourself, you can easily hold space for your little Crab, often a sensitive mush, to share what they're experiencing emotionally, which can't help but bring you closer.

- **When you're tuning into your intuition.** You can naturally model how to trust your inner voice— something your mini Crab is innately adept at as well.

YOU'LL CLASH . . .

- **If you're struggling to understand their moodiness.** Although you're both in tune with your emotions, your Crab can be more delicate than you when they're in their feelings, which could require you meet them with extra TLC.

- **When they want to forge ahead, and you'd rather take it slow.** They'll inspire you to dive into uncharted terrain more readily, while you'll show your Crab the benefits of either sticking to what's tried-and-true or doing your research before making a move.

- **When either of you is feeling more withdrawn while the other craves bonding time.** You both have moments when you need to pull back and go inward and those when you want to feel close and connected. You won't always be in sync, but those instances can offer a chance to work on adaptability.

SCORPIO PARENT & LITTLE LEO

Because you and your baby Lion are both fixed signs, you match each other's dynamism, self-possessiveness, self-motivation, and resolve to cross the finish line of anything you've set your sights on. On the flip side, you both struggle with inflexibility and being open to change, so when stubbornness flares up, you can expect some headbutting. Still, you'll be impressed with how optimistic, buoyant, and sunny your tiny Leo is by nature, and they'll be mesmerized and inspired by the way you innately command power and respect.

YOU'LL CONNECT . . .

- **By pinpointing an ambitious, shared goal and working toward it with laser focus.** You and your Leo are equally determined and capable of applause-worthy follow-through.

- **When you're experiencing the whimsical and otherworldly.** You're drawn to all things spooky and magical, while your Lion is a big fan of fantasy and romanticism, so you'll adore playing dress-up or reading fairy tales together.

- **When you're exploring a new passion.** You both get fired up and "fixed" on your interests and pastimes; exploring those together can present a wonderful opportunity to bond.

YOU'LL CLASH . . .

- **When the way you express emotion is out of sync.** You tend to be more private and quieter about your emotions than your outgoing, boisterous little Lion, and at times they may need you to crank up the volume on your love.

- **If your Lion's push to be in the spotlight feels like an invasion of privacy to you.** Your Leo was born to be onstage and will make that known from the time they're tiny, seeking attention whenever, wherever, and from whomever, which won't always sit right with you. But it's also a chance to foster more mutual understanding.

- **If you're both unwavering on calling the shots.** Your little Lion fancies themselves just as much of a leader and the "boss" as you, which could translate to power struggles.

SCORPIO PARENT & LITTLE VIRGO

While you're comfortable wading into the deep end of emotion, your tiny Maiden is focused on practical details, facts, and figures. But you have a great deal in common too—specifically, sleuthing skills and an unflinching devotion to each other. You can teach your mutable earth sign how to train their focus on a particular goal and block out any distractions that their buzzy ruler, Mercury, makes them more susceptible to. You'll also find that your fixed nature is in sync with their love of routine, and that your baby Virgo can help you adopt a perspective that's rooted in pragmatism.

YOU'LL CONNECT . . .

- **When you break down an ambitious undertaking into practical steps.** Because your Virgo enjoys zeroing in on details, and you're a master of follow-through, you're wonderfully productive as a pair.

- **When you show your Virgo how to tap into their intuition.** When your Virgo toddler can't quite pinpoint why they're cranky, they could be struggling to tune in to and trust their inner voice. But as a water sign who's naturally in touch with your instincts, you can show them the ropes.

- **By demonstrating how much you care.** You and your Virgo tot are equally thoughtful and devoted to bonding time.

YOU'LL CLASH . . .

- **If your fixed nature conflicts with their mutable one.** While your Maiden can easily adapt, you find it tougher to change course midstream. But this could challenge you to be more flexible in order to support your Virgo.

- **When you're leading with your heart, and they're in their head.** Your Mercury-ruled, down-to-earth Virgo is as cerebral as you are connected to your intuition. So quite often,

meeting them where they are might require you to focus on just the facts versus the feelings underlying them. This could be as simple as talking them through the technical steps of a challenging situation (like, say, their first haircut) as opposed to how they could feel during the experience.

- **When your priorities are out of sync.** Your mini Maiden's goal is to gather information in an effort to be of service to others, while you're a strong believer in the idea that knowledge is power. Understanding how their motivation differs from yours can get you on the same page.

SCORPIO PARENT & LITTLE LIBRA

You and your Scales baby see the world in very different ways. While you're most comfortable exploring deep-rooted emotions and, thanks to your co-ruler, Pluto (god of the underworld), uncovering secrets and shining light on anything that's hidden in the shadows, your Libra is airy, social, and most interested in connecting with people in a breezy, intellectual way. They prioritize pleasure over power and, as a cardinal sign, find it easy to dream up big-picture ideas that they're eager to initiate. Nonetheless, you're equally interested in pouring energy into your closest bonds, so even in challenging moments, you'll work to boost mutual understanding.

YOU'LL CONNECT . . .

- **By spending time as a pair.** There's nothing you love more than bonding moments with your Libra, and they're big fans of hanging with you one-on-one.

- **When you funnel your big feelings into eye-catching projects.** Whether you're painting or arranging a bouquet with flowers from your garden, you can show your Scales baby how to work through complicated emotions and tap into their appreciation of art and beauty all at once.

- **When you dream together.** Your Libra can inspire you to think even bigger, and you'll show them the nuts and bolts of working toward the finish line.

YOU'LL CLASH . . .

- **When your little Libra's lightheartedness conflicts with your laser focus.** Your airy child is happy to move from one activity to the next without much deliberation, while you generally choose a game plan and stick to it at all costs. That said, your Scales baby could inspire you to lighten your figurative grip on a particular approach.

- **When your Scales baby wants to be social, and you're feeling more aloof.** Though your default mode is reserved, your Libra thrives when they're surrounded by people. You can create space for them to be social while modeling comfort with solitude.

- **When peace-loving Libra mistakes your fired-up energy for rockiness.** Because your co-ruler is Mars, you can be passionate, and at times, your little one might misread this tone as a sign of discord. Noting that you're only excited and explaining why could calm their nerves.

SCORPIO PARENT & LITTLE SCORPIO

You and your fellow Scorpion make for one truly dynamic, magnetic, determined, powerful duo. Because you're both so intuitive, it's easy for you to read each other, and because you're endlessly loyal, family-oriented, and passionate, and you prioritize your closest bonds, you'll easily nurture a deep connection. The most challenging aspect of your relationship is the fact that you share the tendency to be inflexible, so if you're unwilling to budge, you'll butt heads instead. On the other hand, seeing your baby Scorp mirror your most stubborn behaviors back to you could motivate you to work on being more adaptable—something your mini you will benefit from seeing modeled.

YOU'LL CONNECT . . .

- **By reveling in mystical stories and routines.** For example, you might enjoy reading detective stories together and learning about the healing powers of crystals.

- **When you spend quality time with your elders.** You and your baby will adore spending special moments with older loved ones and learning about your family tree.

- **When you work through emotional experiences.** You're both comfortable feeling deeply, and your baby Scorp can become even more adept at this by watching how you process and address what's in your heart.

YOU'LL CLASH . . .

- **If neither of you is willing to compromise.** Fueled by Mars, the planet of action, you can both set your sights on a goal and move toward it relentlessly. But if they're zeroed in on a trip to the park, and you've decided to stay in, you may want to prepare for a meltdown.

- **When you struggle to open up.** If you're both finding it challenging to talk through your feelings—as you're apt to do in an effort to appear in control— you might miss out on an opportunity to understand each other better and to bond.

- **When a power struggle breaks out.** Because you and your junior Scorp are co-ruled by control-seeking Pluto, you'll both want to be in charge. Ensuring that there are moments in which your little one gets the reins (like by picking out their own pajamas) can boost harmony.

SCORPIO PARENT & LITTLE SAGITTARIUS

Your baby Archer might be as intrigued as you are befuddled by the way you both present yourselves in the world. While it's challenging for you to switch gears and explore unfamiliar terrain, your fiery, free-spirited Sag lives for it, seeking out eye-opening experiences and welcoming new horizons. You value privacy, often seeming secretive as a result, and your Sag's passion for the truth means they often blurt out sensitive information or observations. But your desire to conquer any challenge complements your little explorer's spiritedness. You'll do well to frame your relationship as an adventure.

YOU'LL CONNECT . . .

- **When you're presented with a specific challenge to address as a team.** Your problem-solving skills and Sag's thirst for knowledge and experience make you an unstoppable duo.

- **Through your shared passion for life.** You and your jovial Jupiterian baby are both go-getters and will admire each other's fire and zest for life.

- **When you're taking bold action.** Although you might like to stick to tried-and-true strategies, your ruler, Mars, does help you to be more action-oriented—a trait you share with your fiery, courageous Archer.

YOU'LL CLASH . . .

- **When you think of bonding time differently.** Ruled by expansive Jupiter, your Archer is comfiest when surrounded by big, open space—literally and figuratively. So while it might sound counterintuitive, you'll foster attachment best by giving them plenty of room to explore.

- **When your communication styles conflict.** Your Archer believes it's honorable to express their opinions and beliefs without a filter, while you take very special care with what you share. Being aware of the motivation behind your Sag's mouthiness could make it easier to understand and handle.

- **When your Archer wants to explore, and you'd rather stick to what you know.** From trying new flavors to checking out different hiking trails, your Sag will perpetually challenge you to desert your comfort zone.

SCORPIO PARENT & LITTLE CAPRICORN

You and your little Sea Goat make quite a powerful pair. Being that you're both goal-oriented and determined to succeed, you can easily put your heads together to master any skill or complete any project you set your sights on. But while you're comfortable getting swept out into the deep end of intense feelings that often serve as fuel for your resolve, your little Capricorn often puts emotionality aside, believing it will interfere with the practical perspective they're more at home with. And as you admire their grounded approach, they'll learn from you how to connect with their spiritual side and inner fire.

YOU'LL CONNECT . . .

- **By working hard to reach your endgame.** Ruled by Mars, you want to come out on top, and your Saturnian little one is always up for doing whatever work is necessary, so there's no doubt the two of you can set and hit the most ambitious of goals.

- **When you bond with older loved ones.** Like you, your Sea Goat respects, looks up to, and is eager to learn from wise senior loved ones.

- **Through rituals and traditions.** Your little Cap will be just as thrilled as you are to bake the cookie recipe that's been passed down for generations or to take that annual summertime family trip.

YOU'LL CLASH . . .

- **When you're unclear on how your little Sea Goat is feeling.** Because you're so comfortable in the world of emotion, your Capricorn's often detached disposition can throw you for a loop. But they're more like you than you may realize. As long as they feel supported, they'll open up in their own time.

- **When your little Capricorn's initiative conflicts with your fixed nature.** Although they'll pursue goals at an unhurried pace, they will move forward without much deliberation, which could leave you scrambling to catch up.

- **If you're both striving to set and enforce rules.** Your Cap, being the precocious kid they are, might create boundaries and regulations for themselves—or for you! Depending on the situation, instead of attempting to out-discipline them, you might instead strive to lighten the mood and infuse the moment with a touch of humor and playfulness.

SCORPIO PARENT & LITTLE AQUARIUS

From possessing a strong sense of self to excelling at follow-through, you and your baby Water Bearer will often see eye to eye. Their forward-thinking, innovative streak, courtesy of their ruler, rebellious Uranus, will impress you, while your passion and dynamism are something they'll strive to pick up from you. But as an air sign, they're more at ease with rational thinking than deep-rooted emotions. And because you are both fixed signs, a stubbornness overload could lead to friction. But it might also fuel breakthroughs that stir you both to be more flexible and open-minded.

YOU'LL CONNECT . . .

- **By holding your ground as a team.** No matter the objective, when you and your fellow fixed sign are on the same page, you'll be committed to seeing it through.

- **By tackling a charitable effort.** Your baby Water Bearer wants to do what's best for the greater good, mirroring your innate empathy. In turn, helping others boosts your bond.

- **When you're open to each other's perspective.** You can teach your mini Aquarius how to tap into their intuition and spirituality, while they'll spark your interest in science.

YOU'LL CLASH . . .

- **When compromise feels out of reach.** If you've both committed to different approaches or ways of thinking, you might find yourself dealing with a standoff that'll require you to ditch the black-and-white thinking and prioritize finding common ground.

- **If your emotionality conflicts with their analytical perspective.** Leading with your heart and intuition may come naturally to you, but it's less so for your mini Water Bearer, who will most value that which they can prove with facts, evidence, and logic. Seeing eye to eye may require you both to get out of your headspace.

- **When your Water Bearer is being especially contrarian.** Whether they're questioning your most strongly held beliefs or simply doling out more than their fair share of toddler nos and whys, your patience could be tested by your baby Aquarian's desire to strike out against anything traditional.

SCORPIO PARENT & LITTLE PISCES

As two water signs, you and your sweet baby Fish have a harmonious bond rooted in comfort with swimming in your emotions. When you're together, you might even find it easier to tap into your intuition, because you both have an elevated capacity to read between the lines. Thanks to your rulers, go-getter Mars and powerful Pluto, you are more action-oriented than your hazy Neptune-ruled little Pisces, so you can give them the tools they need to transform daydreams into something concrete. And they'll guide you toward adopting more imaginative, whimsical thinking.

YOU'LL CONNECT . . .

- **When you're swept up in creativity.** When your artistic instincts meet your baby Pisces's wild imagination, you'll dream up a bevy of inventive projects, which you will happily guide to fruition.

- **When you're casting rationality aside and letting intuition take the reins.** You and your little Fish are equally comfortable tuning in to your heart for answers that your head might miss the mark on.

- **By working through challenging feelings.** Attuning to your little Fish's complex, intensely felt emotions can come naturally. In turn, they'll trust they can open up and process whatever they're going through with your support.

YOU'LL CLASH . . .

- **If your little Fish is being indecisive, and you're already set on a plan.** Your Pisces might need a bit more coaxing than you feel is necessary, but in these moments, it's best to remember that their mutability is at play.

- **If your direct, intense tone overwhelms your baby Pisces.** It's not your nature to beat around the bush—especially when you're setting boundaries—but there will be moments in which your sensitive Fish might require a softer approach to more readily take in what you're saying.

- **When you want to take action, and your Fish's head is in the clouds.** You'll notice that your Pisces often lacks self-motivation, so when you want to get something done, you might need an extra dose of patience and hand-holding.

FIRE + MUTABLE + ARCHER

THE SAGITTARIUS PARENT

With your sun or other placements in the mutable fire sign, you're an independent, philosophical, wanderlust-filled, jovial adventurer who prioritizes truth and knowledge. You pride yourself on being unfiltered, opinionated, and entertaining (especially if Mercury in your birth chart is in the sign of the Archer!). Your parent friends appreciate the hilarity of your bold, no-holds-barred statements. And even though you might reject rose-colored glasses, Sag is ruled by Jupiter—the planet of luck, optimism, and abundance—so you often see opportunity in any conundrum that arises in the midst of your parenting journey. As a mutable sign, you're quick to adapt or learn whatever you must to resolve a dilemma—and if it's one that's horizon-broadening in some way, well, that's even better. You're often fired up to take on more, more, more—quite happily, actually. But like anyone else, you may sometimes find yourself in need of a reset. Try these routines to nurture yourself:

BEST SELF-CARE ROUTINES FOR A SAGITTARIUS PARENT

- Plan a road trip to a location you've never explored before.
- Wander around your favorite natural history museum.
- Listen to a variety of TED Talks to learn about a wide array of topics.
- Watch your favorite stand-up comedian.
- Learn a foreign language (which you plan to put to use during future travel) on an app like Duolingo or Rosetta Stone.

SAGITTARIUS PARENT & LITTLE ARIES

You'll notice that you and your baby Ram are similarly passionate, enthusiastic go-getters who want to be in the thick of everything the world has to offer. That's no surprise, considering you're both action-oriented, fearless fire signs. But while you aim to make the most of the present and hope your baby will do the same, your baby Aries prefers to move on to the next activity, game, or part of their day as quickly as possible. And while you surely love to come out on top, you'll be challenged by instances in which they'd rather win than learn. But because you're both so dynamic, you'll find mutual understanding when you plow ahead as a pair, prioritizing playfulness and your shared sense of gut-busting humor.

YOU'LL CONNECT . . .

- **Through your shared love of life.** You and your spirited, Mars-ruled Ram are equally enthusiastic about pursuing thrills at every turn.

- **By getting out of your comfort zones.** You see the world in the same way others might see an immersive museum exhibit—it's fun and yours for the taking. And your Ram concurs, pumped to follow whatever itinerary you've laid out for them.

- **Through high-energy pastimes.** From sports to entertaining each other with physical comedy, you and your baby Aries usually have a surplus of energy you can expend on having a blast together.

YOU'LL CLASH . . .

- **When your little Ram's preference to keep it simple is at odds with your desire to try something new.** At times, you'll be fired up to try a unique recipe or plan an adventurous day trip, but your tiny Aries would rather keep it simple. In these situations, it may be best to honor their no-muss, no-fuss nature.

- **When you're focused on being right, and your mini Aries wants to win.** Because you're both headstrong in your own ways, you'll find you enjoy the smoothest sailing when you create space for give and take.

- **When your Ram gets confrontational.** You may both be fiery and direct, but your Ram toddler could surprise you with their appetite for conflict and roughhousing. Guide them to channel those impulses into something more productive and educational, like active play that fosters their gross motor skills.

SAGITTARIUS PARENT & LITTLE TAURUS

By seeing the world through a lens that's much different from your own, your fixed earth sign baby will often show you the other side of the coin you may have forgotten to consider. They value coziness and staying close to home, prizing security and, sometimes, their material possessions above all else. As a free-spirited aspiring globe-trotter, you may strive to inspire them to be more adventurous—even if only by taking in different sights and sounds along a previously unexplored walking path or choosing a new song to listen to on repeat. They'll appreciate you catching them if they do shake things up from time to time, and, in turn, they might even motivate you to slow down and embrace simple pleasures over exploration. And because your ruler is lucky Jupiter and theirs is pleasure-seeking Venus, you are both naturally upbeat and bighearted, and sharing those emotions will often bring you even closer.

YOU'LL CONNECT . . .

- **When you go beyond eyes and ears to learn.** While some children are visual learners and others might prefer audio, you'll find that you can lean on all of your baby Bull's keen senses—touch, taste, sound, smell, and sight. For example, you might have them pet the family cat then look at the word cat to begin to recognize the word.

- **When you enjoy travel-related traditions.** Whether you're headed to your go-to summer destination or taking an annual road trip, your baby Taurus will appreciate sticking to a tried-and-true game plan.

- **By goofing around.** Your baby Bull will appreciate your jokes and contribute their own brand of zaniness.

YOU'LL CLASH . . .

- **When you're itching for adventure, and your little Bull wants to hang back.** Urging your fixed Taurus to get out and explore will often take plenty of patience, understanding, and accepting that snuggling up with their lovey often beats taking in new sights.

- **When you see boundaries as restrictive.** You may see structure as more of a drag than your Bull, who's more likely to find it comforting and grounding.

- **When you're faster to embrace change than your tiny Taurus.** You might expect your Bull to be just as quick to change course as you are, but when faced with a switch-up, they'll often need to do it in their own unhurried way.

SAGITTARIUS PARENT & LITTLE GEMINI

You and your Twins baby are opposites, but that doesn't mean you'll butt heads. In fact, you tend to complement each other. You both crave learning experiences and can't help but soak up interesting knowledge everywhere you go. Your little Gemini will show you how to gather information in a more lighthearted way, while you'll model passion and drive. Together, you'll be frequently on the go, social, and perpetually curious about the road you take as a pair.

YOU'LL CONNECT . . .

- **When you shrug off your everyday routine.** From exploring new walking trails to experimenting in the kitchen with unique ingredients, you and your Twins baby will appreciate any opportunity to stretch your wings and go beyond the mundane.

- **When you're able to soak up new information.** As two perpetually curious, lifelong learners, you and your Gemini have lots of museums and educational TV shows in your future.

- **By hitting the road.** You'll likely have never met a little one as eager to get out into the world and travel by car, train, plane, or boat to experience thrilling new places.

YOU'LL CLASH . . .

- **If your Gemini expresses the need for more independence.** Because they'll vacillate between being very attached and more independent, you could be stunned to find that your Twins baby actually is mirroring you in their need for more space. But when you take a step back, you'll realize that you know from firsthand experience the value of being given plenty of room to explore safely on your own.

- **When you're struggling to key into specifics.** Because you're ruled by big-picture Jupiter, you often think in terms of sweeping plans, while your Twins baby is tuned in to the details. Being aware of that can support mutual understanding.

- **If your fire is at odds with their more detached style.** You can't help but form and share impassioned opinions, while your Gemini is airier and more intellectual. Though this might seem different to you, you can certainly learn from your Twins kid's different lens.

SAGITTARIUS PARENT & LITTLE CANCER

Falling under very different elements and qualities, you and your baby Crab have a lot to teach each other. Your sensitive water baby's favorite thing to do is nest, cuddled up close to you and ideally within the coziness of their home. They won't be as much for zipping from one thing to the next and aren't drawn to travel in the same way you are. But you'll see eye to eye when it comes to being go-getters, storytellers, and foodies. By creating space for your Crab to step into these roles, they might just join you on your next big adventure. On the flip side, seeing life through their lens could lead you to find more to love about staying in.

YOU'LL CONNECT . . .

- **When you're learning about the world through story time or entertainment.** Your water baby is a curious explorer in their own right; they'd just prefer to learn and grow while snuggled up in your arms.

- **When you experiment in the kitchen.** You'll find that food almost always inspires your tiny Crab to mix things up. Just know that while they're open to new flavors, textures, and types of dishes, they'll always have go-to comfort foods.

- **When you urge them to initiate an ambitious plan.** You can nudge your Crab out of their shell by tapping into their cardinality. Offer a few activities or places to visit, then let them take the reins.

YOU'LL CLASH . . .

- **If you're on different pages emotionally.** Your propensity to say exactly what's on your mind without factoring in diplomacy or to raise your voice because you're feeling fired up could result in a tidal wave of emotions from your highly sensitive baby Crab. While you are passionate about being truthful and direct, holding space for your Cancer's big emotions might require adopting a softer approach at times.

- **If your needs aren't in sync.** Your need to maintain your free-spiritedness could be at odds with your sweet Crab's need to be very close. This could require coming up with activities (like babywearing on a hike) that boost happiness for you both.

- **When you're craving different surroundings.** While your little Crab will be happy to accompany you just about anywhere, there will be times they'll just want to get back to the space they'll almost always see as the most comfortable and tranquil: home.

SAGITTARIUS PARENT & LITTLE LEO

As two fire signs, you and your little Lion are equally passionate, action-oriented, and adventurous. You frequently entertain each other, make each other laugh, and can't help but prioritize having a good time. One potential challenge: You're both highly opinionated, and when you don't see eye to eye, neither of you is apt to shy away from making your thoughts and feelings known. Thankfully, you're both up for tackling any tension that's brewing head-on.

YOU'LL CONNECT . . .

- **By seeing who can make the other laugh more.** You're both comfortable entertaining others and can't help but strive to, but you're especially pumped to send each other into a fit of laughter.

- **When you're taking action.** As a dynamic duo, as soon as you've made up your minds on an action plan, you'll agree on moving forward—decisively, confidently, and as fast as possible.

- **When you're pursuing lots of fun.** You and your Leo baby are similarly invested in enjoying yourselves no matter where you are and especially when you're together.

YOU'LL CLASH . . .

- **When your Lion bristles at your directness.** Although you're both assertive, your little Leo might find it tough to cope with your truth telling, as they'll often see it as abrasive and disruptive of their sunny state of mind.

- **When your little Leo acts like they're above chores or other necessary work.** Their regal attitude could have you shaking your head and doing your best to bring them back down to earth.

- **If you're equally fired up but on different pages.** When you have a fun activity in mind that looks nothing like what your Leo was hoping for or vice versa, tempers could flare.

SAGITTARIUS PARENT & LITTLE VIRGO

You and your tiny Maiden can show each other an entirely different perspective. As two mutable signs, you're similarly adaptable but see conflicting aspects of life as important. For instance, although menial, everyday tasks might make your eyes glaze over, because you'd rather be out in the world, you may be surprised to find just how comforted your baby Virgo is by routine, to-dos, and minutiae. They can show you the beauty of zeroing in on the specifics in order to reach the finish line on a goal, and you can model dreaming in a bigger, bolder way.

YOU'LL CONNECT . . .

- **When you're learning something new.** You tend to prefer to soak up knowledge through experiences, and your little Mercury-ruled Virgo enjoys reading and talking about new concepts. Fusing the two methods will bring you together.

- **When you meet people together.** When your outgoing fieriness joins forces with your Maiden's communicative nature, you'll be one of the most popular pairs on the playground.

- **When you can make everyday errands and chores more thrilling.** Your little Maiden doesn't mind pitching in around the house, but transforming a task into a game (tell your Virgo they'll earn points for each toy they pick up and put away, and once they hit a certain goal, they'll win an extra bedtime story) can promote bonding.

YOU'LL CLASH . . .

- **If your Virgo takes one of your signature truth bombs to heart.** Because your little Maiden is sensitive and runs the risk of being self-critical, they could be easily hurt by words they interpret as harsh.

- **When you're thinking in sweeping terms, and your Maiden is focused on the details.** This side effect of your having such different lenses could lead to misunderstanding, but it could also make you a formidable team.

- **If you're ready to make a move, and Virgo is still mulling their options.** You understand wanting to research before you get the ball rolling, but you might not see why your baby Maiden needs so much information. Your best bet: Support their desire to gather info while explaining that they can keep doing so even once they're pushing forward.

SAGITTARIUS PARENT & LITTLE LIBRA

Not only do you and your tiny Scales baby adore getting out into the world and socializing but you both also aim to pinpoint the truth and defeat injustice in any situation. Your Libra baby will look up to your ability to tell it like it is, and you'll appreciate how diplomatic they can be. At the same time, they may bristle at your unfiltered, highly opinionated side, particularly if they fear it'll lead to a confrontation. Similarly, you could be frustrated at times that they're so devoted to looking at both sides of an issue they struggle to form a strong opinion. But doing your best to understand each other's perspectives can be truly eye-opening.

YOU'LL CONNECT . . .

- **When you're exploring.** You'll find that your airy Scales baby is as up for impromptu adventures as you are.

- **When you're in big groups.** Because your Libra is such a social butterfly, and you appreciate any opportunity to entertain others, you'll love planning or attending parties as a duo and enjoying plenty of playdates with your Scales baby's friends.

- **When you're in the moment.** You and your little Libra are both pros at being present and finding a way to have fun, even if you're in the midst of something monotonous like waiting in line or folding laundry.

YOU'LL CLASH . . .

- **If you're fired up, and your Scales toddler is craving more balance.** Your need to say what's on your mind—filter-free and often at top volume—could cause your Libra to jump into peacemaking mode by urging you to shush or trying to turn your attention to something lighter.

- **If your shared penchant for going with the flow impedes your ability to complete a task.** Your baby's airiness and your mutability could cause you to lack the kind of grounded focus you might need to reach the finish line.

- **When you wish your mini Libra would take a stand.** You're so passionate about your ideals and opinions that your airy baby's breeziness might be confusing, but they may also inspire you to embrace objectivity from time to time.

SAGITTARIUS PARENT & LITTLE SCORPIO

You and your baby Scorpion find each other's perspectives equal parts fascinating and confusing. While you're on a perpetual mission to explore uncharted waters, your little Scorp is comfiest sticking to what they know—and they're as passionate about that as you are about seeking adventure. And while you don't mind saying exactly what you're thinking in any given moment, your water sign baby is deeply private. Nonetheless, because they count go-getter Mars among their ruling planets, they're action-oriented like you—and can be fiery to boot. When you lean on this commonality, you can achieve anything you set out to tackle together.

YOU'LL CONNECT . . .

- **Whenever you're able to go big and bold.** Your big-picture focus, courtesy of Jupiter, and your baby's passionate energy, stemming from Mars, make it possible for you to dive into large-scale challenges without batting an eyelash.

- **When you're tackling a specific challenge.** Because you'll embrace any test or trial as an opportunity for learning, and your Scorp is a natural investigator, you'll make a truly effective problem-solving team.

- **When you see eye-to-eye on taking the reins as a duo.** You and your passionate tiny Scorpion will bond over your shared drive to lead and set trends, inspiring others to follow in your footsteps.

YOU'LL CLASH . . .

- **If you'd prefer to connect differently.** You believe in giving your baby lots of freedom and space to explore, but as a sensitive, fixed water baby, they'll crave more closeness—such as skin-on-skin time and extra snuggles—than you may realize.

- **When you express yourselves in conflicting ways.** While your instinct is to speak your mind without hesitation, your highly private Scorp is innately uncomfortable with wearing their heart on their sleeve and might have trouble understanding why you do.

- **When you're hoping your Scorpio baby is up for exploration but they'd rather focus on the familiar.** To you, moving past the well-trodden path is necessary for personal growth, but your Scorpio believes pouring their passion into what they already know and love is what will get them furthest. Your best bet: striking a balance between these two viewpoints.

SAGITTARIUS PARENT & LITTLE SAGITTARIUS

When you and your fellow free-spirited, fiery little Archer come together, you can expect overflowing wanderlust, adventure-seeking, and lots of opportunity for hilarity. You know full well that your tiny explorer needs lots of freedom and space to thrive, which will help them feel seen. And they'll be gleeful that you can easily turn even the most mundane moments into a dazzling festivity. You'll just want to watch out for the fact that you both have a predisposition to take everything to a fiery, Jupiterian extreme, so you could find it useful to model and initiate grounding practices alongside your mini Sag.

YOU'LL CONNECT . . .

- **Whenever you're able to shrug off the mundane.** You and your baby Archer live for eye-opening moments, so any chance to explore something new—whether you're on your first long-distance trip or checking out a new playground—can bring you closer.

- **By learning about truth and justice.** Whether you're reading your Sag toddler books about game-changing leaders (like Sojourner Truth and Mahatma Gandhi) or talking about how you as a family can serve your own community, you'll be fired up to make a difference as a pair.

- **Through hands-on experiences.** Science experiments, playing in the sand at the beach, or collecting leaves around your neighborhood can tap into your shared love of learning by doing.

YOU'LL CLASH . . .

- **If your shared focus on fun prevents you from reaching the finish line.** You and your little Archer may believe there's no such thing as having too good a time, but your baby's tendency to shrug off bedtime or chores in lieu of play will serve as a reminder that you'll both be happiest when you find a balance between recreation and responsibilities.

- **When you veer into fiery, mouthy overload.** You're often the one dishing out the unfiltered truth bombs, but when your tiny Archer serves up their own, you could be caught off guard, equally amused and aggravated.

- **When you have your hearts set on different adventures.** If your Sag toddler is pumped to go to their favorite museum but you've decided that this weekend's devoted to a road trip, you might face a meltdown.

SAGITTARIUS PARENT & LITTLE CAPRICORN

You and your Sea Goat baby each have your own way of moving through life. While your little earth sign is pragmatic, reserved, serious, goal-oriented, and perpetually aiming to earn recognition for their hard work, you're in the moment, outgoing, and boisterous, and prize adventure and learning opportunities over achievement. Given this dynamic, you might occasionally find yourself questioning who's the parent and who's the kid. But you can show your Sea Goat how to embrace playfulness and spontaneity more readily, while they'll impress you with their work ethic and grounded, precocious point of view.

YOU'LL CONNECT . . .

- **When you can highlight each other's strengths.** For instance, once you've hyped up a particular activity or task, set a goal for your Sea Goat to achieve. When you lean on your individual strengths, you'll feel most effective and connected.

- **When you value each other's point of view.** You can easily admire and applaud your little one's industriousness, and they'll be enthralled by your effortless optimism and bravery.

- **Through active adventures.** You and your tiny Sea Goat both enjoy being presented with a physical, preferably outdoorsy challenge like checking out a hiking trail or making your way through an obstacle course.

YOU'LL CLASH . . .

- **When you wish your little Sea Goat would lighten up.** At times when you're striving to set the stage for a spontaneously fun, upbeat time, your serious, often stoic Sea Goat might not show the level of enthusiasm you'd hoped for. But that's not to say they won't appreciate the effort.

- **If you're conveying how you care in different ways.** You tend to make grand, warm, showy gestures to express your love, while your baby Capricorn will be more reserved and traditional, preferring to be read their go-to bedtime story or offered a favorite snack.

- **If your paces are out of sync.** You'll often dive into a task or challenge without much preparation whatsoever, but your Cap prefers an approach that's slow, steady, and calculated.

SAGITTARIUS PARENT & LITTLE AQUARIUS

You and your airy Water Bearer have an easygoing bond based on similar interests and points of view. Your mini Aquarius collects friends everywhere they go and is happiest when playing as part of a group, and you'll set a fun-loving, entertaining, spirited tone at their endless playdates. Your passion for justice jibes with their interest in taking action for communal good. You might face rockiness when they struggle to be open-minded—especially when you're attempting to guide them through what you were hoping they'd see as an exciting learning experience—but in general, your relationship is rooted in mutual understanding.

YOU'LL CONNECT . . .

- **By motivating each other.** You both bring unique ideas to the table and are eager to get them done.

- **When you're unapologetically yourselves.** Whether you're supporting your Water Bearer tot's desire to wear their Halloween costume to the grocery store in May, or they're gleeful that you're using a different language, you'll appreciate each other's passion for being true to oneself.

- **By finding ways to give back.** Your urge to stand up for what's right, and your Aquarius's humanitarian instincts will inspire you to be active, aware, and involved in your community as a pair.

YOU'LL CLASH . . .

- **When you're fired up about an adventure, and your Aquarius has their own plan in mind.** Although they're a social air sign, your baby Water Bearer's fixed nature means it's tough for them to embrace the unknown, which you're boundlessly enthralled by. Give them time to wrap their head around the unfamiliar.

- **When you're not sure how to respond to their contrarian retorts.** As easily as you'll dole out a blunt statement, your Water Bearer toddler could cut you with an out-of-the-blue, antagonistic remark rooted in wanting to be different. You can easily meet their rebellious streak with a sense of humor.

- **If your "bigger is better" philosophy isn't working for your tiny Aquarius.** Thanks to Jupiter's influence, you celebrate being over-the-top, often expressing yourself boldly. But your Water Bearer tends to be more reserved. So you could see them exhibit seriously sassy "threenager" behavior in response to your grandiose style.

SAGITTARIUS PARENT & LITTLE PISCES

You and your whimsical Fish baby are similarly adaptable and wired to dream big. But given your direct nature and their sensitivity, some moments will call for putting in extra work to fully understand each other. While you may be self-motivated, your Pisces baby, possessing such a delicate heart, will require tender, gentle coaxing from you to get a move on. But they'll learn from and admire your relentless brio and bravery. And you'll be fascinated by their deep empathy and beautiful imagination.

YOU'LL CONNECT . . .

- **Through beloved traditions.** From holidays to birthdays and family rituals, you and your Fish both find comfort in spiritual celebrations and special occasions.

- **When you help your Pisces make the most of their imagination.** It's easy for your little Fish to get swept up in daydreams, and when you bring your optimism and drive to the mix, the two of you can create something concrete.

- **When you go on free-spirited adventures, ideally near water.** Both you and your Pisces love being in the moment and find inner peace by being in wide open nature, and trips to a nearby beach or lake will bring your little Fish even more joy.

YOU'LL CLASH . . .

- **If your tone feels too harsh.** While you believe it best to avoid beating around the bush with your Pisces, they will likely respond best to sensitive information delivered as warmly as possible.

- **When you're fired up, and they're in their feelings.** While your mini Pisces will be enthralled by your go-getter, buoyant approach, they may occasionally need to tend to big emotions before they can get on board with your game plan.

- **When your little Fish is struggling with courage.** Although you want to support your Pisces's wild imagination, you could find it frustrating if they seem more interested in dreaming than doing. Thankfully, by setting an example and championing their skills, you can empower them.

THE CAPRICORN PARENT

Influenced by the sign of the Sea Goat, thanks to your sun or other personal placements falling in the cardinal earth sign, you're goal-oriented, hardworking, often serious, and pragmatic. Ruled by taskmaster Saturn, you thrive when you're putting your nose to the grindstone in an effort to tackle a particular challenge. It's through this lens that you'll support your little one in pursuing their own ambitions. And because you're rather traditional, you may find comfort in utilizing tried-and-true parenting strategies passed down by your caregivers. Known to be loyal, reliable, and direct, you're the one your parent friends and loved ones often lean on for practical advice. Your little one will see you as a grounded, guiding force who can teach them the magic and power of Saturnian structure, organization, boundaries, and persistence. You may be happiest when you're hard at work, but even you need—and deserve—a time-out from toil. Try these routines to nurture yourself:

BEST SELF-CARE ROUTINES FOR A CAPRICORN PARENT

- Go hiking on a scenic trail.
- Tend to your garden.
- Experiment with specialty coffees and slow-brewing methods like pour-over.
- Dive into a meditation lesson on an app like Headspace or Calm. Even better if it is part of a series that you'll feel accomplished completing.
- Check out a rock climbing gym.

CAPRICORN PARENT & LITTLE ARIES

As two cardinal signs, you and your little Ram both come up with big sweeping visions that you're excited to take on and push relentlessly to the finish line. While you're both focused on success, the paces at which you'll pursue it are quite different. You believe in moving toward your goal in a steady, practical way, while as a result of their Mars rulership, your Ram is fast, furious, frenzied, and competitive. Likewise, your mini Aries may want to rebel against rules and limitations they perceive as a hindrance to progress whereas you see them as constructive. But by keeping an open mind about each other's approaches, you'll be a powerfully dynamic pair.

YOU'LL CONNECT . . .

- **By supporting your little one's self-motivation.** You not only see but applaud your baby's drive, which will only serve to boost their confidence and bond with you.

- **When you model perseverance, and they impress you with their impulses.** You can teach your baby Ram all about putting in the time to see a plan through, while they'll prove there are pursuits in which speed and playfulness can come in handy.

- **When you bond over taking charge.** You're both natural leaders, and when you see your similarly ambitious Ram grab the reins, your heart can't help but swell with pride.

YOU'LL CLASH . . .

- **When your dispositions feel out of sync.** Your reserved, unflappable nature might strike your frisky, fiery little Aries as uptight, and you might wish there were a way to turn their aggressive nature down a tick.

- **If you're promoting structure and rules, and your Ram's independent streak kicks in.** Your rambunctious child will pick a battle against anything they feel is standing in their way, including—and perhaps especially—the carefully thought-out guidelines you've set in place to help them thrive.

- **When your Ram isn't as interested as you are in putting in the work to reach their goals.** Your little Ram wants to be declared number one but isn't as committed as you are to putting their nose to the grindstone to hit that goal. For that reason, you'll want to connect the dots between effort and reward.

CAPRICORN PARENT & LITTLE TAURUS

You and your fellow earth sign naturally see eye to eye, as you're both down-to-earth, eager to set goals that you can work diligently toward slowly and steadily, and value staying calm, cool, and collected even in the face of an uphill battle. Because your tiny Taurus isn't quite as self-directed as you are, they'll be happy that you're there to offer just the right amount of hand-holding to encourage them along. And once they get going, they'll amaze you with their fixed energy-fueled resolve.

YOU'LL CONNECT . . .

- **Tracking progress on a big-picture goal.** You and your little Bull move at a similar pace toward long-term aspirations, and you'll enjoy setting up systems to show your progress. For example, your child might want to save up to buy a toy they've set their sights on, and you can help them track how much they've stashed away in their piggy bank. Early financial lessons are of particular interest to you both!

- **When you're tackling everyday responsibilities.** You and your tiny Taurus especially enjoy taking care of tasks that keep your home comfortable and aesthetically appealing, like making sure the dog's bed is free of crumbs and using place mats on the dinner table.

- **By creating beautiful gifts for each other.** Your little Taurus will often channel their artistic Venus-influenced eye and keen senses into gifting, offering up a flower or papier-mâché sculpture, and as a similarly tactile earth sign, you'll return the favor, perhaps knitting them a blanket or growing their favorite fruit in your garden.

YOU'LL CLASH . . .

- **If you find yourself having a power struggle with your stubborn Bull.** While you both have pretty long fuses, you might be challenged to maintain your chill when your Taurus believes they should be calling the shots.

- **When your energies are mismatched.** Your Bull prefers low-key activities like listening to relaxing music while baking or napping with you versus being on the go. So when your cardinality is showing and you're itching to take care of business, they might need some coaxing to get on board.

- **When you're exhausted.** Because you and your tiny Taurus can be so easily consumed by tasks you take on together, you might realize that you haven't had a moment to rest, which could spur grouchiness all around.

CAPRICORN PARENT & LITTLE GEMINI

Your wide-eyed, communicative Gemini will certainly teach you how to see the world from an unfamiliar vantage point. While you prefer to take your time hitting specific goals, climbing up the mountain one small but crucial step at a time, your tiny multitasking Twins baby is wired to soak up all the information possible in order to share it with others ASAP. After all, just as their ruler, trickster Mercury, moves quickly, so does your Gemini. Structure and boundaries could be a hard sell to your airy kid. But they'll appreciate your willingness to help them come up with a strategy for enacting their endless ideas, and you'll find their information-gathering and social skills useful when you're working toward your own goals.

YOU'LL CONNECT . . .

- **When you're researching a shared goal.** Though you and your Gemini tot take different approaches to gathering information, you both find the merit in soaking up knowledge, especially while holding a specific intention—like planning a family trip or finding a dinner recipe—in mind.

- **By working on an ambitious project as a team.** You can show your Twins kid how to channel their boundless energy into concrete results.

- **By prioritizing playfulness with family.** From board games to outdoor activities, you equally appreciate any opportunity to kick back and bond with loved ones.

YOU'LL CLASH . . .

- **When your pace feels too slow for your multitasking Twins kid.** While you value adopting a slow, controlled pace, your baby prefers to flit from one activity to the next and may be frustrated if they feel anchored for too long.

- **If your Gemini tot laughs off boundaries.** Show them that rules can be freeing and even the key to having more fun. For example, if they know they have to be tucked in no later than 7:00 p.m., they can be sure to make time for all three bedtime stories they want to hear.

- **If your Twins baby is feeling more social than you are.** You tend to be more reserved than your airy little one, but because they crave—and learn best from—nurturing connections, dedicated playdates and time out exploring the world can help them thrive.

CAPRICORN PARENT & LITTLE CANCER

Although you and your baby Crab are opposites, you share an ability to dive into anything you've set your mind on, given that you're both cardinal signs. This means you're both up for putting in the work to better understand each other. Intent on hitting your goals and appearing in control, you tend to put your feelings on the back burner in order to stick to the task at hand, but your Cancer tot can't help but allow their feelings and intuition to lead the way. You can show them how to focus on what they want to achieve and channel their emotions into the work they'll need to do to get there. And experiencing their sensitivity, sentimentality, and sweetness firsthand could inspire you to be more accepting of your own emotionality.

YOU'LL CONNECT . . .

- **By talking through big feelings.** You can help your Cancer baby with the vocabulary they need to communicate what they're experiencing emotionally, and in turn, you might find that you're more inclined to open up as well.

- **When you're kicking off—and pushing forward—on a big project.** Because you share the ability to take the initiative, diving in won't be an issue, but you can also model diligence and endurance for your sensitive Crab.

- **By championing each other's big-picture dreams.** You'll both admire how the other pinpoints and pursues their ambitions.

YOU'LL CLASH . . .

- **If you're struggling to get in sync emotionally.** Whether you find yourself wishing your Crab could prioritize the practical route over their feelings, or they're having trouble connecting with you when you're reserved, being on different pages offers a chance to learn more about each other— and yourselves.

- **If you both want to dive into conflicting pastimes.** You may not always agree on how to best expend your fired-up, go-getter energy, presenting a chance to strive for a compromise or make room for two different game plans.

- **When you show you care in different ways.** You might show your Crab how loved they are by preparing their favorite snack or making sure they're properly bundled up when it's chilly out, but they'll crave—and offer up— more closeness, cuddle sessions, and I love yous.

CAPRICORN PARENT & LITTLE LEO

Your spotlight-loving, outgoing, sunny baby Lion might seem as though they have a whole different skill set and priorities from you, but look a bit closer, and you'll find that you have more in common than you realize. Equally driven, you both crave recognition for your strengths and passions. Although your paces may be unalike—you're deliberate and steady, while your dynamic, fiery Leo would prefer to get wherever they're going sooner versus later—and you show how you feel in very different ways, you can help your Lion be more grounded as they pursue their ambitions, and they'll show you how fun and productive it can be to get fired up.

YOU'LL CONNECT . . .

- **By aiming for applause.** You and your little Lion will love to join forces on a project that's sure to earn you recognition, whether that's performing a dance for family or baking up a batch of brownies.

- **When you're mapping out your aspirations.** You're both so driven, and your most vibrant conversations may center around what you want to accomplish as a pair and how you plan to get there.

- **By modeling what leadership involves.** You and your Lion are natural-born leaders, and you can coach them on what it means to set a positive example and how to collaborate with others.

YOU'LL CLASH . . .

- **If your Lion's playfulness is at odds with your need for efficiency.** For instance, you could be frustrated if you're checking out at the grocery store and have asked your little Leo to help you place lighter items from the basket on the checkout counter, but they've decided to put on a show instead of sticking to the task at hand.

- **If you don't understand your Leo's desire to command the spotlight.** Being the center of attention isn't your jam, and you might struggle to connect with the attention-seeking aspect of your Lion's personality. But they'll always appreciate your effort to support their play for the spotlight.

- **When you can't agree on who's calling the shots.** Your confident Lion might lightheartedly scoff at the boundaries you set, believing they know what's best for themselves. Meeting them with a playful, creative reward for positive behavior may be more effective than striking a stern tone.

CAPRICORN PARENT & LITTLE VIRGO

You and your Maiden make quite the practical, earth sign pair. You're both goal-oriented, organized, and analytical. You'll admire your Virgo baby's attention to detail, desire to contribute to everyday tasks, and thoughtfulness, and they'll appreciate your drive, confidence, and wisdom. Because it can be tough for you to wear your heart on your sleeve, your sensitive, Mercury-ruled Virgo might nudge you to talk more about emotions, and by believing in them and their ambitions, they'll grow up to be even more self-assured and driven.

YOU'LL CONNECT . . .

- **When you're breaking down an ambitious project.** Virgo likes tending to detail, preferring to be in the weeds, and you move at a steady pace to hit the finish line, so together, you're an effective duo.

- **By checking off practical tasks.** From tackling a mountain of laundry to walking the dog together, both of you derive a sense of accomplishment from taking care of your business.

- **By letting loose.** You're prone to forgetting to make time for relaxation. By adding fun to the agenda, you'll set a positive example for your hardworking Virgo, and you'll both get a well-deserved break.

YOU'LL CLASH . . .

- **If you're both exhausted.** You and your Maiden are driven to get a lot done, but your mental energy runs quite high, and if either of you needs downtime, stormy moods could ensue.

- **If your baby Virgo is zeroed in on a particular need, and you're looking at the big picture.** Whether it's getting the temperature just right in their bedroom or asking for a specific lovey to cuddle, details matter a ton to your tiny Maiden, while, as a cardinal sign, you tend to be thinking about the greater landscape (for example, might a sleep regression be around the bend?). Making room for the minutiae can help you get on the same page as your Maiden.

- **If your values are out of sync.** While you prioritize recognition and achievement, your Mercury-ruled Virgo cares more about communication and proving themselves useful, which you'll want to bear in mind when they express their interests and aspirations.

CAPRICORN PARENT & LITTLE LIBRA

As two cardinal signs, you and your social Scales baby are always dreaming up thrilling ideas and plans to make them a reality. But while you prefer to take a no-nonsense, scrupulous approach, your Venus-ruled baby would rather apply their creativity and charming social skills toward hitting their goals. They're also lighthearted, and as an air sign, prone to experimenting with one interest one minute and another the next. But when it comes to playing mediator or taking action that they believe will result in a greater sense of harmony for others, you'll notice that they're just as serious as you.

YOU'LL CONNECT . . .

- **When you both adopt a can-do attitude.** No matter what bold undertaking you and your Scales baby have set out to achieve, you'll appreciate each other's drive to get it done.

- **When you're rooting for each other.** You'll applaud your Libra's ability to endear themselves to just about anyone, while they'll admire your fortitude.

- **When your Libra shows you the beauty of working one-on-one.** While you might be fine with flying solo, it's your Scales baby's natural inclination to partner up, so carving out special time to dream and do together can bring you closer.

YOU'LL CLASH . . .

- **If you're in a goal-oriented headspace, and your Libra wants to let loose.** Some moments might call for bridging the gap between your desire to achieve and your airy baby's craving for social play.

- **When you've set out a practical strategy but your Libra needs to take their own path.** Whether you're working on baby-led weaning or tackling simple chores around the house, your Scales kid may lack your focus, potentially getting sidetracked by something that seems like more fun. You can bring them back to the task at hand by initiating a playful game or engaging conversation.

- **When your Scales kid is feeling more outgoing than you.** Getting on the same page socially can be tough for you and your Libra, but if any little one was to be open to negotiating a compromise, it would be your balance-loving child.

CAPRICORN PARENT & LITTLE SCORPIO

With a shared zeal for setting lofty goals and working hard to hit them, you and your little Scorpion are an impressive duo. Although you're similarly driven, your fixed water sign baby is comfortable exploring their deepest emotions while you'd prefer to focus on the rational, concrete aspects of life. But talking about how you feel can be a challenge for you both, because as reserved and stoic as you are, your Scorp can be incredibly private. They'll look to you for lessons on how to get grounded and more logical, while you'll learn the magic of connecting to your spirituality from them.

YOU'LL CONNECT . . .

- **By being equally ambitious.** Because your little one's sign is co-ruled by go-getter Mars and transformative Pluto, and taskmaster Saturn rules Capricorn, neither of you shies away from a challenge. In fact, the bolder an undertaking, the better.

- **Through quality time with grandparents and older loved ones.** You and your Scorp share a strong reverence for elders.

- **By embracing family traditions.** As the fixed water sign, your little Scorp has an abiding respect for rituals—like carving pumpkins in the fall or visiting a favorite blueberry farm every summer—which you also appreciate as an old soul.

YOU'LL CLASH . . .

- **When your Scorp is being aloof.** You can relate to them being so reserved, but you might also be a bit unsure how to proceed if they're clearly holding in big emotions.

- **When your go-getter nature is at odds with** your Scorpio's fixed tendencies. While you'd prefer to try a new experience, your mini Scorp will stand their ground on the food, activity, or routine they already know and love.

- **If you're both vying to be in charge.** Even when you've laid out the boundaries and rules for them, your confident Scorp tyke has an astonishing ability to assume power in a quiet, crafty way, which could throw you for a loop and cause you to rethink how to best put guardrails in place for them.

CAPRICORN PARENT & LITTLE SAGITTARIUS

You'll find that there's much you and your adventurous mini Archer can teach each other. While you value putting in hard work and being recognized for it, your Sag often aims to entertain and explore in an effort to experience life. Boundaries are Saturn's realm, but go-big-or-go-home Jupiter would prefer to go boundary-free, so you'll often be bridging the gap between your two conflicting philosophies. But you can also look forward to your baby Archer motivating you to take a more spontaneous, playful approach, while you'll model the merits of putting in the work to fulfill their aspirations.

YOU'LL CONNECT . . .

- **When you go on an adventure.** From babywearing your Archer on a train ride to visit loved ones to teaching them how to ride a bike, you're both empowered to explore uncharted terrain.

- **When you make room for each other's strengths.** Whenever you need a dose of enthusiasm, your little Sag will bring it, and when they need to boil their big ideas down to specific goals, you can guide the way.

- **When you applaud each other's unique perspective.** Even though it's not how they move through the world, your Sag will appreciate your diligence and dedication to reaching the peak of any mountain you climb, and you'll be in awe of their brave spiritedness.

YOU'LL CLASH . . .

- **If you're in a serious mindset, and your Sag just wants to have fun.** You could struggle to get on the same page in moments when you're focused on taking care of business and your Archer is being especially playful.

- **When you're not speaking the same love language.** You show you care in a way that's more reserved and likely more service-oriented than the over-the-top, excitable, and often loud way your Archer expresses affection. But it could still strike you as delightful and inspire you to respond in kind.

- **When your slow, steady pace is at odds with your baby's dynamism.** You'd prefer to take on any endeavor one well-thought-out, pragmatic, controlled step at a time, while your Sag will happily bound right into the unknown. Offering them plenty of opportunities to do so—as safely as possible, of course—will be key to seeing them bloom.

CAPRICORN PARENT & LITTLE CAPRICORN

As two no-nonsense, driven, and traditional-minded Sea Goats, you and your baby will have no trouble setting ambitious intentions and then taking whatever time is required to reach the finish line as a like-minded pair. You'll get a kick out of what an old soul your little one is—much like you were at their age, no doubt—and smirk when they try a tone that's somehow even more professorial and grown-up than yours. The main challenge you and your tiny Cap could face: Your mutual resistance to hitting pause on work from time to time could cause you to get tuckered out and cranky. But when you see your own diligent work ethic reflected back by your Sea Goat, you could be stirred to prioritize more fun and rest for you both.

YOU'LL CONNECT . . .

- **Through your shared industriousness.** Whether you're tackling a puzzle or chores around the house, you and your Sea Goat will be motivated to get from point A to point B to cultivate a sense of accomplishment.

- **By taking your time.** Whether you head out on a leisurely walk or build a castle with blocks, you both believe that by taking it slowly and steadily, you'll probably be even more satisfied once you reach your destination.

- **When you applaud each other's achievements.** No one knows how much you value being recognized and respected for your hard work like a fellow Cap.

YOU'LL CLASH . . .

- **If you get stuck in a seriousness rut.** Your shared pragmatism and work ethic are commendable, but by feeding off each other's sense of duty, you might forget that having fun is just as important.

- **If you can't see eye to eye on what to pour your energy into.** Your Cap tot might be fired up to play ball in the

backyard, but you've decided to organize the playroom. Giving your baby Cap plenty of space and time to initiate activities and feel like a leader in their own right is integral to nurturing their confidence.

- **If you let your ambitions overshadow anything else.** It could be easy for you to both be so focused on hitting a particular milestone or completing an impressive project that you forget to enjoy the journey and your shared experience, which could spur frustration between you.

CAPRICORN PARENT & LITTLE AQUARIUS

You and your Water Bearer baby will find each other both exciting and challenging. While you appreciate boundaries and traditions, thanks to your ruler, Saturn, your tiny Aquarius is guided by game-changer Uranus, which spurs them to march to the beat of their own drum, rejecting convention at every turn. You could be left shaking your head at your airy baby, who believes every rule you set was meant to be broken. But by establishing boundaries that leave them with plenty of room to rebel, you'll help them funnel their innovative thinking into productive results.

YOU'LL CONNECT . . .

- **By learning about science.** You appreciate working hard to gather data, while your research-oriented Water Bearer might as well have been born wearing a lab coat.

- **By pursuing unconventional activities.** Your tiny Water Bearer will appreciate your willingness to dive into out-of-the-ordinary activities, like purposely scribbling outside the lines.

- **When your Aquarius can encourage you to innovate, and you can help them set goals.** Viewing the world through your Water Bearer's eyes, you'll see the merits of trying an idiosyncratic approach. Meanwhile, you can show them how to pursue progress one practical step at a time.

YOU'LL CLASH . . .

- **When your Aquarian's high social energy conflicts with your rigorous schedule.** As far as your Water Bearer's concerned, the more the merrier, but you'll often want to cut playdates short to get on with your to-dos.

- **If your Aquarius is continually testing your limits.** There may be times when your Water Bearer pushes your buttons and boundaries because they find it fun. Meeting them with a sense of humor—the quirkier, the better—can help.

- **If you're up for something new, and they're stuck on what they know.** Although Aquarius has a rep for being forward-thinking, and Cap's often typecast as stodgy, don't forget who's the initiative-taking cardinal sign (you!) and who's the fixed sign (your Water Bearer). This means you may sometimes be the one proposing an adventure while your Aquarius tot argues for watching their favorite movie for the gazillionth time.

CAPRICORN PARENT & LITTLE PISCES

On the surface, it might seem like you and your baby Fish are radically different, as they're dreamy and sensitive, and tend to sit back and see what happens as opposed to jumping to action. But the truth of the matter is that you can offer your Pisces tot down-to-earth, security-boosting support that will make them feel like they can transform their most whimsical daydreams into something real. Your imaginative Fish can also show you the benefits of more fully embracing your spirituality, creative instincts, and most complex emotions.

YOU'LL CONNECT . . .

- **When you can bring structure to your Fish's creative dreams.** In moments when your Pisces struggles to figure out where to go with their imaginative impulses, you can steer them in a productive direction.

- **By cozying up.** From baking to caring for plants and pets, you and your little Pisces both have a penchant for making sure your home is comfy and serene.

- **When you're learning about the past.** From reading bedtime stories inspired by history (one of your favorite topics)

to poring over family photo albums, you and your escapism-loving Fish will both enjoy feeling as though you've been swept up in a time machine.

YOU'LL CLASH . . .

- **If your Fish is feeling blue, and you're striving for a concrete fix.** When it feels like even the most logical solutions aren't comforting your Pisces, you could be frustrated. Often, what they'll need even more than a fix is for you to validate their emotions and reiterate that you're there as they work through them.

- **If your Pisces is sensitive to your tone.** Even if you felt like you were only reiterating a rule or boundary, your delicate Fish might find your self-expression overly stern and harsh. Try a softer approach.

- **When your little Fish is adrift in their imagination, and you're insisting on a reality check.** Bringing your dreamy Pisces back down to Earth can be challenging. But it's also important to pick your battles, because sometimes the rational take could stand to fall by the wayside for the sake of your Fish's creativity.

THE AQUARIUS PARENT

Born with your sun or other personal placements in the sign of the Water Bearer, you're forward-thinking, humanitarian, possibly a bit eccentric, and occasionally contrarian. Though you're individualistic and proud of being a bit quirky, you're also happiest when fostering connections to your community. As far as you're concerned, it takes a village to not only raise a child but also tackle all the causes that are close to your heart. As the sign associated with the Eleventh House of Friends, you have a parent friend group that's wide and diverse. Ruled by revolutionary Uranus, you have a progressive, future-minded take on everyday parenting challenges, whether that's using the latest tech or championing cloth diapers or gentle parenting practices. By looking up to you, your baby will learn how to give back to others, cherish platonic bonds, strike out against convention, embrace an evolved point of view, and proudly stand in their sense of self. To cope with daily stressors and to feel more vital, you'll gravitate to practices that are unconventional, high-tech, and innovative. Try these routines to nurture yourself:

BEST SELF-CARE ROUTINES FOR AN AQUARIUS PARENT

- Go for a walk or run while listening to your favorite podcast.
- Wander around a local science museum or planetarium.
- Catch up with friends in your go-to group text.
- Volunteer at a local charity, like food bank or clothing donation center.
- Express your individuality by experimenting with your personal style.

AQUARIUS PARENT & LITTLE ARIES

When you're out in the world with your baby Ram, the two of you are bound to make quite the impression on others as a personable, high-energy duo. Like you, your fiery tot is independent and driven to be a trendsetter. While you both move at a fairly snappy pace, your Aries could challenge you to keep up. And while you're breezier than most of your fellow fixed signs, it can be tough for you to switch gears, which your Aries would love to be doing in perpetuity. But overall, given your Ram's playful fire and your social airiness, you can't help but make each other laugh and enjoy many adventures together.

YOU'LL CONNECT . . .

- **When you come up with sweeping challenges, and your Aries steps up to the plate.** As an innovative Aquarian, you can easily propose thought-provoking activities (like science experiments or bird-watching) that will engage your rambunctious Ram.

- **When you're equally inquisitive.** While you're more science-minded and your tiny Aries would prefer to *do* versus hypothesize, you both have an insatiable appetite to explore the world around you.

- **When you celebrate your free-spiritedness.** Much like you, your little Ram is fiercely independent, and you'll encourage them to own what makes them an individual with all their might.

YOU'LL CLASH . . .

- **When they're being competitive and you want to collaborate.** You could be presented with an uphill battle when trying to teach your Aries the value of teamwork and they're more interested in striving to be number one.

- **When your Ram is easily distracted, and you're deeply invested in the particular task at hand.** Your excitable Ram is always looking for a new undertaking, which could irk you when you want to stick to the project you're already in the weeds on.

- **When you and your Aries are moving at different paces.** Your baby Aries wants to be perpetually on the go, and though you don't mind moving at a quick clip, you can get sidetracked by socializing. Expect mini meltdowns at the park when they're over you having a schmooze fest with one of your many friends.

AQUARIUS PARENT & LITTLE TAURUS

While you prefer the unconventional approach, your baby Bull defaults to what's familiar and comfortable, perhaps even traditional. Buzzing from one social commitment to the next lights you up, whereas your Taurus would prefer to be cozy at home. You both forge ahead until you've completed any task you've taken on, but you'll usually take very different routes to your endgame. But seeing the merits of each other's perspectives can make you both even stronger and capable of hitting any goal you set together.

YOU'LL CONNECT . . .

- **When you're spending quality time with your nearest and dearest.** You and your Venus-ruled Bull both value building and nurturing your bonds.

- **When your strengths shine.** You'll admire how grounded and persistent your Taurus is, particularly when you're tackling a creative project, and they'll be impressed with your eye for innovation.

- **When you're self-aware and even a little self-deprecating.** Noticing just how alike you are, especially when you're both digging your heels in, can lead to lots of giggles.

YOU'LL CLASH . . .

- **When your out-there style isn't in line with your Bull's sensibilities.** When you urge your Taurus tot to wear their hair in an unconventional way or finger paint instead of using crayons, they may be less than thrilled. It's an opportunity to let them find what speaks to them—even if it's different from what speaks to you.

- **When you want to shake up your Taurus's routine but they push back.** You could get frustrated if you try to introduce a new activity, food, or social routine that you think is exciting, and your Bull takes longer to get acclimated than you might have anticipated. But if you take a step back, you may realize that you actually can relate, since you share that fixed energy.

- **When your mutual stubbornness flares up.** If you both resolve not to budge or can't see the nuance of a particular disagreement, you could be at a standstill.

AQUARIUS PARENT & LITTLE GEMINI

As two air signs, you and your tiny Twins kid are very much in sync. You both thrive when you're being social, learning, and gathering info from as many sources as possible. But while you're rather stubborn and resolute as a fixed sign, your mutable Gemini can struggle with uncertainty and a scattered attention span. You'll help them with follow-through, and in turn they'll show you the merits of their lighthearted, playful point of view.

YOU'LL CONNECT . . .

- **When you're surrounded by friends and family.** You and your Gemini will forever be fans of big groups and lots of liveliness.

- **When your shared high mental energy soars.** Any intellectual pursuit from brainteasers to jokes based on wordplay will provide hours of entertainment and stimulation for you and your Twins child, especially as they get older.

- **When you're exploring uncharted terrain.** Whether you're taking a train trip or browsing gadgets at the mall, you both find it thrilling to experience and learn something new, especially when it comes to technology and travel.

YOU'LL CLASH . . .

- **When your fixed nature is at odds with your Twins child's indecisiveness.** Your Gemini baby wants to take in all the info and consider all the options, and still, they might not be able to reach a conclusion—well after you've already made up your mind. You'll do best to empower them to reach a decision whenever they're ready.

- **When your Gemini's lack of focus impedes progress.** Whether you're checking off to-dos or playing a game together, you might find it challenging when they struggle to zero in on the task at hand. They could end up being more engaged if there's plenty of room for them to explore.

- **If your tone suddenly feels too strict.** Because your breezy Gemini baby would generally prefer to keep the mood light, airy, and communicative, they may bristle when your Uranian-fueled stormy side shows up.

AQUARIUS PARENT & LITTLE CANCER

You and your little Crab offer each other truly unique—and often contrasting—perspectives. Your emotional Cancer is in tune with their feelings and intuition, while you often prefer to lead with your head over your heart. Finding common ground might be a challenge when it comes to revealing your emotions. But while you might express your compassion in different ways, it's also a trait that can bring you together.

YOU'LL CONNECT . . .

- **When you care for others.** You and your Crab can't help but pour energy into showing up for those in need. You'll enjoy being part of any charitable effort.

- **When you unpack big emotions.** Because you're more intellectual than emotional, you can help your Cancer tot take a step back from their, at times, overwhelming feelings and find the best language for processing their most heartfelt emotions.

- **When you celebrate free-spiritedness.** Thanks to your devotion to individuality, and your Crab's ability to tune in to and follow their heart, you can both appreciate the importance of being true to yourselves.

YOU'LL CLASH . . .

- **When your Crab wants to stay home, and you're feeling more social.** While your Cancer tot craves lots of comfort food, warm snuggles, and one-on-one time with those they love, you like to get out to a parent-and-baby play class or meet friends at the park, so you'll need to find a balance between sticking close to home and being out in the world.

- **When you're leading with logic, and they're consumed by emotion.** You tend to default to a rational headspace, and your baby defaults to a deeply feeling one, so bridging that gap is key to bonding.

- **When your preference for the unconventional doesn't resonate with your Crab.** While you might be singing the praises of an eccentric outfit you saw on social media or a little-known indie rock band you learned about from a friend, your Cancer kid will embrace whatever speaks to their heart, regardless of whether it's popular.

AQUARIUS PARENT & LITTLE LEO

Though you're both fixed signs, you and your baby Lion are opposites. While you embrace the most rational point of view, your sunny Leo often sees the silver lining of any situation. Their positivity might rub off on you, allowing you to embrace the bright side more readily, while your humanitarian perspective can inspire your Lion to think about the world outside of themselves. As two strong-willed personalities, you'll have your disagreements, in which one or both of you might dig your heels in, but you're resolutely committed to smoothing over any bumps in the road.

YOU'LL CONNECT . . .

- **When you're socializing.** You are both friend magnets—whether it's stopping to chat with someone in the neighborhood or throwing a big party, your highest energy as a pair will flow when you're surrounded by others.

- **When you're fostering your Lion's sense of community.** Whether you're volunteering at a local organization or donating to a food bank, you'll show your fiery baby how satisfying it can be to show up for others.

- **By talking through your Leo's big dreams.** Even when they're tiny, you'll get the sense that your ambitious Lion plans to aim for the stars, and you can help them come up with a logical game plan for making any major aspiration a reality.

YOU'LL CLASH . . .

- **If you're both refusing to back down.** While you're both prone to black-and-white thinking and digging your heels in, you'll express it differently. Your little Leo will be passionate and loud when defending their position, and you'll tend to get quiet and stoic. While it can be challenging, simply being aware that you're equally stubborn can make it easier for you to navigate conflict.

- **When your Lion wants to command the spotlight.** While teaching your Leo about cooperating with and acknowledging the needs of others is undoubtedly important, offering them plenty of time to shine on their own is especially integral to nurturing their confidence.

- **When you're dealing with your Leo's domineering side.** Your fiery natural-born leader will want to take the reins almost every chance they get, potentially resulting in power struggles.

AQUARIUS PARENT & LITTLE VIRGO

You and your baby Maiden are equally driven to learn as much as you can about the world around you, then channel that knowledge into helping others. You'll notice that your Virgo tot tends to get stuck in the weeds a bit more than you, and they're also less decisive but more adaptable. You can foster their focus and self-assurance, while they'll offer you the most grounded point of view. Together, you'll find that you're always coming up with inventive ideas that—thanks to your baby Maiden's work ethic and your follow-through—usually come to fruition.

YOU'LL CONNECT . . .

- **When you rely on technology to learn.** Whether you're teaching them about colors or a new language, leaning on tech will make the experience more enriching for you both.

- **When you're in a pragmatic headspace.** Count on your analytical Virgo to get it when you want to take any uphill battle one logical step at a time.

- **When you join forces to be of service to others.** Your Virgo instinctively wants to do their part for any group effort, and you aim to champion the greater good, so as an altruistic duo, you can make a difference in your family and your community.

YOU'LL CLASH . . .

- **When you're struggling to wrap your head around Virgo's indecisiveness.** Because you tend toward decisiveness as a fixed sign, you'll struggle to relate to your mutable Maiden's hemming and hawing. But these moments can be an opportunity to encourage them to tune in to and trust their budding inner voice.

- **When your Virgo wants to switch gears quickly, and you're not quite there yet.** Mercury's energy—and thus, your Maiden's nature—is quick and curious, so when your Virgo has had enough of a particular game or project, they might be ready to move on to the next thing, while it can take you time to change course.

- **When you speak different love languages.** While you are both intellectual, your little Maiden will—often quietly—wish for plenty of warm, supportive, affectionate words and quality time. Snuggling during story time and liberally sprinkling I love yous can go far in increasing their emotional confidence.

AQUARIUS PARENT & LITTLE LIBRA

You and your fellow air sign baby often see eye to eye—from striving to connect and collaborate with different types of people to seeking out games that challenge all the senses. But while you're most interested in being involved with groups, teams, and community efforts, your Scales baby prefers socializing one-on-one, which could encourage you to mix up how you're planning playdates and other activities. They might not fully understand your need to avoid anything you see as conventional (whether that's a popular teething toy or a tradition like getting a smash cake), and you might not always get why they shy away from conflict, but as two idealistic, inquisitive air signs, you usually find it effortless to get in sync.

YOU'LL CONNECT . . .

- **By tending to your friendships and making new ones.** You and your Scales tot are undeniably two of the most social signs, so when you're out in the wild, people can't help but be magnetized to your friendly orbit.

- **When you satiate your shared curiosity.** You'll grow even closer to your Libra baby while enjoying opportunities to learn in an active, experiential way.

- **When you're sharing idealistic views.** Both you and your Libra believe the world could be a better place and want to do your part to make that so.

YOU'LL CLASH . . .

- **When your contrarian tendencies are at odds with your Scales baby's desire for tranquility.** Because you prize sticking to the facts over keeping the peace, you won't steer clear of argumentatively defending what's rational in your view. But in some moments, you may want to go the diplomatic route for your conflict-averse Libra.

- **If you're not on the same page about what kind of activity to dive into.** As inventive as you are, artistic projects aren't as enticing to you as science-minded ones. But your Venus-ruled tyke will appreciate your efforts to bridge the gap between their interests and yours.

- **When you're moving slowly, and your Libra is in go-getter mode.** Once your Scales baby has made up their mind and is ready to go on a new undertaking, they'll be hard-pressed to slow down, whereas you'll need a bit of time to warm up.

AQUARIUS PARENT & LITTLE SCORPIO

From possessing a strong sense of self to generally seeing any undertaking through to the finish line, you and your Scorp tyke share the usual fixed sign traits. But you're also quite different in that while you're driven by rationality, your little water sign is frequently consumed by their emotions. They'll be intrigued by your inventiveness, and you'll be mesmerized by how quietly passionate they can be about anything they're truly interested in—from daily walks around their favorite pond to working meticulously with a new building block set. Because you're both so prone to inflexibility, you may get stuck in black-and-white thinking, but working through your differences is sure to lead to growth.

YOU'LL CONNECT . . .

- **When you commit.** Whether you've decided to meet a milestone or team up while playing a game, when you and your little Scorpio are in, you're all in, and no one can sway you from seeing it through.

- **When you're exploring empathy.** Although you tend to express it in a more cerebral way than your little Scorpio, you're both compassionate and will put your heads together to determine how best to show up for your VIPs and strangers alike.

- **When you can each see the world from the other's vantage point.** If you're open to it, your Scorp will inspire you to tune in to and trust your instincts, and you'll offer them a valuable forward-thinking perspective.

YOU'LL CLASH . . .

- **If you're struggling to cooperate.** You're both reluctant to change course when you've made up your mind, so instances where you're not in sync could lead to gridlock. The silver lining: Your Scorp's stubbornness could motivate you to model more flexibility.

- **If your analytical take is at odds with their emotional one.** Your tiny Scorpion is at ease swimming in the deep end of their heart. While you prefer to deal with concrete evidence, try to hold space for what they're experiencing.

- **If Scorpio needs more emotional closeness.** Your fixed water sign baby can err toward possessiveness—especially when your attention is scattered—so your challenge will be to strike a balance between meeting their need for bonding time and encouraging independent play.

AQUARIUS PARENT & LITTLE SAGITTARIUS

While your baby Archer may be more outwardly emotional and spotlight-loving than you, you have a harmonious, like-minded dynamic. While you're setting up playdates galore, your similarly social Sag will find it easy to click with just about any buddy they're paired up with. And your knowledge-seeking, naturally philosophical Archer believes in fighting for the greater good just as much as you. While you might not be up for every adventure they daydream about and push for, they'll nudge you out of your comfort zone, and you'll encourage them to consider the logistics of their wildest quests.

YOU'LL CONNECT . . .

- **When you champion each other's boldest visions.** Your inventive, future-minded perspective pairs well with your Sag's fearless, fiery lens.

- **When you embrace your individuality.** Your Sag is outspoken about what they like and what they don't, and you're a champion of originality, so you'll often click when you're marching to the beat of your own drum, whether it's dressing in eccentric outfits for the fun of it, even while running errands, or singing a beloved song at the top of your lungs together in the middle of a park.

- **When you can right a wrong.** As they get older, your tiny Archer will want to address injustices (like local homelessness) with you—a wonderful way to start is by reading books and having age-appropriate conversations.

YOU'LL CLASH . . .

- **When your tendency to stick to what you know conflicts with your Archer's desire to explore.** As a fixed sign, you're comfortable staying on a familiar path (perhaps booking the same vacation rental every year), but because your Sag often wants to check out uncharted terrain, you might want to work on being open to the unknown.

- **When either of you is too direct.** You both value the truth, but you might find that your sassy, blunt Sag tot's words can sting as much as your Uranus-fueled, sharp-tongued quips.

- **When your little Sag is testing your carefully placed boundaries.** Your Archer is as free-spirited as they come, which you admire, but when your Jupiterian kid persistently pushes for more than you've allotted, you'll want to reiterate that the boundaries you've set are for their own good.

AQUARIUS PARENT & LITTLE CAPRICORN

Your differences present an opportunity for you both to learn and grow. While your ruler, electrifying Uranus, is all about shaking up the status quo, your Cap baby is guided by taskmaster Saturn, which oversees boundaries and traditions. You may wonder if your Capricorn is even more of an adult than you are, frequently making up their own rules and regulations—for themselves and others—while you encourage them to embrace a more playful perspective. And yet, they will likely continue to be the most serious, driven little one you've ever met. They'll show you how to blend ambition and pragmatism, while you'll model healthy social skills and empower them to embrace their quirky side.

YOU'LL CONNECT . . .

- **When you spotlight each other's unique skill set.** Your baby's seemingly stern perspective makes them a natural-born leader, and your electrifying tendencies make you a true innovator. Create space for those traits to shine, and you two will be a productive pair.

- **When you're open to the traditional take.** Your tiny Sea Goat will admire how you're so forward-thinking, but they'll also appreciate when you accept their simple preference for plain vanilla ice cream.

- **When your desire to innovate melds with their grounded take.** Whether you're meal prepping or trying a new hiking route, you'll land on the ideal balance of out-of-the-box thinking and a practical approach together.

YOU'LL CLASH . . .

- **When you want to be social, and they'd rather stick to the task at hand.** You might be surprised—and somewhat amused—when your strict little Cap tries to curb you from schmoozing with your friend at the grocery store so you can finish shopping.

- **If your Sea Goat becomes domineering.** As much as you'll want to foster your budding CEO's confidence, remind them that they'll become even better leaders by being a team player.

- **When your fixed nature conflicts with their cardinality.** You might be cool sticking with your regular Saturday afternoon errands followed by pizza, but your industrious, initiative-taking Sea Goat may thrive if offered the opportunity to take on a new project or an unfamiliar challenge.

AQUARIUS PARENT & LITTLE AQUARIUS

You and your fellow futuristic, humanitarian, inventive Water Bearer make one truly social, independent, open-minded duo. You'll get a kick out of how idiosyncratic, colorful, and free-spirited your Aquarius tot is—and of course how much they remind you of yourself. Like you, they'll say no for the sake of rejecting the status quo as they're just as contrarian as you are. The good news is that because you have firsthand, lifelong experience with this perspective, you know better than anyone how to support your mini Aquarius and help them feel seen for the unique nascent idealist they are.

YOU'LL CONNECT . . .

- **By giving your Water Bearer baby plenty of breathing room.** When you provide your tiny Aquarius with plenty of time and space to explore and come up with ideas and opinions on their own, they'll feel seen and respected for who they innately are.

- **When you talk about your beliefs.** You and your Aquarius kid see the world for what it could be. This is an easy topic to cover and connect on, especially when you model how you work to make your ideals a reality, perhaps by composting or raising money for a local nonprofit.

- **By rejecting the status quo.** From your love of power clashing to your disdain for that pop hit everyone's listening to over and over, you will both be on a fun-loving mission to be unapologetically, uniquely yourselves.

YOU'LL CLASH . . .

- **When you both struggle to adapt.** With double fixed energy swirling between you, at times it may be tough for either of you to adapt. But in an effort to model flexibility for your baby Aquarius, you might be inspired to let go—at least a bit.

- **When your Water Bearer rejects rules for the sake of it.** You may intimately know what this is all about, but that doesn't make it any less frustrating when your Aquarius scoffs at your boundaries because they don't want to seem like they're conforming.

- **If one of you is craving more warmth.** Though you're generally in sync on how you express affection—in an aloof, cool, intellectual way— there may be times when one of you wants to feel closer than the other, so you'll need to strike a balance between making room for your independent nature and showing how much you care.

AQUARIUS PARENT & LITTLE PISCES

Daydreaming is one of the main pastimes you have in common. That's because while you're inventive, they're imaginative, which means you can help them turn whatever their mind conjures up into a reality. But while your goal is to channel your creativity into a practical outlet, your Pisces is far less rational-minded. Sensitive and empathic, they're often adrift in their deeply felt emotions, which can be tough for you to wrap your head around as such an analytical person. But let your Fish pave the path to connecting even more deeply with your heart and intuition, and you'll model how they can make logical moves toward achieving their dreams.

YOU'LL CONNECT . . .

- **When your baby Fish can help you go with the flow.** You might wish you could be more adaptable at times, and your mutable tot can show you the way.

- **By exploring emotions from both a rational and heartfelt point of view.** You can help your Fish pause to process their feelings from an objective standpoint, while you'll learn from them how liberating it can be to experience emotions for what they are.

- **By caring for others.** Whether they're making an effort to conserve water or donating toys, your little Fish wants to heal the world as much as you do.

YOU'LL CLASH . . .

- **When your little Fish is off in the clouds.** When their imagination takes over, your dreamy Pisces might have trouble engaging with you in that game of patty-cake or Simon Says. A gentle tone and light sense of humor can urge them to join you back on Earth.

- **If you're struggling to see all sides of an issue.** Your empathic Pisces is perhaps overly tuned in to—and wants to tend to—everyone's energy and emotions, whereas you can be very attached to your own way of thinking and feeling. You can help them be more clear on how they truly feel, while they'll inspire you to open your heart to others' points of view.

- **When your love languages aren't in sync.** As an emotional water sign, your Fish will openly share how they feel through lots of hugs, kisses, and snuggles, while, as a mentally charged air sign, you're more cerebral. Upping your bandwidth for expressing your own warm feelings—and encouraging your Pisces's sweet expression—will only benefit your bond.

WATER + MUTABLE + FISH

THE PISCES PARENT

With your sun or other personal placements in the sign of the Fish, you're empathic, intuitive, and a dreamer. You feel deeply, have an inherent ability to read between the lines, and can struggle to not take on other people's energy as your own. This means you often need to guard your sensitive heart so as to not be swept out to sea by your or anyone's emotions. Ruled by mystical Neptune, you're in tune with your spiritual side, have a vivid imagination, and are naturally artistic, all of which serve you well when you're connecting with your little one through make-believe. Because you're so innately tender and compassionate, your friends know they can rely on you to commiserate with them and talk through some of their greatest challenges. And by watching you, your baby will learn how to care for themselves and others, tap into their inner voice, and explore and better comprehend their feelings through art, music, dance, or any other creatively fulfilling outlet. Because you may easily take on other people's stress as your own, finding time to tend to your needs can keep you feeling your best. Try these routines to nurture yourself:

BEST SELF-CARE ROUTINES FOR A PISCES PARENT

- Take a hatha yoga class, which combines poses with breathing techniques to calm and center the body and mind.
- Spend time in water, whether a nearby lake or community pool.
- Try Reiki, a Japanese form of energy healing.
- Meditate with Pisces-ruled crystals like aquamarine or amethyst.
- Watch a classic film you've always loved.

PISCES PARENT & LITTLE ARIES

Your Ram is a frequently fired-up, speedy little go-getter, while you like to take a slower pace and go with the flow. Whereas you're sensitive and gentle, they are direct, even brash. For these reasons, you'll often feel like you're speaking different languages and moving through the world at conflicting paces, but by remaining open and curious, your impressive Aries can show you how to bravely step into your power, while you'll model empathy and the splendor of not only acknowledging but sitting with their emotions.

YOU'LL CONNECT . . .

- **When you teach them patience.** Because they'd prefer to be moving on to the next activity ASAP, waiting is not your Aries's forte, but you can show them how to tap into their imagination to entertain themselves in those moments when the cookies need a few more minutes in the oven or their sibling is not ready to head out the door.

- **By coming up with ambitious plans.** Pairing your artistic brain with their intense one can make it easy for you to dream up and dive into a major undertaking without hesitation.

- **When you help your Aries connect with their emotions, and they inspire you to pursue your dreams.** Looking to each other for inspiration and motivation can lead to magic for you both.

YOU'LL CLASH . . .

- **When you're particularly sensitive, and they're being especially feisty.** Your Aries tot wants what they want when they want it, and their occasionally demanding nature could be a lot for you at times. Encouraging them to use words like please and thank you can go far.

- **When they're ready to take action, and you're not quite sure how to proceed.** While you're waiting to see how you feel before you can move forward, your Aries will already be miles ahead if they have their way. The best way to cope: doing your best to speed up a bit while encouraging them to slow down and think before hitting the gas.

- **When their competitive streak is at odds with your empathic view.** Your Ram will pull no punches while aiming to be number one, and you're often on a mission to protect others emotionally, so you'll want to teach your Aries how to be a good sport from the get-go.

PISCES PARENT & LITTLE TAURUS

If there were a prize for the sweetest snuggle bugs, you and your baby Bull would win it by a mile. You're similarly sensitive and both fans of taking it easy, reveling in the dreamiest, prettiest aspects of life. You'll find that you appreciate your tiny Taurus's practical, grounded perspective, and they're eager to venture into whimsical territory with you. Your baby earth sign may inspire you to work through your emotions in a tactile way—like crafting or baking—and you'll help them feel more at ease exploring their spiritual side.

YOU'LL CONNECT . . .

- **When you prioritize their sense of security.** Even more than other kids, your Taurus's main objective is to cultivate a feeling of safety and security, which you'll do for them in spades, whether by comforting them after a bad dream or reminding them that you have their back when they're in an unfamiliar situation.

- **When you channel big feelings into creative outlets.** No matter how intense the emotions you're dealing with, you know that art is truly therapeutic, and your Venus-ruled kid agrees.

- **When you take a step back from the daily grind.** Both you and your baby Bull appreciate—and benefit from—dedicated, restful breaks to recharge.

YOU'LL CLASH . . .

- **When they struggle to express their emotions.** Your peace-loving, Venus-ruled child has a long fuse. But they will occasionally lose their cool as much as any tot, and when they do, they may have trouble recognizing and expressing their toughest emotions. Thankfully, you're uniquely qualified to help them do just that, given your emotional intelligence.

- **When your Taurus refuses to budge.** As a mutable sign, you're adaptable, which could lead to frustration when your Bull's fixed nature makes it difficult for them to accept change. Thankfully, because neither of you is exactly in a rush, you have the patience required to guide them through a gear shift.

- **When you're in the moment, and their minds are made up.** At times, your tiny Bull expects a particular tried-and-true routine, while you're more apt to go with the flow. You may find that adhering to a bit more structure can preempt crankiness.

PISCES PARENT & LITTLE GEMINI

Thanks to your shared mutability, you and your Twins baby are similarly adaptable. While you're often wrapped up in what's going on in your heart, your effervescent air sign baby is preoccupied mentally. With their affinity for information gathering, super-social energy, and desire to be on the go, they'll motivate you to move at a quicker pace and express yourself in different ways, and given your comfort with the emotional, intuitive side of life, you'll show them how to get out of their head in order to more readily recognize and honor their feelings.

YOU'LL CONNECT . . .

- **When you combine their love of language and your vivid imagination.** Whether you're making up a bedtime story one-on-one or regaling family members by sharing an experience you had together, you and your Twins baby are a natural storytelling duo.

- **When you nurture their emotional intelligence.** Because your Twins kid is so cerebral, they're more at ease with intellectual pursuits than tuning in to their heart, but you can make discussing feelings a regular part of your dialogue.

- **By fostering self-expression.** Encouraging your curious Gemini to get swept up by their imagination, as you're apt to do, allows them to tap into their most playful, creative side.

YOU'LL CLASH . . .

- **When you're on different wavelengths.** Between your dreaminess and your airy kid's scattered energy, it can be easy for you to feel like you're speaking two different languages or missing what the other is saying. Thankfully, you're a pro at slowing down and seeing the world from their perspective, which can make all the difference.

- **If you're both struggling to make up your minds.** As two mutable signs, you'll find it easy to change course midstream, but you can also have trouble focusing and making decisions.

- **When you're emphasizing dreaminess and creativity over the facts at hand.** Your Gemini baby, with Mercury as their guiding force, is perpetually gathering information, which may require you to put imaginative pursuits on hold so you can more fully engage with their preferred mentally charged activity.

PISCES PARENT & LITTLE CANCER

You and your fellow deeply feeling, empathic, intuitive water baby enjoy a natural harmony. As a cardinal sign, your Crab tends to be more action-oriented than you, and as a mutable one, you have an easier time embracing the moment. You'll be impressed by your Cancer's ability to tap into their feelings to fuel their dreams, and they'll be excited by the depth and complexity of your emotional understanding and imagination. As a sensitive, compassionate pair, it's easy for you to ensure that the other feels seen.

YOU'LL CONNECT . . .

- **Without words.** Given your shared empathy, you and your baby Crab might often feel like you have the ability to read each other's minds.

- **By enjoying the therapeutic benefits of being in or near water.** Whether you're bathing your Cancer baby or dipping your toes in the surf, spending time together in your element can only bring you closer.

- **When you're expressing emotions through a creative outlet.** You and your similarly artistic little Cancer may enjoy making up songs, dances, or plays.

YOU'LL CLASH . . .

- **When your Cancer's cardinality is at odds with your mutability.** Your Crab may get impatient if they can't move the ball forward on an activity or project in a timely manner, which may be the case if you're caught up in considering all the angles of the situation. Sticking to just the facts can help you simplify your thought process, so you and your Crab can get down to business.

- **When your Crab withdraws.** You understand what it's like to be swept up in challenging emotions, but you might not be sure how to react when your Cancer retreats into their shell. While you may be saddened that they've gone silent, these moments ultimately call for leaning on your innate empathy.

- **If your little Cancer's clinginess gets too intense for you at times.** You love feeling close to your sweet Cancer kid, but in moments that they get possessive, you'll want to set boundaries that allow them to feel connected and grant you enough space for self-care.

PISCES PARENT & LITTLE LEO

While your mini Lion moves through the world with a bold, optimistic brand of spirited self-confidence, often knows exactly where they're headed, and isn't a fan of diverging from their set path, you're more passive, influenced by the energies around you, and open to seeing where the tide might lead. But you both prefer to see the whimsical side of life. You'll demonstrate the benefits of getting caught up in your imagination and embracing emotion over action, and they'll be your greatest cheerleader and the pint-size embodiment of empowerment and pure joy.

YOU'LL CONNECT . . .

- **When you're creating something your Leo can show off.** You'll both find a particular sense of satisfaction from pouring your artistic skills into a project you can display (like a suncatcher or clay sculpture).

- **When you take a break from your routine.** Your fun-loving Leo will be as excited as you are by a family trip to the beach or an afternoon picnic with you.

- **When you're onstage together—or you set the stage for your Lion.** Whether you enter your Leo toddler into a costume contest or applaud their impromptu dance imitating the penguins at the zoo, you'll bond over your shared love of performance.

YOU'LL CLASH . . .

- **If your Lion misinterprets your indecisiveness as not having their back.** When your Leo makes up their mind, they are hard-pressed to change it, and proud of what they want to do, so if you're wishy-washy on it, they might feel slighted. It could help to reassure them that you're on board with their passion but just want to get a sense of the specifics.

- **When your Leo is feeling social, and you're in a reserved mood.** Whether you're overwhelmed or tired as a result of absorbing everyone else's emotions, you might want to skip that party or trip to the park your Leo was fired up about. If you do, compromise by presenting them with a self-expressive, active pastime like having a family sing-along.

- **When your Leo is struggling to adapt.** Once your mini Lion is set on a particular flavor, outfit, or lullaby, they won't be eager to consider an alternative. While you may initially be aggravated by their obstinacy, show them that there's a lot of fun in trying something new.

PISCES PARENT & LITTLE VIRGO

You and your little Maiden, both possessing big hearts, want to pour your energy into supporting others. But because you're opposites—your Virgo, the practical, cerebral mutable earth sign, and you, the dreamy, emotional mutable water sign— you might not always see eye to eye on how to achieve the same goal. Yet you each bring skills to the table that the other wants to hone. You'll be captivated by the way your Mercury-ruled Virgo focuses on details, soaks up tons of info, and communicates, while you can model for them the Neptunian ability to tap into and listen to your intuition and trust your heart over your head.

YOU'LL CONNECT . . .

- **By blending facts and fantasy.** When your Virgo is enthralled by a particular subject—say, a place you've visited on vacation or a historical figure—they'll get a kick out of learning everything there is to know, then taking it to a more imaginative place, like writing and acting out a play that incorporates the facts you've gathered.

- **When you pair up to lend a shoulder to someone who's struggling.** You and your Maiden are both deeply empathic, so whenever a friend, neighbor, loved one, or pet needs a little extra TLC, you can easily join forces to show up for them.

- **When you apply your strengths to supporting each other.** Your down-to-earth Maiden may show you how to be more present and grounded, while your compassion and warmth can boost their ability to believe in themselves.

YOU'LL CLASH . . .

- **When you struggle to understand each other.** When you're in an imaginative headspace and your Virgo is thinking in practical terms, confusion could be a sign it's time to take a step back and clarify what you want to accomplish together.

- **When you're both being sensitive.** Your little Virgo might take issue with a specific word or tone you use, and you might be stung by their budding critical nature. These moments could present you with the opportunity to hone your communication.

- **When you're dealing with mutability overload.** If you're both considering all angles of a particular scenario and struggling to make up your minds, you could find yourself at a standstill.

PISCES PARENT & LITTLE LIBRA

You and your Scales baby may not share an element or quality, but you definitely understand each other's desire to make the world a tranquil place. You often want to channel your ability to understand and process heavy emotions into healing others, while your conflict-averse Libra will do all they can to bring more balance to any situation. And as a cardinal sign, they're go-getters who will impress you with their talent for taking the reins in a lighthearted way. Meanwhile, you'll help your tiny social butterfly cultivate as much comfort with their inner world as they have with the external, social landscape they're so drawn to.

YOU'LL CONNECT . . .

- **When their Venusian pursuits meet your Neptunian pleasures.** Thanks to your respective rulers, you're both drawn to visual and performance art, which appeals to your Libra's eye for beauty and can feel like a dreamy escape to you.

- **When you tap into your imaginations for the sake of harmony.** From enjoying soothing music to making a bouquet to use as a dinner centerpiece, you and your Libra are both gifted at infusing any moment with beauty and serenity.

- **By embracing simple pleasures.** From enjoying a delicious cookie to observing a bird in the yard, you are both captivated by special everyday moments.

YOU'LL CLASH . . .

- **When you keep sweeping a conflict under the rug.** Because you're both so sensitive to conflict, you'll often go out of your way to preempt or smooth over disagreements, which might feel best in the present but could lead to pent-up feelings and more stress. This tendency could inspire you to tackle an issue head-on from the start.

- **When your energies aren't in sync.** Perhaps they're charming visitors, and you're feeling emotionally exhausted from entertaining, or they're pushing to FaceTime the grandparents, but you don't have the bandwidth. Getting on the same page might require firing yourself up to be on their super-social level.

- **If your Libra interprets complicated emotions as negative.** As an incredibly emotionally intelligent empath, you're uniquely qualified to help your Scales child recognize and work through big feelings.

PISCES PARENT & LITTLE SCORPIO

You and your fellow intuitive water sign Scorpion are particularly attuned to your own emotional states and each other's feelings. You admire your baby Scorp's investigative prowess, and they're mesmerized by your never-ending compassion and creativity. Whether you're talking about a beloved family holiday or coming up with your own special traditions, you'll rarely question that your Scorpio is taking spiritually meaningful moments to heart in the same way you do. And because your Scorpio is such a go-getter, their passionate approach to life can energize you, while you'll model adaptability that will allow them to be even more in touch with their imagination.

YOU'LL CONNECT . . .

- **When you dream together.** Letting your mind wander to whimsical places might be your specialty. Your Scorpio can do the same, but because they're more action-oriented, they'll benefit from your guidance on swapping the concrete for the imaginary.

- **When you trust your inner voices.** You are both extraordinarily capable of letting your gut lead the way, so if there's ever a question of how best to proceed, encourage your Scorp tot to check in with themselves.

- **By facing fears.** From scary dreams to preschool jitters, your Scorpio might get freaked out and struggle to move past eerie feelings, but with your ability to hold space for any distress, you'll illuminate your little one's path out of the shadows.

YOU'LL CLASH . . .

- **When you're finding it tough to help your Scorp go with the flow.** You could be caught off guard by your fixed-sign kid refusing to go to tumble class or insisting on playing Elmo's "Brushy Brush" over and over. Remind them how empowered they'll feel if they get outside of their comfort zone.

- **When your Scorp demands the reins.** Being the heartfelt mush that you are, you might run the risk of getting bulldozed by your pint-size yet power-seeking Scorpion. Although you want to keep the peace, there may be moments when you need to remind them of their boundaries.

- **If your Scorpio acts possessive.** Meltdowns may be fueled by your fixed water sign being a Velcro baby who doesn't understand that you're a bighearted healer who distributes a fair share of healing energy to everyone in your orbit.

PISCES PARENT & LITTLE SAGITTARIUS

If there was ever a child who could show you that your wildest Piscean daydreams can become a reality, it's your fearless baby Archer. Although you may share the ability to adapt on the fly, your tiny Sag is every bit a direct, adventurous, and driven firecracker who will say exactly what they want, which could both thrill and, at times, shock you. While you are sensitive and respect others' sensitivities, your Sag is on a mission to pinpoint and celebrate the truth of any matter, even if it means blurting out an observation that stings. You'll help them not only to get in touch with and honor their own complicated emotions but also to more readily pick up on what's in other people's hearts, and they'll leave you feeling electrified by their admirable confidence, courage, and sense of humor.

YOU'LL CONNECT . . .

- **When you go big with special occasions.** Your celebration-loving Sag knows how to have a good time, and you adore exercising your artistic muscle by designing an Instagram-worthy cake or compiling a themed playlist.

- **When you pair your dreaminess with your Sag baby's optimism.** Whether you're pondering ideas for a family vacation or planning a memorable snow day activity, you'll be motivated by your Archer's joie de vivre.

- **When you're willing to shrug off what feels familiar to embrace the unknown.** Whether they're bounding around a playground or blurting out their opinion, your Sag tot's bravery could freak you out—but also motivate you to move beyond your comfort zone.

YOU'LL CLASH . . .

- **If your Sag's over-the-top approach requires reining in.** Whether it's more snacks or playing music at top volume, more always seems better to your Jupiterian kid. You could be torn between letting them be themselves and firmly holding much-needed boundaries.

- **When your Sag blurts out their truth, and it stings.** Your fiery toddler could leave you feeling emotionally wounded when they speak their mind filter-free.

- **When you have different ideas about what an adventure looks like.** To you, doing a creative project is thrilling, but your Archer wants to be thrown into the middle of an eye-opening experience, like a farmers market or a road trip to Grandma's.

PISCES PARENT & LITTLE CAPRICORN

In many ways, you and your baby Sea Goat have contrasting priorities. While you're guided by your heart, they tend to brush big feelings aside in an effort to stick with the tactile world. And when you're tuning in to the energy of a given moment to decide how to proceed, they're determined to move slowly and steadily toward whatever objective they're currently focused on. In turn, your wise little Cap will teach you that it can be beneficial to bring more structure and pragmatism into your dreamy world, and you'll encourage them to honor their emotional selves, pointing out that it can only serve to make them more successful.

YOU'LL CONNECT . . .

- **When you combine their industriousness and your whimsy.** Whether you're constructing with LEGOs or making a fort out of cushions, you and your diligent Cap will bond by engaging in pastimes that involve both building and dreaming.

- **When you carve out time for relaxation.** Your assiduous Cap will believe it's best to be busy all the time. Prioritizing chill-out sessions instills a lifelong healthy habit for your Sea Goat.

- **By escaping to the past.** While you may not be able to jump in a DeLorean going eighty-eight miles per hour, you and your Sea Goat can still take a step back from your everyday reality to explore a different era or your own family history. You'll both be captivated by photo albums or stories that bring you back in time.

YOU'LL CLASH . . .

- **When you're confused by your Capricorn's seeming stoicism.** It can be tough for you to understand why your Sea Goat shuts down when it's clear they're angry, sad, or just plain exhausted, but moments like these allow you to gently remind them that it's not only OK but preferable to work through uncomfortable emotions versus sweeping them under the rug.

- **If your practical Cap gets impatient with your dreaminess.** Your Sea Goat is one of the most grounded kids of the zodiac, while you're very imaginative, so this difference is bound to result in headbutting.

- **When your Sea Goat is on a mission, and you're letting it flow.** Your cardinal earth sign wants to reach the peak of any mountain they set their sights on, whereas you're happy to see where the tide takes you. Acknowledging your different motivations can promote mutual understanding.

PISCES PARENT & LITTLE AQUARIUS

You and your little Water Bearer might see the world in your own ways, but you're both extremely inventive. Neither of you is a stranger to getting swept up in fantastical thinking, but while you dream for the sake of it, your baby Aquarius would prefer to use their imagination to solve problems and connect with others. You might be awestruck by your innovative Water Bearer as they work through a puzzle or a brain game—one that perhaps they came up with themselves! As they encourage you to consider the analytical angle of a particular situation, you'll show them that there's also merit to mystical aspects of life they can't see, touch, or prove.

YOU'LL CONNECT . . .

- **When you jointly push your shared dreams across the finish line.** Your artistic eye and your Aquarian's desire to follow through means that whether you're tackling an art project or experimenting in the kitchen, you can achieve the results you aimed for.

- **When you can both talk about—and allow yourselves to experience—emotions.** Your scientific Aquarius questions everything, including how they feel, which you'll entertain, while also encouraging them to embrace what's in their heart.

- **By getting creative with giving back.** You and your similarly altruistic Water Bearer can apply your vivid imaginations to coming up with many charitable ideas.

YOU'LL CLASH . . .

- **If your Aquarius takes aim at your daydreams with their contrarian streak.** Whether you've planned a day at an amusement park or proposed a make-believe game, your Water Bearer will likely opt to stick with reality rather than suspend their disbelief. Instead of pretending to be a wizard or unicorn, they might say they're a scientist or doctor.

- **When your Water Bearer's locked into their definitive perspective.** Your Aquarius may decide that they'll never go swimming again or that they'll only use red crayons. You can meet this obstinacy with a sense of humor.

- **When you express affection differently.** When it comes to showing their love, your independent Aquarius likely won't adore the abundance of snuggle time or mushy language. Airy and aloof, they would rather help you with a chore or entertain you with jokes than show you how much they care.

PISCES PARENT & LITTLE PISCES

As two emotionally intelligent, empathic, and even somewhat psychic Fish, you and your tiny Pisces are one of the most creative, sensitive parent-kid duos around. You intimately understand your Pisces's sensitivity to all the energy around them, so when they're struggling to process what they're picking up, you can walk them through teasing out and tending to their own feelings. And because you're both up for seeing where the tide takes you, neither of you will have to speed up or slow down to accommodate the other. Knowing how easy it is for your little Fish to get swept out into a sea of emotion, you'll nurture them with your limitless stores of compassion and the grounding tricks you've learned over the years.

YOU'LL CONNECT . . .

- **When you explore artistic outlets to see which resonates.** Because pouring your emotions into a creative pursuit is so therapeutic for you both, you'll enjoy trying a few—painting, drama, dance, or singing—to land on the ones that you most love doing together.

- **By finding comfort in imagination.** Whether you're getting lost in a bedtime story or pretending you're dolphins while splashing around in a pool, taking even the tiniest break from reality will feel like a dream getaway for you and your baby Fish.

- **When your Pisces leans on you to work through any feeling.** Your Fish will find a lot of comfort in knowing you can help them process even their deepest, most complex emotions.

YOU'LL CLASH . . .

- **When you're both tapped out.** Your shared sensitivity to your environment can lead to feeling run-down after a frenetic day, which could end up with your baby Fish being fussy, you being cranky, and you both potentially taking it out on each other.

- **If you're struggling with a lack of motivation.** As two mutable, dreamy Pisces, you could occasionally find it tough to get going, preferring to stay cocooned in your domestic sanctuary. But too much downtime can result in frustration and restlessness.

- **When you're irritated by a reality check.** Whether your little Fish is having a tough time hitting a milestone or you're overwhelmed by the mental load, having to hit pause on daydreaming in order to tend to an everyday challenge can make for grouchiness all around.

PRO TIPS FOR YOUR BABY-RAISING TOOLBOX

Maybe you're raising a fixed Leo who loves to be in charge but loathes diverting from their game plan, a mutable Pisces who would rather float around in their feelings than make a decision, or a cardinal Aries who dives into an endeavor headfirst but isn't the biggest fan of follow-through. Whatever their starry blueprint looks like, you've likely already noticed that the qualities of your little one's astrological placements shape how they see and interact with the world. For that reason, holding their main qualities in mind can help you to support their budding voice, appetite for knowledge, and journey from one milestone to the next.

One way to do that: Consider these tips and tricks, tailored to each quality—cardinal, fixed, and mutable—from Bonnie Compton, a child and adolescent therapist, parenting coach, and author of *Mothering with Courage*, and London King, a doula and childbirth expert, both of whom aim to support parents in holding space for their child to grow into the wonderfully unique person they're meant to be.

PARENTING PRO TIPS FOR CARDINAL SIGN BABIES

Consider trying these expert-backed strategies for supporting your Aries, Cancer, Libra, or Capricorn child's self-expression, learning, and growth.

Reframe boredom as an opportunity. Because your little one is a natural-born leader and initiator, they enjoy starting activities. This means that when a game or toy begins to lose its luster, your cardinal sign baby or toddler will be more likely than other kids to grouse of boredom. But try to avoid perpetually seeking alternatives that will "stick," says Compton.

"Boredom can actually spur creativity in these little ones," she notes. "Left to their own devices, they'll initiate another type of play." You'll just want to be sure they have access to age-appropriate toys, games, or even simple play objects like a ball that they'll be apt to go after with their signature dynamic energy.

Couple novelty with continuity. Cardinal sign little ones love feeling a sense of accomplishment but may be prone to losing interest midway through an undertaking. You can keep them engaged by making a detail of the process new and different, says King. "For example, when you're striving to encourage follow-through, use stickers that come in a variety of colors, textures, and shapes, and they'll be excited to keep 'the shiny' coming," says King.

Foster their independence while setting boundaries. Possessing innate independence, cardinal sign kids will start vying for power early on. That's why Compton says you'll want to allow them to take the lead when possible.

"Your 1-year-old may want to climb up the stairs—instead of saying 'no,' let them do so as you stay and watch, support, and guide them," advises Compton. "Or if you have a toddler, ask them if they want to climb up into their car seat or if they'd like you to put them in it. It may take longer, but you're fostering their independence."

They'll also assert their desire to be in command. For instance, your cardinal toddler may declare that they want a red cup only to be granted their wish and immediately demand a blue cup. "They're exerting their will, but they can become overwhelmed and scared if they have too much power," she points out. "They want to know their caregiver is in charge."

Compton recommends setting a boundary by saying something like, "You chose the red cup, so we're going to set the blue cup aside, and we'll use it tomorrow."

PARENTING PRO TIPS FOR FIXED SIGN BABIES

Tap these expert ideas for supporting a Taurus, Leo, Scorpio, or Aquarius child's self-expression, learning, and growth.

Present alternatives without forcing the issue. When your fixed toddler is determined to do something their way, or not at all, you can gently remind them that there are other options. Compton gives the example of a 9-month-old sitting on your lap and persistently reaching up for your cup or glass. "Of course that's going to result in them spilling, so you can say, 'No, you can't have my glass, but this sippy cup with a lid is going to be a great way for you to drink your juice!'" she suggests.

Or perhaps your fixed toddler insists on watching the same show or listening the same song they've enjoyed for days in a row. "They'll do this because it creates stability," says Compton. "You can acknowledge how they feel by saying, 'I know you love Luca, and you can watch it again tomorrow, but today we're going to try something different.'" And then you can give them two or three choices to pick from.

Reframe a plan B. More so than a cardinal or a mutable child, a fixed toddler might be beside themselves when faced with the unfamiliar. Say their lovey happens to be out of commission because it is in the wash. Moments like these can be an opportunity to reframe the backup plan as an opportunity for them, says King. She recommends saying something like, "I know you miss your lovey, but it needs to take a bath when it's a bit dirty—just like you! But I wonder if maybe you have another stuffed animal that could be lonely tonight?" That can be heart-opening for your little one and strengthen their flexibility.

Offer them a "time off" space. Although toddlers of all signs will inevitably throw tantrums, fixed kids might have a tough time letting go. That's why it can be so helpful to offer them plenty of ways to self-soothe.

King recommends teaching them a mindfulness practice, which they can rely on through childhood and beyond. "Encourage them to take their shoes off and walk in the grass, then focus on how the prickly blades feel on their feet," she advises. Or urge them to feel the wind or sunshine on their face—all while breathing it in. This focus shift can quickly help them feel calmer, says King.

Mindfulness breaks or time-offs serve as a reset, says Compton. "Remind them that tomorrow is another day," she advises. "And they get a chance for a do-over."

PARENTING PRO TIPS FOR MUTABLE SIGN BABIES

Try these expert suggestions for supporting a Gemini, Virgo, Sagittarius, or Pisces child's self-expression, learning, and growth.

Consciously connect. While this could be a heartfelt way to connect with any sign, mutable babies would especially benefit from a trick King swears by called "timer eyes." "How often do you really fixate face-to-face with your baby without making funny sounds and faces? Try setting a timer on your phone for one to two minutes, and just look into your child's eyes. It's a soothing way to deepen familiarity and connect while promoting focus," explains King.

Slow down. While your mutable sign child might find it tough to make and stick to a decision, they're also especially openminded, curious, and adaptable. You can nurture these traits and promote your child's creativity by carving out mindful moments.

If you're out on an evening stroll and your child notices a dandelion sprouting in a sidewalk crack, try not to hurry them along, suggests Compton. "Let them be curious—even within a structured time frame. You can say, 'We're going to explore for the next 10 minutes, and then we're going into the house to get ready for bed.'"

Foster confidence in their decision-making and inner voice. Behind a mutable toddler's indecisiveness is often a struggle to trust themselves and listen to their intuition.

Compton gives the example of a toddler who was gifted money for their birthday, put it toward a toy, and then ended up questioning whether they made the right choice. In this case, the best thing you can do is acknowledge how they're feeling. "Say something like, 'I know you're disappointed or confused, but there will be more birthdays and opportunities to buy a different toy,'" advises Compton.

This can help them move past the moment while acknowledging and validating their emotions. "It's in our nature to want to be seen and heard," notes Compton. "If they're told they're wrong, they second-guess themselves."

SIBLING SIGN COMPATIBILITY

If you're raising more than one baby by the stars, you can get a sense of how they'll connect and clash by matching their sun signs—as well as other placements.

KEY

For more information on the below, please see "The Aspects" on page 25.

☌ **Conjunct:** Your two little ones have a lot in common—possibly so much at times that it results in head-butting.

⊻ **Semi-sextile:** Lacking the same element or modality, these siblings don't share the same needs or energy, so they might have to work to understand each other. Still, seeing the world through their sibling's eyes could lead to growth.

✳ **Sextile:** These siblings' basic energy is in sync, which makes it natural for them to forge a friendly, easygoing bond.

□ **Square:** These kids share the same modality but not the same element and might feel a natural tension that can fuel conflict or brilliant action.

△ **Trine:** These siblings share similar needs, emotional wiring, and a harmonious bond.

⊼ **Quincunx:** Because these two children move through the world in different ways, patience and open-mindedness can preempt annoyance between them.

⚬─⚬ **Opposite:** Though their differences may make it tough for them to get in sync at times, they are like two sides of the same coin and balance each other out.

	Aries	Taurus	Gemini
Aries	☌	⊻	✳
Taurus	⊻	☌	⊻
Gemini	✳	⊻	☌
Cancer	□	✳	⊻
Leo	△	□	✳
Virgo	⊼	△	□
Libra	⚬─⚬	⊼	△
Scorpio	⊼	⚬─⚬	⊼
Sagittarius	△	⊼	⚬─⚬
Capricorn	□	△	⊼
Aquarius	✳	□	△
Pisces	⊻	✳	□

Cancer	Leo	Virgo	Libra	Scorpio	Sagittarius	Capricorn	Aquarius	Pisces
□	△	⊼	⊶	⊼	△	□	✳	⊻
✳	□	△	⊼	□	⊼	△	□	△
⊻	✳	□	△	⊼	⊶	⊼	△	□
♂	⊻	✳	□	△	⊼	⊶	⊼	△
⊻	♂	⊻	✳	□	△	⊼	⊶	⊼
✳	⊻	♂	⊻	✳	□	△	⊼	⊶
□	✳	⊻	♂	⊻	✳	□	△	⊼
△	□	✳	⊻	♂	⊻	✳	□	△
⊼	△	□	✳	⊻	♂	⊻	✳	□
⊶	⊼	△	□	✳	⊻	♂	⊻	✳
⊼	⊶	⊼	△	□	✳	⊻	♂	⊻
△	⊼	⊶	⊼	△	□	✳	⊻	♂

OUTRO

Raising a little one is no doubt one of the most thrilling and ever-evolving adventures of your life. No matter how much you read, how many friends you talk to, or how many TikToks or YouTube videos you watch before welcoming your baby, parenting requires throwing your hands up and accepting that you have no choice but to learn on the job. And as you've likely gathered over the course of reading this book, your greatest teacher will be your child themselves.

I fully believe that parents welcome the baby they're meant to have—the child who's astrologically wired to guide you through lessons your own birth chart calls for. Maybe they will mirror your own stubborn, fixed sign tendencies back to you, encouraging you to be more flexible. Or perhaps they'll offer a wise-beyond-their-years, pragmatic, grounding contrast to your fiery, passionate disposition.

No matter how their birth chart manifests, you'll constantly be reminded that your baby is distinctively themselves. Even if you appreciate your baby as a separate, whole person, it can be tough to see them begin to individuate. But by parenting them through the lens of astrology, it's easier to see why they must—and how they will—be their own person. After all, they have their very own astrological blueprint and, in turn, journey to experience in this life.

My most heartfelt wish is that this book leaves you feeling confident and equipped with knowledge that will make the highs and lows of parenthood more inspiring than challenging. The truth is, even before you uncovered the secrets of your baby's natal chart, you already had everything you needed to raise an amazing little human. But with astrology in your parenting toolbox, you'll be even more empowered and prepared for whatever's down the road.

RESOURCES

BOOKS

ON ASTROLOGY & RELATED SPIRITUAL PRACTICES

Astrology for Happiness and Success: From Aries to Pisces, Create the Life You Want—Based on Your Astrological Sign! by Mecca Woods

The Essential Guide to Practical Astrology by April Elliott Kent

The Inner Sky: How to Make Wiser Choices for a More Fulfilling Life by Steven Forrest

Moving Beyond: Access Your Intuition, Psychic Ability and Spirit Connection by Fleur Leussink

Sun Signs by Linda Goodman

Your Body and the Stars: The Zodiac As Your Wellness Guide by Stephanie Marango and Rebecca Gordon

ON PARENTING

Gentle Discipline: Using Emotional Connection—Not Punishment—to Raise Confident, Capable Kids and *The Gentle Parenting Book: How to Raise Calmer, Happier Children from Birth to Seven* by Sarah Ockwell-Smith

Mothering with Courage: The Mindful Approach to Becoming a Mom Who Listens More, Worries Less, and Loves Deeply by Bonnie Compton

WEBSITES AND APPS

My site, maressabrown.com. Calculate birth charts and access a library of my most recent horoscopes and astrology, parenting, and lifestyle articles.

Astrodienst (astro.com). Here you can calculate a range of astrology charts and purchase accompanying reports.

Big Sky Astrology (bigskyastrology.com). My mentor April Elliott Kent's website, on which you can find astrology essays and how-tos and order various personalized reports.

Cosmic Kids (cosmickids.com). This website and YouTube channel offers a vast array of yoga and mindfulness sessions for children.

TimePassages (available on iOS and Android). Created by Astrograph.com, this is the best astrology app for beginners, offering a personal astrology dashboard generated from your child's or your own chart as well as tailored interpretations.

PODCASTS

Big Sky Astrology Podcast with April Elliott Kent. Veteran astrologer April Elliott Kent breaks down the week's astrological weather and more.

Ghost of a Podcast. Astrologer, psychic medium, tarot reader, and animal communicator Jessica Lanyadoo offers weekly astrological advice and horoscopes.

Parent Footprint with Dr. Dan, hosted by Daniel B. Peters, PhD. "Dr. Dan" is a psychologist, author, and parenting expert; this podcast is aimed at helping parents, children, and families realize and achieve their full potential while living with intention and purpose.

ACKNOWLEDGMENTS

Creating *Raising Baby by the Stars* has been a whimsical, educational journey and long-held dream come true that wouldn't have been possible without many wonderful people:

Elise Ramsbottom, my sunny and perpetually supportive Leo former editor, who made it possible for me to achieve a goal I've had since I was five years old when she invited me along for this fantastic ride. My editor, Shoshana Gutmajer, whose thorough, thoughtful edits and Sagittarian thirst for astrological knowledge are endlessly appreciated. My copy editor, Amélie Cherlin, whose notes and enthusiasm were so valued. And the talented team at Artisan Books: Sibylle Kazeroid, Nina Simoneaux, Suet Chong, Jennifer K. Beal Davis, Donna G. Brown, and Diana Valcarcel.

My parents, Stuart and Irene, and my brother, Elliot, who've always championed my aspirations, and my sissypants, Emmie, whose Aquarius sun sits opposite my Leo ascendant, so it's no wonder she's my beloved sister *and* my brilliant best friend. And the ultimate matchmaker-turned-aunt, Jill Becker Wilson.

My always encouraging therapist, Peggy Matson, who has held space for me to step into my sense of self—and, in turn, the best chapter of my life so far.

My mentor and technical editor, April Elliott Kent, whose starry wisdom and gorgeous writing make me feel like the luckiest astrology student.

Loving friends who've enthusiastically believed in me for many years—some of whom are gentle parents I greatly admire. Especially grateful for you, Colleen Clohessy, Andrew Kudla, Lisa Crilley, Joann Wolferman, Caitlin Devan, Dion Lim, and Meredith Grubbs.

My dear friend Sheri Reed, a Scorpio word magician and the best managing editor of all time. Thank you from the bottom of my heart for being up for teaming up for over a decade.

Astrologers whose work, wisdom, and positive perspectives are a gift: Stephanie Campos (chart twin!), Narayana Montúfar, and Rebecca Gordon.

Parenting tip queens Bonnie Compton and London King, whom I am honored to include in this book.

My beloved fellow Virgo and former *Parents* senior editorial director Julia Dennison. I'm filled with gratitude for your friendship and support. The dynamic team at Care.com I'm so thankful to work with.

My generous editors/friends at the publications I contribute to (especially Melissa Bykofsky, Anna Halkidis, Melissa Mills, Amber Leventry, Kylie Gilbert, Lauren Mazzo, and Sade Strehlke), whom I can't thank enough for helping me build a career that's surpassing my most vivid junior high daydreams. My favorite Emerson College professor, Jeffrey Seglin, who championed my writing.

Most of all, thank you to my partner, my love, Kyle, who inspires me daily with his compassionate heart, bright optimism, and charismatic drive and has taught me what a true partnership looks like and what it feels like to be seen, and to be loved for exactly who I am. Because I'm fortunate enough to call you my rock, I know more than ever that (as a wise man named Doc Brown once said) if put my mind to it, I can accomplish anything.

INDEX

Maressa Brown is a journalist and astrologer who has written parenting, astrology, pop culture, and general lifestyle content for nearly two decades. She is a regular contributor to *Parents* magazine, resident astrologer for *InStyle* and *Shape*, and senior editor for Care.com whose writing has also appeared on What to Expect digital, in the *Washington Post*, and on PopSugar.com, Horoscope.com, Astrology.com, and more. A graduate of Emerson College, Brown is a member of the International Society for Astrological Research and the Authors Guild. She lives in Los Angeles. You can find more about her work at MaressaBrown.com.